Hello, Cruel World!

ALSO BY MELINDA WENNER MOYER

How to Raise Kids Who Aren't Assholes

'The latest book by science journalist Melinda Wenner Moyer should be top of your pile. Designed as a research-backed guide to help parents equip their children with the tools they need to thrive. The chapters are short and readable, broken down into bite-sized sections, each giving you one piece of advice and the science to back it up. Moyer oozes empathy and can help you take a kids'-eye view on even their most infuriating behaviours.' **Catherine de Lange, *New Scientist***

'There are some books that I return to time and time again to help me with parenting – and life itself. *Hello, Cruel World!* is destined to become one of those well-thumbed manuals. The three biggest messages from [it] are to listen more than you lecture (and when you introduce rules, explain why); comfort more than you chide; and prepare more than you protect. These messages feel crucial if we want our children to feel compassion towards themselves and other people.' **Genevieve Roberts, *The i Paper***

'A much-needed manual for building character in kids. Melinda Wenner Moyer is a leading voice on parenting, and her book is packed with evidence-based, non-obvious practical advice for nurturing resilience, kindness, critical thinking and well-being.' **Adam Grant, #1 *New York Times* bestselling author of *Think Again*, and host of the podcast *Re:Thinking***

'In *Hello, Cruel World!*, Melinda Wenner Moyer tackles the most pressing and controversial issues in modern parenting with remarkable clarity and depth. Her strategies, rooted in cutting-edge science and real-world experience, help parents understand how to foster compassion and resilience, navigate the social media landscape, engage with kids in ways that will reduce bias and polarization, teach key information literacy skills, and more. *Hello, Cruel World!* is an essential roadmap for parenting in the 21st century – an indispensable guide for any parent trying to raise a confident, compassionate, self-aware child in today's tumultuous climate.' **Tina Payne Bryson, Ph.D., *New York Times* bestselling co-author of *The Whole-Brain Child***

'Melinda Wenner Moyer has done it again. A timely companion to her best-selling *How to Raise Kids Who Aren't Assholes*, *Hello, Cruel World!* might be my new favorite parenting book. It's eminently readable and grounded in both solid research and the reality of modern parenting. If you've ever wondered (or worried) about how to guide your kids through the challenges of making friends, making smart choices around drugs and alcohol (even when their friends aren't), and staying competent, kind, and curious amidst the chaos of life, this is the book for you. If I could pick one book to put in the hands of every parent, this would be the one!'
Carla Naumburg, PhD, author of *How to Stop Losing Your Sh*t with Your Kids*

'It can be terrifying to make decisions as a parent in an increasingly overwhelming world full of bias, polarization, and disinformation. But having this book on my shelf just made the job easier, because Melinda Wenner Moyer brings her impeccable scientific reporting skills to grapple with all of the big questions that keep us up at night – and her solutions and strategies are realistic and empowering for parents and kids alike. *Hello, Cruel World!* is required reading for any parent hoping to raise good humans today.' **Virginia Sole-Smith, *New York Times* bestselling author of *Fat Talk: Parenting in the Age of Diet Culture***

'Melinda Wenner Moyer is a great writer – funny, sharp, and always impeccably researched and scientifically accurate. This new book is a masterclass for parents who want to help kids navigate the messy, imperfect world outside our homes and beyond our control.' **Michele Borba, Ed.D., author of *Thrivers***

'If you're confounded by our culture and want to raise children who can not only navigate our world but evolve it for the better, *Hello, Cruel World!* is an essential guide. It's science-based, profound, and intuitive, and full of techniques to apply not only to our parenting, but to ourselves.'
Elise Loehnen, *New York Times* bestselling author of *On Our Best Behavior*

Hello, Cruel World!

SCIENCE-BASED STRATEGIES FOR RAISING TERRIFIC KIDS IN TERRIFYING TIMES

Melinda Wenner Moyer

The information in this book may not be suitable for everyone and is not intended to be a substitute for medical advice or medical treatment. You are advised to consult a doctor on any matters relating to your health, and in particular on any matters that may require diagnosis or medical attention. Any use of the information in this book is made on the reader's good judgement after consulting with his or her doctor and is the reader's sole responsibility.

Published by arrangement with G.P. Putnam's Sons, an imprint of Penguin Publishing Group, a division of Penguin Random House LLC. First published in the United States in 2025.

First published in in the UK in 2025 by Headline Home
An imprint of Headline Publishing Group Limited

This paperback edition published in 2026

1

Cataloguing in Publication Data is available from the British Library

Paperback ISBN 978 1 0354 2340 8
ebook ISBN 978 1 0354 1663 9

Offset in 8.56/14.89pt Bogue Slab by Six Red Marbles UK, Thetford, Norfolk

Printed and bound in Great Britain by Clays Ltd, Elcograf S.p.A.

MIX
Paper | Supporting responsible forestry
FSC® C104740

Headline's policy is to use papers that are natural, renewable and recyclable products and made from wood grown in well-managed forests and other controlled sources. The logging and manufacturing processes are expected to conform to the environmental regulations of the country of origin.

Headline Publishing Group Limited
An Hachette UK Company
Carmelite House
50 Victoria Embankment
London EC4Y 0DZ

The authorised representative in the EEA is Hachette Ireland, 8 Castlecourt Centre, Dublin 15, D15 XTP3, Ireland (email: info@hbgi.ie)

www.headline.co.uk
www.hachette.co.uk

For all our children

Contents

PART II
Connect

PART III
Cultivate

Hello, Cruel World!

Introduction

I can't remember exactly when the insomnia started, but it was not long after my kids stopped yelling for me in the middle of the night. I remember feeling such relief at the possibility of finally, again, enjoying restful slumber, only to discover that my brain had other plans. At least once a week, something would rouse me at an ungodly hour—my house creaking, my dog snoring, my bladder protesting—and suddenly I was wide awake, mind buzzing, thinking about all the scary things going on in the world. Eventually, my thoughts veered to worrying about my kids. Was I letting them watch too much YouTube? Were they resilient enough? How could I turn them into critical thinkers? Would they, too, battle anxiety in the middle of the night?

Lying in bed, I tried all the remedies: deep breathing, counting sheep, body scans, CBD tinctures. Sometimes I resorted to Xanax. Usually, after an hour or two, I could fall back asleep. But I knew the scene would repeat itself soon enough, like a dystopian version of *Groundhog Day*.

There have been tough times all throughout history, of course, but it feels to me—and I'm sure I'm not alone in this—that many issues and threats our children will have to manage weren't nearly so bad for us. They will have to contend with worsening political polarization, disinformation, climate change, gun violence, radicalization, and economic inequality, to name but a few.

Whenever I'm panicking, I ask myself if there's anything I can do to feel more in control. Often, the answer is *research*. So, fueled in large part by the fears I have on behalf of my kids, I dove deep into data and scientific studies to try to find out if there were things I could do as a parent to help prepare them—and I was relieved to discover that the answer was *yes*. This book is a guide to all the strategies I uncovered: a handbook for raising kids who will be able to navigate the unique set of challenges they will face in this complex world.

Our Kids Are Struggling

Even if you don't lie awake at night worrying about your kids like I do, data shows that Gen Z and Gen Alpha are suffering right now in ways their elders did not. According to the Centers for Disease Control and Prevention (CDC), suicide attempts among youth have increased over the past decade, with more than one in five teens—and nearly one in three teen girls—reporting that they have seriously considered attempting suicide. Deaths due to drug overdoses among adolescents more than doubled between 2019 and 2023.

Anxiety rates and sleep deprivation among youth have been on the rise, too, with fewer than one-quarter of adolescents meeting recommended sleep guidelines. Perhaps as a result, many kids today don't feel like they can handle the obstacles life throws at them. In a large 2023 survey conducted by the Boys and Girls Clubs of

America, nearly 70 percent of youth said it was either "sort of" or "very" true that when something important goes wrong in their life, they can't stop worrying about it and they try to keep other people from finding out. As US Surgeon General Vivek H. Murthy recently wrote, "The challenges today's generation of young people face are unprecedented and uniquely hard to navigate. And the effect these challenges have had on their mental health is devastating."

Of course, not every kid is struggling—and some of the observed rise in youth mental health problems may not reflect true increases, but rather the fact that a higher proportion of kids and teens today are being screened and diagnosed (and, hopefully, treated) for mental health issues now than in the past. Still, I hear from hundreds of parents weekly as they engage with my Substack newsletter, and they are concerned, if not downright terrified. We all want to know the same thing: How can we help our kids?

To that end, many of us are desperately trying to chip away at the world's problems before our kids grow up. We vote, volunteer, attend marches and rallies, give money to charity, install solar-energy panels, and call our representatives. Some research suggests that contemporary motherhood causes women to become more politically active and left-leaning; I've felt this change in myself, in large part because I want to make the world better for my kids. As one mother put it to me, choosing to become a parent is a decision parents make on behalf of their children—our kids have no say, after all, in whether they are born—so it can feel like our responsibility to make sure we are not bringing them into a world that isn't worth living in. We do everything in our power to make things better, and we *are* making a difference. I firmly believe that.

Dealing with "a World Full of Assholes"

That said, we're not going to be able to solve all the difficult problems of the world before our children grow up. And we know that some things may keep getting worse before they get better—including how we, as a society, treat each other. When author Ryan Holiday interviewed me for his podcast *The Daily Stoic* about my book *How to Raise Kids Who Aren't Assholes*, he essentially said: Not raising assholes is important, but how are our kids going to deal with a world *full* of assholes? How do we raise our children to deal with them and all the terrible things they do? Throughout their lives, not only will our kids have to manage all sorts of problems but they'll also have to cope with all sorts of people. What can we do to set them up to succeed?

Hello, Cruel World! contains my answers to those questions. We can be activists in our parenting by preparing our children for the seemingly impossible world they are going to inherit—so that they can not only handle it but change it for the better. We can teach them the skills they will need to take care of themselves, fight for what they believe in, manage uncertainty, build healthy relationships, and bridge divides. We can help them think of themselves as part of a larger whole. We can show them how to set boundaries, care for others, and take responsibility for their actions.

Over the past several decades, researchers in many fields—psychology, sociology, education, information and media literacy, communications, adolescent mental health, and addiction, among others—have been studying how various skills and strengths develop in children and teens and what parents, teachers, and other adults can do to foster them. To uncover their hidden gems, I read thousands of studies, interviewed hundreds of researchers and therapists, and traveled to several locales to observe promising research-based interventions so that I could share with you some of the key things parents can do to raise kids who can handle what life throws at them.

I know, I know; the last thing we all need is more work to do. "I get overwhelmed when I begin listing out all of the things I'm responsible for teaching," one mother lamented in a recent discussion thread in my newsletter. "Wow, it's a lot." But here's some good news: Many of the parenting strategies I uncovered in my reporting are relatively easy to implement and free—yes, some require a time investment, but many simply involve being intentional about our choices and the kinds of conversations we have with our kids. Some strategies actually involve stepping back—not giving our kids everything they want and granting them more responsibility and independence, which can decrease our workload rather than increase it. Many of the strategies can also, over time, help kids become more generous, helpful, and resilient—which, I daresay, could make parenting a much more enjoyable experience, too.

I organized the key skills our children need today into three categories, which form the three sections of this book. In part I, "Cope," I explore the science of teaching kids how to take care of themselves and manage uncertainty and challenges. I discuss the best ways to protect children's mental health and prevent substance use and addiction. I dig into the science of fostering healthy resilience, including why and how our parental instincts sometimes undermine it rather than strengthen it. This section also includes a science-based exploration of how to help kids learn to treat themselves with compassion. And I explore the value of helping kids set careful boundaries so they can find balance in our ever-intensifying grind culture.

In part II, "Connect," I discuss how to help kids connect with those around them in ways that can bring society together rather than further drive it apart. In this section, I dive deep into the science of building strong relationships, exploring why kids often struggle to cultivate authentic connections and what can be done about it. I talk about the emerging science on the development of polarization and what we can do to ensure that our kids approach the world with curiosity and inclusiveness rather than judgment and fear. I also share the latest research-backed approaches for building empathy and compassion.

Finally, in part III, "Cultivate," I dig into the science of teaching kids how to engage with the world around them in ways that will keep them safe and healthy and cultivate a better tomorrow. I explore what we can do as parents to instill financial literacy as well as an understanding of the causes of inequalities and what could be done to address them. I discuss the latest science on social media and technology and how we can help kids understand and manage it. And I explore the research on helping kids think critically and accurately evaluate the information they come across, including where it comes from and whom it serves.

You can use this book however you like. There's no need to read it from start to finish; if there's a particular skill on your mind, or one your child struggles with, feel free to jump straight to the relevant chapter. I've included approaches that can work with kids of a variety of ages, from preschool through the teen years. You'll notice, too, that there is some overlap, in that the same strategies occasionally appear in multiple places. Although this might make for a little redundancy, I find it reassuring: It means that, according to the research, some parenting approaches strengthen numerous skills.

There's No Magic Bullet—and That's a Good Thing

To be clear, there is no one-size-fits-all approach for raising kids who can handle the complexities of the world today. What helps one child may not help another. Research can give us only averages—information about what helps or hinders groups of kids, and often there's lots of variation within them. So as I share the research and its implications, I implore you to take the advice that feels like it will be a good fit and leave the rest. If you try something and it doesn't work, it's not a sign that you've done something wrong or that there's something wrong with your kid. It just means that your child is not average—and that probably comes as no surprise.

The research on parenting has historically suffered from a number of limitations that could make its conclusions less useful for some families, too. Much of the literature has included only families from Western, educated, industrialized, rich, and democratic countries (the acronym for which is "WEIRD," which fits because most of the world does not fit into these categories!). This means that results from many studies may not be as helpful for children growing up in other cultures.

Another big problem is that the vast majority of studies involving parents and kids have included mothers but not fathers. To be fair, this is not entirely scientists' fault—fathers are less likely than mothers to volunteer for parenting research unless researchers specify that they want *only* dads, which few do. This could mean that some science-based strategies could work better for mothers than for fathers. We just don't know.

None of this means that the research on parenting is useless—it just means that, like anything else, it's not perfect. Despite its flaws, science is still the best tool we have for whittling away at the truth and helping us understand the kinds of strategies that are useful for most parents and kids. This literature can also help us separate the good parenting advice from the bad. And if you want to read more about any of the science or statistics I've cited, there's an extensive notes section at the end of the book that includes more than three hundred citations.

Yet the goal isn't—and should never be—perfection. I'll admit: I have mixed feelings about parenting advice, which is ironic given that this book is full of it. That's because advice inadvertently implies that there is one "right" way to parent, that every parent-child interaction should be optimized, and that parenting mistakes are to be avoided.

None of these things are true. There are many wonderful ways to parent, and there are countless constructive ways to engage with kids on any particular topic or in any particular situation. I also believe that, as parents, we don't have to (and even shouldn't) put our children first all the time, and that it can be helpful when we mess up.

I know this might be hard to believe. Over the past few decades, middle- and upper-class parents have been putting more and more time, money, and effort into raising their kids. Experts have referred to this trend in different ways, but one term that has stuck is "intensive parenting." It's been spreading to other socioeconomic classes, too: In a 2019 study, sociologist Patrick Ishizuka, then at Cornell University, surveyed a nationally representative sample of more than 3,600 US parents. Whereas working-class parents used to adopt a more hands-off approach with their kids, emphasizing safety but allowing for independence, his survey found that parents of all social classes now believe that intensive, child-centered parenting is the best way to raise kids.

There's nothing wrong with being a thoughtful, supportive, and conscientious parent. But there's a difference between focusing on the big picture and obsessing over the details. This book is focused on the big picture—what the research tells us about the types of conversations we should ideally have with our kids, the frameworks we might want to consider using, the values and priorities we may want to emphasize. But there is plenty of wiggle room. And that's important, because no two kids are the same, no two parents are the same, and no two families are the same.

It's also crucial that we give ourselves grace. One thing that's become increasingly clear from the science is that when we put too much pressure on ourselves, we (and our kids) can suffer. In a recent study, researchers conducted in-depth interviews with mothers who were experiencing parental burnout and concluded that "the fear of not being a good enough mother is central to the experience." If we believe that every interaction with our kids has to be just so, we are more likely to feel inadequate, burned-out, and exhausted. We are then less likely to make thoughtful parenting decisions. We may also increase the chance that our kids will veer toward perfectionism and feelings of inadequacy themselves.

One day, while driving my kids to day camp, I asked them: *Do you think it's useful for you when you see me mess up?*

My then eleven-year-old practically yelled in response: *YES! Oh yes, Mom, it's so helpful.* He said it's powerful to know that everyone, including grown-ups, makes mistakes.

My then seven-year-old daughter added that when I apologize after making a mistake—such as if I yell at her when I probably shouldn't have—it makes her feel much better.

When we make mistakes, we show our kids that failure and struggle is not a sign of ineptitude. It's a sign we are human. We all fail; we all make bad choices; we all forget things; we all react in less-than-constructive ways because our feelings get the best of us. This is important for kids to know. Plus, these errors are opportunities for problem-solving and learning. When I screw up—and believe me, it's often—I try to explain to my kids what the experience has taught me, and how, maybe, I can avoid it next time. Mistakes give us chances to model accountability, too. Few things are as powerful to kids as their parents' heartfelt apologies.

This book, then, isn't about precision or perfection—if anything, it's about the opposite. I think of it as a research-based guide to help parents center big-picture parenting goals and strategies, which sometimes get overshadowed by the chaos of day-to-day life and our immediate worries. Ultimately, I suspect that we all want the same things for our kids: that they grow into resilient, healthy, compassionate, and wise human beings. I have been so grateful to discover through my reporting that many of these gigantic, seemingly impossible goals are, in fact, within reach. My hope is that this book will help you raise kids who will not just survive but thrive in this challenging world—and, hopefully, transform it into a more welcoming, more wonderful place.

PART I

Cope

1

"I Hate Myself!"

Fostering Self-Compassion

Recently, a good friend told me a story involving her nine-year-old daughter, Charlie. One evening, my friend heard Charlie chiding herself over and over again: "I'm the worst human. I hate myself. I'm terrible!"

My friend—who also happens to be a fantastic child psychologist—listened, empathized, mirrored Charlie's words, and snuggled with her. In other words, she tried to do everything "right." In response, Charlie started crying even harder. "And now you're being so nice to me!" she wailed. "That makes it even *worse*!"

It can be both heartbreaking and infuriating to hear children berate themselves. Sometimes, the things they say are patently ridiculous. My daughter will sometimes do something totally innocuous and age-appropriate, like spill orange juice on her shirt, and then start sobbing and declaring that she's the absolute worst person in the world. With these kinds of oversize reactions, I worry how she'll treat herself when she faces bigger challenges or makes more meaningful mistakes.

As it turns out, self-compassion might be one of the most important, if not *the* most important, skills we can instill in our children. Because the fact is, life is not going to be easy for most of our kids. What will determine how challenges and hiccups affect them is, in large part, their self-compassion—or lack thereof. It's "one of the biggest gifts you can give your child," said Kristin Neff, a psychologist at the University of Texas at Austin and the author of the book *Self-Compassion.*

If you're skeptical, I get it—there are lots of common misconceptions about self-compassion that might be lurking in your head, some of which I'll address shortly. But suffice it to say that if you were thinking about skipping this chapter, please reconsider.

Why Self-Compassion Matters

First, let me define self-compassion, because it's often misunderstood. According to Neff, self-compassion is, quite simply, compassion directed inward. It involves being aware of and touched by our own suffering, regardless of whether that suffering is caused by our own mistakes or things outside our control. It involves being supportive to ourselves in our toughest moments and not judging ourselves too harshly.

As you probably already know if you've ever done something dumb, it can be really hard to practice self-compassion in the moment. It's a lot easier to think *Oh my god, I'm such an idiot!* than to treat yourself with kindness. Ask me about the time I dented my brand-new car thirty-six hours after driving it off the lot. I definitely did not offer myself a hug or tell myself that everybody makes mistakes. I'm pretty sure I called myself a total asshole.

Here's what self-compassion is not: It is not self-pity. It is not self-indulgence. It is not absolving yourself of blame or refusing to take responsibility. It doesn't cause people to become lazy and self-indulgent and do nothing but sit on the couch and eat chocolate. If anything, self-compassion achieves the *opposite*: It helps us accept that we are imperfect, yes, but also makes us more willing to work to grow and do better. (For the record, though, sitting on the couch and eating chocolate is perfectly fine, and I think we should all do it more often.)

Self-compassion is linked with many broad benefits.

Self-compassion is an incredibly helpful skill, though some of its benefits might, at first, seem surprising. Most of the research on the topic has been conducted among adults, but over the past fifteen years, researchers have started digging into how self-compassion affects kids and teens. And pretty much every study that's been done suggests that self-compassion is powerful.

Studies have found that self-compassionate adolescents are, for instance, more resilient—they can bounce back more quickly and easily in the face of challenges and they are not as harshly affected by stress as other kids are. Self-compassionate kids are also less likely to have symptoms of anxiety and depression than other kids and have greater psychological well-being overall.

If we teach kids self-compassion and they can bring these skills with them into adulthood, they reap even more benefits. Adults high in self-compassion better handle bad experiences and are generally less anxious, depressed, stressed, and suicidal than other adults are. They are less perfectionistic and have more intrinsic motivation.

Self-compassionate adults tend to exercise more, are more likely to seek medical care when they need it, have safer sex and healthier romantic relationships, and have overall better physical health. Sounds pretty good, right?

Some research has linked self-compassion to compassion for others, too, suggesting that when we treat ourselves well, we can treat other people well, too. It makes sense: "If your own emotional needs are being met, then you're more willing, or you're more able, to give to others and be there for others," said mindfulness and self-compassion teacher Karen Bluth, a fellow with the Frank Porter Graham Child Development Institute at the University of North Carolina at Chapel Hill.

Some researchers even go so far as to argue that we as parents can make the planet a better place by helping our kids learn self-compassion. "To the degree we can help more children be kind and loving to themselves, I think it could totally change the world," said Wendy O'Leary, a certified mindfulness meditation teacher and parent educator based in Massachusetts. "It's what gives me hope in the midst of the chaos that we see around us."

If self-compassion is that powerful, why is it so damned hard to master?

I've long been befuddled as to why self-compassion is so hard when it's clearly so helpful—and why self-criticism, the opposite of self-compassion, is often our go-to choice instead. Why do we so frequently talk shit about ourselves—and why do our kids do it, too?

Researchers theorize that self-criticism has become part of the human condition because it's been evolutionarily advantageous. Much as dogs instinctively know to lie down and show their bellies to more dominant dogs, we humans evolved a tendency to recognize, and sometimes loudly vocalize, our weaknesses so that those around us will like and accept us. "We're trying to prevent the group members from either kicking us out, which evolutionarily would mean death, or harming us in some way," Neff explained to me. Over evolutionary time, these tendencies likely served our ancestors well, helping them survive and pass the predilection for self-criticism on to their children, their grandchildren, and eventually to us and our kids. And now, here we are—raising kids who collapse into self-reproaching tears when we ask them if they've brushed their hair.

There may be other reasons why we lack self-compassion, too. Sometimes we say bad things about ourselves in front of our friends—*I look so bad in this outfit!*—so that they can contradict us and make us feel better. Also, if we regularly talk to ourselves in unkind ways, it may feel less hurtful—or at least, less surprising—when other people treat us poorly, too. In this way, self-criticism can be a twisted form of self-care, Neff explained. We do it because we're trying to keep ourselves safe. So it makes sense that kids, who feel especially vulnerable, might lean into this tendency even more.

If we're wired for self-criticism, is there any point in trying to swim against the tide? Thankfully, the research suggests that it is, indeed, possible to teach people—including our kids—how to be more self-compassionate. But first, let me explain what self-compassion requires.

THE KEY COMPONENTS OF SELF-COMPASSION

Over the years, Neff and her colleagues have identified three key components of self-compassion.

1. **Noticing your feelings in the moment.** This is often referred to as "mindfulness," and I think of it as simply being

aware of, and accepting of, our feelings. As Neff explained in her book, observing feelings requires turning our attention away from our circumstances and mistakes—which we often focus and ruminate on when we're upset—and instead acknowledging that we're having a hard time. It involves taking the time to turn attention inward and reflect on how we feel. Doing this helps us see our current situation more clearly and pulls us away from obsessive thoughts about our current predicament or the mistakes we think we've made.

2. **Recognizing the shared human experience.** The word "compassion" comes from the Latin for "suffering with," so an essential part of self-compassion is recognizing that we are not alone in our struggles and that being a human means being flawed. It involves reminding ourselves that other people have made the same mistakes and have experienced the same pain and hardship. Often, when we berate ourselves, we feel the exact opposite: that we're the only ones in the world who could be so stupid—but, of course, that's never true. (Although I don't know anyone else who has dented a new car within thirty-six hours, just saying.)

3. **Treating yourself kindly.** When you practice self-compassion, you treat yourself with gentle kindness and understanding in hard situations rather than beating yourself up. It's hard, because often, when we make mistakes, we tell ourselves we don't deserve to feel better. We can think about this part of self-compassion as being akin to "treating yourself as you would a friend." If your friend spilled orange juice on their shirt, what would you say to them? Probably not "You're the worst person in the world."

> Maybe, instead, something like "Oh, shoot, that sucks. I hate it when accidents like this happen." This part of self-compassion involves actively comforting ourselves and being touched by our own pain. It also requires asking ourselves what we need and how to address those needs. In other words: What can we do to make ourselves feel better?

Teaching Self-Compassion to Our Kids

To help our kids practice self-compassion in tough moments, we have to help them tap into these key components. Here's how to do that.

1. Practice self-compassion yourself.

In my interviews with self-compassion experts, they emphasized one point over everything else: You can't nurture self-compassion in your children if you don't practice it yourself. "Modeling self-compassion is a really important way—probably the most important way—for parents to instill self-compassion practices in their kids," Bluth said. Kids can learn more from what we do than from what we say. So even if you tell your kids to treat themselves kindly, the message probably won't sink in if you call yourself a jerk every time you burn dinner.

To get better at self-compassion, you'll need to internalize and actively practice its three components—noticing your emotions, tapping into a sense of shared humanity, and treating yourself kindly. In her wonderful book *You Are Not a Sh*tty Parent*, clinical social worker Carla Naumburg recommended another step, too:

staying curious. Curiosity is the antidote to judgment, she wrote, so when we struggle, it can be helpful to come at the situation with curiosity—to try to understand why things are so hard and why things happened the way they did.

If I'm upset that I burned dinner, and I try to get curious about why it happened, I might realize that while I was sautéing the chicken, my kid was asking me to help him with his homework. Then my dog started chewing on my shoe and I had to wrestle it out of his mouth and—oh, right, I also only got four hours of sleep the night before. I realize that it's no wonder the chicken got charred—and perhaps I should feel grateful that I didn't burn the house down, too. Suddenly, I feel a lot less angry at myself.

Another concept that's worth keeping in mind is that imperfect parenting can be more valuable to children than "perfect" parenting is (not that there really is such a thing). In 1953, pediatrician Donald Winnicott proposed the concept of the "good enough mother," arguing that it's good for kids when mothers (ahem, but let's expand this to all caregivers, shall we?) are imperfect and, at times, inattentive—because imperfect parents help children learn to manage frustration and problem-solve. Put another way, every time I burn dinner, I'm actually building my kids' tolerance for displeasure and discomfort. So there.

It's especially important to practice self-compassion when our kids push our buttons. You probably won't be able to support your toddler during their third grocery store meltdown if you haven't first taken a second to recognize that the situation is difficult for *you*, too. Self-compassion provides comfort and calmness, which is exactly what we need when our children start throwing cereal boxes in aisle three.

Still, there's a difference between knowing how to practice self-compassion and actually doing it. It may take more than just reading this chapter to maintain a regular practice. If it's a struggle for you, consider taking an online self-compassion workshop; the Center for Mindful Self-Compassion, which was cofounded by Neff and clinical psychologist Christopher Germer, offers regular classes (centerformsc.org). Becoming better at self-compassion will not only likely help you in myriad ways, but it will help you help your kids, too.

"You can't really teach it to your kids," Neff said, "unless you know from the inside what it's like."

2. Help your child notice, recognize, and label feelings.

Self-compassion is defined as the ability to treat yourself kindly when you are suffering. So in order for kids to practice it, "they need to be aware of what they're feeling when they're feeling it," Bluth said.

At first this may sound silly. Don't all people—even little kids—notice their feelings? To some degree, yes. But often, kids *feel* their feelings without *noticing* them. They aren't able to create the space needed to step out of their emotional state and think *I am feeling frustrated right now.* Yet we know from the research on self-compassion that the ability to notice our feelings, and to distinguish between them, is critical. Research suggests that many adults lack the ability to identify their own distinct emotions—so this is a skill that we should help our kids start building in childhood.

Thankfully, it's not that hard. The key is to be thoughtful about how we respond to our kids' emotions and how we talk about emotions in general.

First, when kids have big feelings, it's helpful to acknowledge, label, and validate them aloud. "Name the emotion for your child so that they learn how to name it for themselves," said Christopher

Willard, a psychologist and self-compassion expert who teaches at Harvard Medical School. You might say something like *I sense that you're feeling embarrassed right now.* Try to be granular with your labels to help your kids learn words for the many feelings that aren't always talked about, such as hopelessness, remorse, disgust, alarm, dread, boredom, and annoyance. (If your kids are anything like mine, as they learn more and more emotion words, they'll start correcting you: *No, Mom, what I'm* actually *feeling right now is despair.*

Ask your kids what they're feeling in their bodies, too, so they can start to link body sensations with emotions. O'Leary explained to me that kids are often much better than adults at doing this—they might notice that every time they are sad, they feel an aching in their chest—so getting them to pay more attention to these relationships can help them recognize what they're feeling in tough moments. They might notice *Oh, my chest hurts*, and then realize *Okay, I must be feeling sad.* This practice doesn't just teach them about emotions; it can also make struggling kids feel better. Research suggests that when you name the emotion you are feeling, the emotion immediately becomes less intense.

To this end, one helpful exercise for older kids and teens (and adults!) is the body scan, which involves using your body to tune in to your emotions. Have your child sit down in a comfortable place, close their eyes, and breathe slowly. Then have them focus on a particular body part—start with the top of the head and move down—and notice any sensations they feel at each spot. Have them slowly move their scan to other regions—the face, neck and shoulders, chest, abdomen, back, buttocks, legs, ankles, feet and toes. Encourage them to focus on sensations, such as heat or tightness, which are often associated with different emotions.

When my kids were younger, their dad and I used to play a "guess the emotion" game with them to increase their emotional granularity. Whenever we were at a restaurant and were waiting for our food—in my opinion, there are few things harder than keeping small, hungry children quiet and calm—we would go around the table one at a time. The first person would silently choose an emotion to act out in front of the others, and we would take turns guessing what feeling they were trying to embody. Then we'd move on to the next person and so on. Not only did the game introduce the kids to new feelings—I would shout out things like "elated!" and then explain what it meant when I saw my kids' baffled looks—but it also taught them what different feelings look like in terms of facial expressions and body language.

One thing to keep in mind, though, is that kids sometimes have trouble recognizing and naming their own feelings until around the age of eight, when they develop what is known as metacognition, or an awareness of what they are thinking and feeling, said Jamie Lynn Tatera, a certified mindful self-compassion teacher and the creator of the Self-Compassion for Children and Caregivers program. In other words: The process of learning about emotions takes time. Still, we can help kids develop the foundations of this skill by labeling their emotions for them when they're younger and helping them learn what different emotions look like.

As parents, we should also try to resist the desire to reassure our kids in ways that are invalidating. I don't know about you, but when my kids are upset—and especially when they're more upset than I think they should be—I tend to want to minimize their negative feelings by saying things like *You're okay!* or *It's not that big of a deal.* We do this for loving reasons—we don't like to see our kids unhappy, and we think that reassuring them is the best way to make them feel better.

But when our kids struggle and we say things like this, we are essentially telling them that they're wrong to feel the way they do, which can be dismissive and deflating—and make it more likely that they'll either amp up their feelings to get more of a reaction out of us or beat themselves up for feeling the "wrong" thing. "We have to cultivate our ability to be with their discomfort, so that we can help them learn how to hold it and hold it with self-compassion," O'Leary explained.

Plus, when we respond to our kids' feelings dismissively, we encourage them to suppress or repress their emotions next time—and studies show that these emotional regulation strategies ultimately backfire, causing people to feel worse than they did before. A 2023 study found that when people habitually judge their negative emotions as bad or inappropriate, they are more likely to experience symptoms of anxiety or depression and to feel less satisfied with their lives compared with people who don't make negative emotion judgments. I know it may seem counterintuitive, but giving your kids permission to experience the full landscape of emotions can make them more resilient and self-compassionate—not less.

3. Help your child understand that everyone hurts.

When kids and teens suffer, they may feel like they are the only ones in the world who've ever felt that way. That's why one of the most common things parents hear from teens is *You just don't understand!*

These feelings, unfortunately, make kids feel even more isolated and ashamed. So it's useful to help them recognize that mistakes and pain are part of the human condition—that in their toughest moments, they are actually the opposite of alone, because pain is something that everyone experiences.

How can we do this? O'Leary said that after validating our kids' feelings, we can say something like *I can imagine anyone in that situation would be feeling pretty bad*, or *It makes sense that you feel this. People often feel that way when something like that happens.* The idea is to zoom out and help your child see that what they're feeling is normal and that others have felt that way, too.

Tone of voice and word choice matter a lot here, because it's easy to sound dismissive when trying to communicate this concept to kids. If I snap at my daughter, *I'm sorry you're sad, but this happens to everyone*, she'll probably interpret my comment to mean that I think she's overreacting. Using a softer, more empathetic voice, and replacing "but" with "and" can help: *That sounds really hard. And I can imagine anyone in that situation would feel the same way.*

We can build this sense of a shared common humanity in other moments, too. When we read books with our kids, or watch shows or movies with them, it can be a helpful exercise to press pause and say something like *I get why this character is feeling hurt*, or *I can imagine she must feel quite angry right now.* When we highlight others' emotional experiences in front of our kids, we help them realize that everybody has tough moments.

Sharing details of your own struggles—and failings—can make a difference, too. Of course, you don't want to burden your children or make them feel like they are responsible for your emotional well-being. But it is helpful for kids to learn that we screw up and have bad days, too. Tatera explained to me that when we make these kinds of admissions to our kids, they often feel less shame when they encounter similar problems.

4. Teach kids to treat themselves kindly and to recognize and respond to their needs.

In addition to validating our kids' feelings and helping them feel less alone, we should also nurture the third component of self-compassion: helping our kids treat themselves lovingly.

At its core, this aspect of self-compassion involves fostering a sense of intrinsic self-worth. It's "creating an environment where the child feels loved and supported just as they are," Tatera said. Often when kids—and adults—struggle, and especially if that struggle is rooted in a mistake, they assume they don't deserve to feel better. (I mean, *shouldn't* I feel like an idiot after denting my car?!) But self-kindness involves helping our kids recognize that no matter what has happened or what they've done, they deserve love and kindness. It also involves recognizing that growth is not about changing who they are but about helping them become the best version of themselves.

One way to do this is to remind our children, regularly, that we love them unconditionally. Often we assume that our kids know this already—but research suggests they may not. Kids who feel pressured by parents to excel or achieve, for instance, sometimes internalize that their parents don't love them for who they are but rather for what they accomplish, which can erode their self-esteem. Communicating our unconditional love can be as simple as regularly telling our kids *I will always love you—no matter what you do or don't do.*

This isn't the same thing as telling our kids they're perfect or holding back from communicating to them that they are making less-than-ideal choices. Tatera explained to me that some parents go out of their way to ignore their kids' transgressions or always clear them of blame, which prevents kids from being able to see themselves clearly and learn important lessons. That's not love or kindness; that's overprotection, and it's harmful. It's "our responsibility as parents to help our kids know about ways that they fall short and that might be causing problems," she said. These conversations can be hard, but they are also essential. Ideally, in these moments we should communicate to our kids that we love them exactly the way they are, but that we want to help them make better choices. In this way, we separate their identity from their behavior.

Another way to help kids feel worthy of kindness—even in their darkest moments—is to cultivate in them a growth mindset rather than a fixed mindset. (For more on growth mindset, see chapter 2.) When we praise kids for ability or intelligence, saying things like *You're so smart* or *You're a natural at gymnastics*, we cultivate a fixed mindset, instilling in our kids the idea that traits such as intelligence and gymnastics ability are things people are born with—either you have them or you don't, and there's not much you can do if you're not naturally gifted. When kids have a fixed mindset, they tend to internalize challenges and mistakes as deep failures—as evidence that they don't have the ability that they hoped they had. It can cause them to beat themselves up when they fail.

A growth mindset, on the other hand, involves praising kids for effort and tying effort to outcome. Instead of saying *You're so good at gymnastics*, a parent might say, *You are doing so well in gymnastics because you've been practicing so much*. With a growth mindset, kids think of effort as a means to improvement, so they also see challenges or failures not as signs of ineptitude, but rather as opportunities for growth. Mistakes become less toxic, which means that kids are less likely to berate themselves when they make them. A growth mindset suggests to kids that "I can learn, I can be flexible, I can change, I can do better, my brain can change—and I'm worthy no matter what," Willard explained.

What should we do when we hear our kids engaging in negative self-talk? It may help to ask them if that's how they would treat a friend in the same situation. You can also emphasize that what they're feeling is temporary and will likely pass. When my friend's twelve-year-old, who sometimes struggles with self-compassion, says, "I hate myself," my friend encourages them to add the phrase "right now"—as in, "I hate myself . . . *right now.*"

Helping kids treat themselves kindly also involves helping them recognize what they need—and that they have some agency in fulfilling those needs. That might involve saying something as simple as *What do you need right now? Would a hug help? Or some alone time?* When kids are upset—even when they blame themselves—we want them to consider and pursue what will make them feel better. They may not immediately know, and that's okay; the goal is to help them recognize that no matter what they are dealing with or what they have done, they still deserve to treat themselves with loving-kindness.

Teaching your kids to practice self-compassion isn't about teaching them to reject responsibility or to absolve themselves of blame. It's about teaching them that they can accept blame and recognize their mistakes, while also knowing that they are still worthy of love, compassion, and nurturing—orange-juice-stained shirts, car dents, and all.

KEY POINTS

1. To teach kids self-compassion, parents need to practice self-compassion themselves.
2. Help kids notice, recognize, and label feelings.
3. Communicate that everyone hurts and makes mistakes.
4. Encourage kids to treat themselves kindly and to respond to their own needs. Tell them you love them unconditionally.

2

"I Give Up."

Nurturing Healthy Resilience

The kids are not all right.

In 2023, according to the CDC, four out of ten US high school students—and more than half of all high school girls—reported feeling "persistent feelings of sadness or hopelessness," an increase of more than 33 percent from 2013. One in five had seriously considered suicide. In a 2021 meta-analysis of twenty-nine studies involving nearly eighty-one thousand international youth aged eighteen or younger, researchers reported that one in five kids now experiences symptoms of anxiety—a near doubling in prevalence compared with before the pandemic.

We have to take care when interpreting data like these, of course, because statistics can be misleading. It could be that society's collective focus on youth mental health in recent years has helped a higher proportion of struggling teens get properly diagnosed—in other words, the rising numbers may in part reflect an increase in detection rather than a true increase in cases. Among other things, the passage of the Affordable Care Act enabled broader coverage of screening and diagnostic coding for mental health problems in medical settings. Some of the increase could be due to *overdiagnosis*, too: All this talk about kids' declining mental health could be causing some kids and teens to think they are suffering from a mental illness when perhaps they are not, in what some have referred to as the "medicalization of sadness."

Still, there's no question that the mental health of kids and teens is less than stellar these days—and that many kids also struggle with resilience, or the ability to handle, adapt to, and bounce back from challenges. Overnight camp directors have noticed that more kids today than in the past choose to go home early because they are less willing to tolerate the discomforts of being away from home. Teachers have told me that kids are more dependent on help than they used to be. Child psychologists have lamented that their young patients refuse to try hard things unless they are certain they will succeed. A school administrator recently told me that more kids are unwilling to try out for sports teams unless they have already been identified by an adult as having promising talent.

These trends seem to start young. Child-development specialist Claire Lerner, who has been working with children under seven for more than thirty-five years, said that she's seen a sharp decline in young kids' ability to manage everyday challenges. "Children are much less mature and self-confident and are much less comfortable with and adept at the self-care, self-help skills that you would typically see," she explained to me recently. Some of these skill deficits are almost certainly linked to the pandemic, but the changes, she said, started well before it.

Older kids—including college students and young adults—seem to be struggling with resilience, too. College professors have lamented to me that parents often call to haggle over their kids' grades or to complain that their kids' tests or classes are too hard. When Boston College psychology professor Peter Gray participated in a meeting on the topic of resilience, he was told by the head of counseling services at a university that many more students were making emergency counseling calls than in the past because they didn't know how to manage everyday problems. Two students, for instance, had called because they'd found a mouse in their apartment. They also called the police, who apparently set up a mousetrap for them.

I want to pause for a minute here to point out that these changes are not necessarily all bad. It may be that kids today feel more comfortable showing their feelings. If children of yore felt compelled by societal pressures to suppress feelings of confusion, frustration, or sadness, and kids today don't, then it may look like kids have become more fragile, when in fact they've just become more open and expressive.

Parents and teachers have also told me that kids today are more likely to communicate their needs and ask for help when they need it—and although those could be perceived as signs of fragility, I think they could be signs that kids are developing stronger self-advocacy skills, possibly because they are growing up in a culture that is showing them more respect. Kids used to be told that they should be seen but not heard. Now many kids grow up knowing that their voices matter—and that is undoubtedly a good thing.

Still, there is a difference between asking for help when you truly need it and asking for help because you *perceive* you need it but really don't. Many kids ask for help not because they couldn't have theoretically handled a situation but because they haven't been given the chance to develop necessary skills.

"They don't seem to realize they are capable of trying hard things on their own," said educator Stacy Boyd, the founder of Brooklyn Wild, an organization that offers play-based after-school programs for kids in Sunset Park, Brooklyn. "The idea of failing in a low-stakes way and then trying again is not their first instinct." Perhaps, Boyd said, this is because the kids want to do things the "best" or "right" way from the start—or maybe it's because they are used to having adult help.

In these situations, kids do okay when they get the help they need. But what happens when they have to face a challenge alone? I want my kids to be able to ask for help, sure—and I also want them, eventually, to be able to handle reasonable challenges without assistance. When kids constantly rely on others to do things for them or fix their problems, and they one day face a challenge nobody can help with, they may feel impotent or helpless. Instead, I want my kids to think: *Okay, this is tough. But I bet I can figure it out.*

Before I move on, I want to acknowledge the fact that some people—maybe some of you!—do not like the word "resilience," and I think that's in part because it has come to mean something it shouldn't. Resilience is sometimes characterized as the ability to endure and shrug off anything—but that's not what it is. Healthy resilience is not about pretending you're fine and powering through. It's not about masking feelings—but rather about respecting, understanding, and managing them.

Helping Too Much

Why are kids today more likely to avoid challenges or cower in the face of them? There are, I'm sure, many reasons. But researchers say that one key cause is that we, as adults, have become increasingly overprotective. We do not give kids enough opportunities to do things on their own, face challenges, and take healthy risks.

There are many reasons for these shifts. One problem is that we're all so damned busy. Think about how many times you've stepped in to help your child fasten their seat belt or tie their shoes because you just don't have the extra two minutes required to let them do the task alone. Yet our meddling, while totally understandable and sometimes unavoidable, not only denies kids the opportunity to get better at various skills but also teaches them that efficiency and perfection are more important than slow and steady progress. We "don't have time to let them fail," Boyd said—and this communicates to kids that if they can't do things perfectly the first time, they should probably not even try and should ask for help instead.

We have also become more fear-focused as a society in recent decades, which causes us to meddle in an attempt to keep kids safe. We are preoccupied with the future, constantly thinking about what could happen next, both to us and to our kids. Because the government provides little support for parents, and many parents raise kids without the support of extended family, the burden of childhood safety feels like it falls more squarely on parents' shoulders, amping up these concerns. Sociologists such as Anthony Giddens have written extensively about these modern cultural conditions, calling the landscape a "risk society."

Perhaps it's more accurate to say we're preoccupied with *some* risks, yet we are perfectly happy to ignore or gloss over others. When writing about the idea of the risk society, sociologist Ulrich Beck noted that risks "are particularly open to social definition and construction." In her book *Worried About the Wrong Things*, Jacqueline Ryan Vickery, director of research for the Youth Media Lab at the University of North Texas, pointed out that there are inherent risks in everything kids do—they can die or get hurt falling down the stairs or choking on food, yet we don't discourage kids from using stairs or eating. We often latch onto scary statistics about, say, kidnappings or social media without considering the broader risk context. "Statistics are a way to identify and quantify harm and can also be used to incite fear," she wrote. And scared parents tend to overprotect their kids.

We can't ignore the impact of generalized anxiety on our parenting, too. In the US, anxiety has been increasing among adults in recent years and was certainly exacerbated by the pandemic—and anxious parents often make overprotective parenting decisions, limiting kids' choices and activities because they are afraid something might go wrong. This might manifest as "'You can't go to a sleepover because it's dangerous," or "You can't go to this park,'" said Golda Ginsburg, a psychologist who is the principal investigator of the Child/Adolescent Anxiety and Mood Program at UConn Health. Other parents may let their kids do things but constantly warn them to be careful. (I'm guilty of that one, for sure.)

Our anxiety often tells us that our kids can't deal with things that they can, in fact, handle perfectly well. A good friend of mine recently invited a five-year-old over for a drop-off playdate. A few days before, the mom texted to ask if she could stay the whole time because her daughter was "feeling nervous." When the duo arrived, the girl skipped off and never looked back—yet the mom still wouldn't leave.

In addition to worrying about our kids' physical safety, we worry about their emotional safety, too—probably in part because we have seen all the terrifying headlines about kids' disintegrating mental health. This worry causes us to scramble to address our kids' needs and wants and to make them feel better when they are or could become upset. We immediately jump in the car to pick up our kids if they say they want to leave a sleepover (been there, done that), rescuing them from their discomfort rather than helping them get through it. We send them tons of care packages at sleepaway camp (been there, done that, too) because we don't want them to feel sad and miss us. (This is sometimes called "snowplow parenting," based on the idea that these parents clear obstacles and discomfort from their kids' lives just as snowplows clear snow.) Schools and camps sometimes jump on the bandwagon, too, giving out participation trophies to buffer kids against the short-lived sadness of having lost.

We might see these reactions as good and kind, but looked at another way, they rob kids of essential, resilience-building experiences and set our kids up to struggle more, not less. That's in part because, as the psychologist Lisa Damour has said, mental health is not about feeling good all the time. Mental health involves feeling emotions that are appropriate to the circumstances and having the tools to cope with them. The way kids can discover how best to cope with loss or distress, she said, is through practice—by regularly experiencing pain, frustration, sadness, and all the other uncomfortable emotions, trying out different healthy coping strategies, and learning over time what works.

When we jump in and try to protect our kids from uncomfortable feelings, or try to make those feelings go away as quickly as possible, we deprive them of these growth opportunities. "We know it's unhelpful," Ginsburg said. Kids need to "feel the anxiety, learn that they can work through it." Research on college students has found that compared with other young adults, those raised by over-involved parents are more likely to experience symptoms of depression, drink alcohol, and take pain pills recreationally. Young adults of hyper-involved parents also tend to feel less motivated and perform less well in school compared with kids whose parents are less involved in their lives.

In constantly hovering and protecting, we send kids a clear message: We think they are incapable. As childhood-independence advocate Lenore Skenazy and psychologist Camilo Ortiz wrote in a 2023 *New York Times* op-ed, "What's missing today isn't just the thrill of climbing trees or playing flashlight tag. It's that when an adult is always present—in person or electronically—kids never really get to see what they're made of." When researchers at the University of Illinois surveyed elementary school students, asking them how they would feel if their parents helped them and made decisions for them, the kids (especially older ones) overwhelmingly said that they would consider their parents' help to be a sign that their parents thought they were incompetent.

Teaching Our Kids Resilience

This doesn't mean, of course, that it's good for kids to experience trauma. But experiencing hard things can actually *decrease* the risk of trauma. In her book *The Emotional Lives of Teenagers*, Damour explained the difference between trauma and healthy distress. The distinction is not defined by the experience itself—we know that the same experience can be traumatic for some people and not for others—but in its *emotional impact*. Trauma occurs when an individual suffers greater emotional stress than they can tolerate. And what determines how much they can tolerate? Lots of things, including their past experiences. When we allow kids to encounter discomfort and shore up their coping skills, we can actually *reduce* the chance that their difficult experiences become harmful.

Here's how to do it.

1. Let kids play—on their own.

Jack Shonkoff, the founding director of the Center on the Developing Child at Harvard University, has described resilience as a mastery of one's environment: It involves having the skills to cope with what's going on around you. These kinds of skills don't develop in a vacuum; they require kids to be regularly exposed to new situations so that they can figure out how to manage them—and, of course, kids must recognize that they *can* manage them.

One of the best—and most innate and natural—ways that kids expose themselves to these kinds of resilience-building contexts is through play. Free, independent play—not to be confused with organized play such as soccer or Monopoly—develops a multitude of skills. Because free play does not have a priori rules, kids typically have to make up their own rules and structures as they go, which is a highly creative process. Kids have to learn to be fair and take turns—they cannot always demand to be Elsa from *Frozen* or soon they will have no playmates. These requirements develop cooperation and delayed gratification skills. And because kids enjoy play, they do not give up as easily in the face of frustration as they might on, say, a math problem—and this perseverance helps them develop emotional resilience, too.

In play, kids also have to communicate their ideas to playmates and cooperate and negotiate with them. Studies show that children use more sophisticated language when playing with others. They can't just get away with asking *Vanilla or chocolate*? as they hand a friend an imaginary cone. They have to provide contextual clues: *Vanilla or chocolate ice cream: Which one would you like?*

Another skill that play helps to foster is self-control. In a

2021 study, researchers observed 132 preschool students during the fall and then the spring to see how frequently they engaged in make-believe play with peers. They also gave the kids tests in the fall and spring to assess their levels of inhibitory control, which is the ability to control their attention, behavior, and thoughts in the face of distractions. The more the kids engaged in pretend play, the more their inhibitory control skills improved over the course of the school year. The researchers concluded, "Social pretend play could be uniquely suited to promote growth in inhibitory control skills."

Interestingly, too, encouraging kids to engage in imaginary play while they are doing challenging tasks may help them persevere longer. In a 2017 study, researchers asked four- and six-year-olds to do a boring but, in their words, "very important" computer task. They also told the kids that they could take breaks whenever they wanted and play games on a nearby iPad.

The children were then split into groups and provided with different resilience strategies to use while doing the boring task. Some were told to think about their thoughts and feelings and to ask themselves the question *Am I working hard?* A second group of kids was told to try to distance themselves from the situation and ask themselves *Is [my name] working hard?* Finally, a third group was told to think about and dress up as an imaginary resilient character—either Batman, Bob the Builder, Rapunzel, or Dora the Explorer. They were told to ask themselves *Is [character's name] working hard?*

The kids who stuck with the task the longest were the ones who engaged in the imaginary play. Researchers believe that this approach works in part because this kind of play involves distancing yourself, psychologically, from things that you want. Taking on a superhero alter ego may have separated the kids from their feelings of boredom so that they could more successfully forgo the lure of the iPad. (Among academics, this effect is referred to as "the Batman Effect," which I love.)

Play also reduces stress, which can boost resilience by helping kids stay calm in tough situations. In one small study, University of Illinois psychologist Lynn Barnett asked anxious kids, on their first day of preschool, to either play with toys or listen to a story for fifteen minutes. Afterward, Barnett assessed the kids' anxiety again and found that the distress levels of the kids who had played had dropped by more than twice as much as compared with the kids who had listened to the story.

How do we ensure that kids get ample playtime? For one thing, we need to give them plenty of unscheduled free time, both by themselves and with peers. But there's more to it than that: We also need to be sure that we don't interrupt them. Boyd, who runs the play-based after-school programs, said that parents often insert themselves into kids' play. "It's hard for the parents to just pause and let them do their thing—they want to jump in," she said. Often they'll ask questions like *Oh, are you building a castle?* But "this just stops the flow of play," Boyd explained, and it can also make kids self-conscious—maybe they were building a boat instead, and suddenly they're wondering if their boat looks too much like a castle. Even if our kids look uncomfortable or frustrated as they play, we should try our best to let them be.

Boyd said that the kids who go through her play-based programs very quickly become more self-confident and resilient. Students who at first complain about or refuse to play in the rain (even with appropriate rain gear) slowly get used to it. Kids who at first constantly ask for help stop asking. They become more autonomous in other ways, too. "I have had parents send me messages saying, 'Oh, after the summer, he would just start making his own lunch to take to school. And he was just so much more independent.'"

2. Don't overemphasize achievement. Nurture a growth mindset.

There's yet another reason parents today are overprotective: We're terrified on behalf of our children's futures. We worry that our kids won't get into college or won't be as financially secure as we were; kids today are far less likely to outearn their parents than kids of the past. So we pressure them to get perfect grades, to excel, and to develop their talents. We do it because we care about them, but unfortunately, this pressure has a downside: It encourages our kids to focus on outcomes and incentivizes them to give up on things when they aren't sure they will succeed.

In our achievement-oriented culture, we often directly communicate to kids that we value outcome over process. We want them to win the competition rather than get third place. We want them to get the highest grade in the class rather than "just" a B. But this emphasis on achievement can create a kind of false binary in kids' brains—either they win it all or they shouldn't even try. This all-or-nothing mindset can cause kids to avoid the kinds of challenging situations that help them grow and learn.

New York City–based clinical psychologist Katie Davis said she sees this kind of thinking frequently in her patients. "They didn't make varsity in tenth grade, then they quit the team altogether, because there's no value to playing on JV. If they're going to be in the ensemble of the school musical [rather than the lead], they quit. There's no point in participating unless they have the title, the recognition, the grades, the name," she said. That "makes it really hard to persevere in the face of challenge. The options are win or do nothing."

As parents, then, we must emphasize the value of doing and experiencing things, even when those experiences don't result in mastery or medals. That requires communicating that we care about learning—not just about grades. And it requires sharing that we are thrilled when our kids try something new or hard, even if they don't succeed. When our kids are inevitably disappointed about not winning or scoring or getting the lead, we should also help them reframe the situation so that they see the value in moving forward anyway. In one small study, Stanford psychologists Carol Dweck and Kyla Haimovitz surveyed seventy-three parents and their fourth- and fifth-grade kids, finding that kids easily perceive when their parents believe that failure is bad and something to be avoided.

One other simple way to communicate the value of trying over succeeding is by using the language of growth mindset. I briefly described growth mindset in chapter 1, but let me take a moment to explain why it's so powerful and also to correct a few common misconceptions.

"Growth mindset" is a term coined by Stanford psychologist Carol Dweck. It's usually described in relation to its opposite, "fixed mindset," which has often been blamed for causing kids to fixate on outcomes and give up in the face of challenges. (Some researchers have recently raised questions about the benefits of fostering a growth mindset in certain contexts, but I still believe it's broadly helpful in most situations when it's used correctly.)

When kids (or adults, for that matter) have a fixed mindset, they believe that ability and intelligence are just that: fixed. They think people are essentially born smart or not so smart, that people are naturally good or bad at things. When we think of ourselves as not very good at math or very good at art, we are thinking in a fixed mindset. Likewise, when we tell our kids they're smart or good at ballet or softball, we are encouraging in them a fixed mindset. We're painting ability and intelligence as black and white—characteristics you have or you don't.

The problem with a fixed mindset is that it backfires when our kids encounter challenges or failures. Let's say you've told your kid that she's great at math, and then she gets a D on a math test. If she has a fixed mindset, she's going to begin to doubt the ability you told her she had. Dweck's research has shown that kids with fixed mindsets are more likely to give up in the face of challenges. In fact, often they give up *before* they fail—when they first sniff out a potential challenge—because they are desperate to preserve their reputation as being smart or skilled. They don't want to experience setbacks or failures, because to them, setbacks or failures are evidence that *they* are failures, and in a fixed mindset world, there's very little that can be done to change that.

One study in particular, published in 1998, really illustrates mindset's power. Dweck and her colleague Claudia Mueller had fifth graders take an intelligence test, and then individually told some of the kids they had done well. But they framed the kids' successes in different ways. To some of the kids, they said, "You must be smart at these problems" (fixed mindset), while they told others, "You must have worked hard at these problems" (growth mindset). Then they asked each of the students if they'd like to do some additional problems, ranging from "problems that aren't too hard, so I don't get many wrong," to "problems that I'll learn a lot from, even if I won't look so smart."

Dweck and Mueller found that the kids who'd been praised for smarts (nurturing a fixed mindset) were more likely to choose the easy problems, whereas the kids praised for effort (nurturing the growth mindset) chose the hard problems.

Interestingly, too, when the researchers later gave all the kids hard problems to see how they handled them, they found that the fixed-mindset kids gave up sooner and said they enjoyed the challenge less. They were also nearly three times as likely as the growth-mindset kids to *lie about how well they'd done* on the problems when talking to peers afterward.

A growth mindset is, essentially, the opposite of a fixed mindset. When people have a growth mindset, they consider challenges and failures as opportunities rather than setbacks—opportunities to learn and grow and get better at things. The best way to foster a growth mindset, Dweck has argued, is to praise kids when they work hard and to tie their improvements to their effort. This last bit is what often trips parents up: They'll praise for effort all day, but they don't take the extra step of helping kids see that purposeful effort results in progress. When your kid's Spanish grade improves, instead of saying, *Wow, you're so good at Spanish*, you could say, *Wow, that good grade must stem from how hard you've been studying*. When your kid does well in a dance recital or in a soccer game, replace *You're so talented* with *All that practice really paid off, didn't it?* Connecting kids' effort to their progress helps them learn to value challenges, rather than avoid them.

What if your kid does well on something after expending little to no effort? You might say something like *I'm glad you got an A on the test, but I wish that you were getting more challenging material in this class, because challenges are how you grow your brain*. And then perhaps brainstorm ways to introduce them to more difficult concepts.

If your kid expends a lot of effort but still doesn't do well, remember that effort itself doesn't necessarily lead to progress; it's productive effort that matters. Maybe your child needs to try out new study or practice strategies. Also, consider that your child could be improving, but the assessments are just getting harder—or it's hard for you to see the progress because it's incremental.

3. Let kids do things on their own.

In October 2023, researchers at C.S. Mott Children's Hospital released the results of a nationally representative poll of US parents of children between the ages of five and eleven. About three-quarters of the parents said that, in general, they made a point to let their child do things by themselves—but their day-to-day decisions told another story. Two-thirds of the parents said they wouldn't let their child walk or bike to a friend's house, and half said they wouldn't allow their child to find an item in the grocery store when they were in a different aisle.

Of course, *of course*, there are circumstances in which these activities could be unwise. Privilege is highly relevant, in that families who live in wealthier communities, which are often safer, understandably feel more comfortable letting their child do things on their own. Race matters, too—consider that Black children and teens are about five times as likely as their white peers to be killed with guns. And some kids may not be developmentally ready for certain activities. I certainly don't question parents for erring on the side of caution when caution is warranted.

Yet it's clear that many parents err on the side of caution when perhaps they needn't. In the Mott survey, only 17 percent of parents of older kids said that their neighborhood was unsafe—yet, still, few let their kids frolic outside alone. Other research backs up the notion that parents today are less likely to let their kids take healthy risks than parents from generations past—they wait until the kids are older to walk to school alone, for instance, and to let them play unsupervised—even though the US is a lot safer today than it was when we were little.

Recently, a good friend told me about a discussion in her local moms' Facebook group. My friend lives in a small rural college town with minimal crime, and a mother had posted asking other parents if they thought it would be okay for her high school daughter to walk around the town during the day with a friend.

The chorus of noes she got in response was deafening. "Too many people, too many things could happen," one woman replied, even though, according to my friend, the town is never crowded and not much ever happens at all.

Why do we do this? For one thing, we detect and respond to social norms. If none of your friends let their kids walk around town with friends, you're probably not going to feel comfortable letting your kids do it, even if you know deep down your kids would be fine. (Plus, they'll have trouble finding a friend who's allowed to go with them!) Even if you know it's perfectly safe, you might worry about being judged by the other parents in your neighborhood if they see your kid ambling down the street by himself. In the Mott survey, 11 percent of parents said they worried about being judged as a bad parent if they let their kids have too much freedom.

This peer pressure can work in so many ways. In addition to shaping what we allow our kids to do, it can also make us feel as if we need to get heavily involved in our kids' school projects because other parents are. It can make us feel uncomfortable letting our kids go to overnight camps, sleepovers, or playdates, too.

Parental fear is also purposefully stoked by politicians, the media, and companies and influencers trying to sell us "solutions." The website of the family monitoring app Life360 claims that 1.9 million passengers are injured in car accidents in the US each year, and that one in three families are victims of identity theft—statistics strategically chosen to ramp up fear so that potential customers will believe they need Life360's extra protection. We are inundated with information designed to make us overprotective.

"Trust is at the bottom of all of this," Skenazy explained. "Do you trust your kid? Do you trust the world? Do you trust your instincts? So much of the marketplace is dedicated to making you not trust—and then the culture gets imbued with a lack of trust and starts confusing trust with neglect."

This is a point I really want to emphasize: Our tendency to overprotect is not our fault. It's driven by a culture that tells us, over and over again and in so many different ways, that we need to hover over our kids to ensure that they stay safe and that they can succeed. Some of us might even live in communities in which granting kids certain freedoms is against the law. Parents have, for instance, been arrested for letting kids play alone in a park. (Thankfully, laws that allow kids to play unsupervised have now been introduced in eight states.)

Still, even when it's legal to let your kids do things, social pressures can be hard to shrug off—so one helpful strategy is to find other families in your community who also value kids' independence. "You need a posse," Skenazy told me. You're much more likely to feel comfortable transgressing social norms if you can find other people bucking the trends, too.

The good news is that parental anxiety eases with practice: The more independence you give your kids, the more comfortable you typically become with it. The first time I let my daughter flip pancakes on the griddle, I was terrified that she'd burn herself, and I'm sure I reminded her approximately 842 times to be careful. Likewise, the first time I let my daughter walk from school to my office alone, I checked my watch every thirty seconds and wondered how long I should wait before going out to look for her. But once she'd accomplished these feats a few times, I noticed that my anxiety eased.

Remember, too, that our children's independence doesn't *always* make our lives easier—but that it's still important for them even when it's unpleasant for us. As Michelle Icard wrote in her book *Fourteen Talks by Age Fourteen*, parents might imagine an independent tween as one who cooks themselves breakfast and does their own laundry—but it can also look like a tween who argues against curfews, closes themselves off in their rooms, and watches adult shows on Netflix. But even these less-than-ideal (to our eyes) forms of autonomy are developmentally important.

"When we don't give kids a chance to test their independence, we deny them the opportunity to practice—and practice is what leads to maturity," Icard wrote.

4. Teach your kids to self-advocate.

To handle certain kinds of challenging situations, kids also need to be able to speak up for themselves and problem-solve. If another kid is playing too roughly with them on the playground, they need to know how to express their boundaries—and if that doesn't work, they need to know how to ask an adult for help. Managing discomfort often involves recognizing your own agency—the fact that you can do something to make the situation better or easier. When kids recognize that they have some power, they become more resilient.

What if you have a kid who's not inclined to self-advocate? My friend Shelly recently told me a story involving her daughter, Anna. Soon after Anna started the second grade, Shelly noticed that she always sprinted down the driveway in the afternoon after getting off the school bus. She then invariably rushed into the bathroom without stopping to say hi. It was clear to Shelly that Anna always really, really needed to pee, so one day, Shelly asked her about it.

"I have never gone to the bathroom at school," Anna confessed to her. "I don't know where the bathroom is, and I'm too scared to ask." It's heartbreaking to imagine eight-year-olds enduring long days at school with full bladders because they don't have the confidence or skills to advocate for themselves. How can we help children like this overcome their fears?

Melissa Giglio, a clinical psychologist who specializes in working with kids with various disorders, including anxiety and mood disorders, said that parents can start by pointing out when their kids make brave choices. Maybe you say, *It was so brave when you said "excuse me" on the bus*, or *It was so brave when you asked your counselor where to put your backpack*. If your child rarely if ever speaks up for themselves, you can start by commending them for other kinds of bravery, like *Congratulations on being brave enough to get through your first day of school!* Once your kid starts to self-identify as courageous, they are often more likely to take risks in other areas, too.

Another tactic Giglio recommends is role-playing. If your child is having trouble speaking up in a particular kind of situation, act it out at home so they can practice. "We want them to be able to learn things that they can say, so that should an incident happen, they have something in their toolbox to pull from," Giglio explained. If they've said it before, even just at home with you, they'll have an easier time saying it to someone else. "Then they can feel good about themselves—that they were able to do something in the moment."

Finally—and this one is tough for me—we should model self-advocacy in front of our kids. If someone cuts in front of you in line at the drugstore when you're with your child, try to speak up for yourself. And if you don't, at least bring it up later—*I really should have said something to that lady, but I got flustered in the moment. What do you think I could have said to her? What could I do next time?*

5. Be supportive—but don't try to "fix" your kids' feelings or coddle them.

One thing that is clear from the research on resilience is that supportive relationships are essential for helping people bounce back from hardship. "Whenever there's evidence of resilience, you can always identify at least one very important relationship that was critical," Shonkoff said in the podcast *The Brain Architects*. "You can't become resilient yourself. You can't will yourself to be resilient. You have to be able to be supported by at least one nurturing relationship."

Such relationships are also crucial for kids' mental health. In a 2022 study, researchers investigated the link between parenting practices and the mental health of sixteen- to eighteen-year-olds, finding that teens whose parents were warm and nurturing—who, for instance, supported them when they were upset—were better at regulating their own emotions and had fewer symptoms of mental illness. Social support likely helps kids for a number of reasons, including by buffering physiological and neurological responses to stressful experiences.

Often, it's a close parent-child relationship that fosters resilience, but friendships can do it, too. (For more on helping kids foster healthy friendships, see chapter 6.) In one small but fascinating study, researchers recruited college students who happened to be passing by a steep hill. They had the students put on heavy backpacks and asked them to estimate the hill's slant in degrees. Some of the students were alone, while others were with a friend. The students who were with friends estimated the hill as being less steep than students who were alone, and the length of time the friends knew each other mattered: Students who had been friends longer perceived the hill as less daunting than those who were with newer friends.

Based on their findings, the researchers surmised that people who go through life without close, supportive relationships "will live in a world where hills are steeper, distances greater, precipices deeper, and other kinds of physical challenges more daunting and demanding."

What does being a supportive parent entail? One thing we know is helpful is to validate kids' feelings. I will never, ever understand why my toddlers turned into demons whenever I closed the car door for them, but in the moment, I always tried to bite my tongue and acknowledge their feelings rather than admonish them. (Some days were more successful than others.) When we listen intently to our kids and respond with affirmations like *Wow, that sounds really frustrating*, or *Ouch, that must have hurt*, we tell our kids that we hear them and believe them. "When people hear you and they say they understand you, you feel trusted, you feel cared for, you feel connected," said Princeton University psychologist Razia Sahi when I interviewed her for a story for *The New York Times*. And then you're better able to cope with your feelings and move on.

What if kids' feelings seem exaggerated or are followed by unreasonable demands? First, it's important to keep in mind that what appears to be no big deal to us can really, truly feel like a big deal to our kids. My kids used to have epic meltdowns when I would cut a sandwich the "wrong" way or peel their banana when they wanted to do it themselves, and they'd often demand a replacement. In these situations, we can both validate their feelings (*Oh, I peeled your banana and you are mad because you wanted to peel it yourself!*) and also not give in to their demands (*But I am not going to give you a new banana. You can either eat this one, or I can save it for later*).

One thing that is often very tempting for parents—but ultimately not very helpful for kids—is trying to "fix" or gloss over children's feelings. When my kids hurt themselves or come to me feeling sad, I often want to tell them things like *You're okay*, or *Chin up, it's not that bad*. I desperately want them to feel better, and I assume that pretending that they are okay will help them get there. But these kinds of responses can, paradoxically, make kids feel even worse, because they minimize or dismiss—when, more than anything else, kids want to be heard and understood.

Sometimes kids struggle with feelings so powerful that these feelings start to get in the way of their daily lives. In these situations, it may be helpful to consult with a professional or to try cognitive behavioral therapy (CBT) techniques at home. CBT involves helping kids develop cognitive and behavioral strategies to recognize and respond to distorted patterns of thinking. I used to talk to my daughter, who struggled with social anxiety, about her "worry brain," explaining that her worry brain was telling her stories that weren't true. She would then use her "thinking brain" to talk back to it and put the worries in their place. I found the *Coping Cat* workbook helpful for introducing kids and parents to CBT strategies for anxiety.

6. Set and enforce rules and limits.

A few years ago, child-development specialist Claire Lerner began working with the parents of a four-and-a-half-year-old boy. The parents were at their wits' end because their son was fully potty-trained at school but demanded their assistance every time he went to the bathroom at home. Clearly, he had the skills to do it all by himself but still, for some reason, craved his parents' help.

The parents had tried asking him nicely. They tried logic. They tried bribery. They tried rewards. Nothing seemed to work—and the harder they tried, the more he dug in his heels.

It's tempting in this situation to think, *Fine, I'll just continue to help him, it's not a big deal*—but in doing so, his parents would actually be holding him back, because they'd be reinforcing his belief that he couldn't or shouldn't go to the bathroom on his own. So Lerner suggested that, instead, his parents should set and hold clear limits, saying something like this: *It's our job to ensure that you do all the amazing things you're able to do as a four-and-a-half-year-old. Going to the bathroom is one of those things, so we're not going to help you anymore. It's your job. And it's totally fine if you don't like it. But this is our new rule.*

Of course, at first, the boy didn't like it. He said, *I'm never going to go the potty!* Lerner, thankfully, saw this coming and advised his parents to reply with something like, *Okay, well, it's your body—you'll have to figure out what to do.* The idea is not to ignore your child's pleas but also not to give in. (Putting the ball into his court, and having him decide how to handle it, also builds confidence, Lerner said.)

Eventually, the little boy did go to the bathroom by himself at home, yet he made it clear he was not happy about it. In typical angry-kid fashion, he banged the bathroom stool and opened and slammed the bathroom cabinets. But within two days, the rage eased, Lerner said, and then he started getting dressed by himself, too. "I see this all the time—they have such a good feeling that they are taking care of themselves. And that's when you see that it's a gift," she explained.

Put another way: Our job is not to make our kids feel safe all the time. "Our job," she said, "is to help our kids feel really good about their ability to take care of themselves."

On the most basic level, when we enforce limits with our kids, we allow them to experience and tolerate discomfort. "The limit enables the child to be more flexible," Lerner said. After all, if you're always giving in to your child's demands, they are never going to learn how to tolerate frustration—which, let's face it, is an inevitable part of life. (That said, rules and limits can affect some kids differently. Neurodiverse children and kids with other developmental differences may have different needs and may benefit from different structures and strategies.)

Sometimes kids reject limits because they are afraid that if they become too independent, they will lose their parents' love and support. So it can also help to reassure kids that you will always love them and be there for them, no matter how old they get or how many things they can do on their own.

What if a limit involves asking a child to do something that, in the end, they actually *can* refuse to do? In these situations, Lerner said, it's helpful to figure out how to stay in charge of the outcome. With older kids, you may have to get creative.

Let's say your rule is that your child needs to get dressed on their own every morning. This is tricky because you can't *force* your child to dress themselves. But what you can do is to offer choices that encourage your kid to adhere to the rule or limit. Perhaps you tell them they can either dress themselves before school or go to school in their pajamas and bring clothes to change into. "You can say: *If you choose not to get yourself dressed, no problem—we'll put some clothes in your backpack, you can go to school in what you're wearing, and if you change your mind, you can change at school,*" Lerner suggested. "Within two days, the kids are getting themselves dressed. And, by the way, they feel amazing."

These same kinds of limits can be applied in many settings. If your kid is afraid to take swimming lessons or refuses to go to school, the limit might be that they have to go (but, of course, you can do things to help them feel more comfortable). "You're not ignoring your child's feelings—you're just saying, *I know this feels uncomfortable, but it's an activity that needs to happen,*" Lerner explained. By helping them work through their fears, you allow them to recognize that they are more capable than they realized.

And again: It's okay if they resist. It's okay if they don't like your rule. "That's one of my mantras to parents—this is going to get worse before it gets better," Lerner said. "They are going to use all the tools in their tool kit to derail the process." They will pull at your heartstrings and make you feel like you're being a terrible, horrible, no good, very bad parent—they want to avoid discomfort, which, fair! Don't we all? Just remind yourself—over and over again, if you need to—that sometimes, what feels loving and kind isn't actually what your child needs in order to grow.

KEY POINTS

1. Many kids today avoid challenges or struggle to persevere in the face of them. Overprotective, achievement-oriented parenting is a contributing factor.
2. Parents should ensure that kids have ample free playtime. Don't meddle!
3. Encourage a growth mindset and don't overemphasize outcomes and achievement.
4. Let kids do things on their own.
5. Accept and validate your kids' feelings, and don't try to "fix" or dismiss them.
6. Set and enforce rules and limits.

3

"Everyone Else Is Doing It."

Preventing Substance Use and Addiction

One day during the pandemic, while attending school over Zoom, the kindergarten son of an acquaintance of mine was learning about the food pyramid—which foods fall into which nutrient categories and so on. Suddenly, and very excitedly, the boy unmuted himself to share a tidbit about his family: "Beer has protein in it," he said, "and my parents eat *lots* of beer!"

If you're a parent who drinks alcohol or occasionally dabbles in recreational drugs—or even if you're a teetotaler—you may have more than a little angst about how to raise kids who make smart choices regarding substances. How do we help our kids understand that some drugs are extremely dangerous, while others may not totally deserve their bad reputation, at least if we use them responsibly? How do we ensure that they learn that certain substances might be safe in small amounts for adults but not for kids, while others aren't safe for anyone, no matter how little is consumed?

Before I delve into this somewhat stressful topic, I want to start with the good news: Far fewer kids and teens are now using drugs and alcohol than they used to. In 1997, the year I graduated from high school, 50 percent of US twelfth graders had reported ever using marijuana, 82 percent had reported ever drinking alcohol, and 30 percent had reported ever using an illicit drug other than marijuana (such as cocaine, heroin, methamphetamines, inhalants like poppers, or hallucinogens). In 2022, by contrast, only 38 percent of high school seniors had reported ever using marijuana and 62 percent had reported ever drinking alcohol. A mere 13 percent said they'd ever used other illicit drugs.

But—is anything about parenting easy?—the picture is not entirely rosy, either. Fentanyl, an incredibly potent synthetic opioid drug that now often taints street drugs, has made it extremely dangerous for kids to dabble in pretty much anything. Between 2019 and 2023, the number of US adolescents who died from drug overdoses more than doubled, and these increases were mainly due to fentanyl. The Drug Enforcement Administration (DEA) reported that in 2022, six out of every ten counterfeit prescription pills they seized contained lethal doses of fentanyl. Many teens have died from fentanyl overdoses after buying what they thought was Xanax, Adderall, or Percocet from friends or dealers.

And although teens are using fewer drugs than they used to, rates of substance use are still worryingly high, especially among affluent adolescents. In work published in 2019, the psychologist Suniya Luthar and her colleagues reported that young women who had attended what they called "high-achieving" high schools—schools with high test scores whose students often attend elite universities—were three times more likely than other young women to be diagnosed with drug or alcohol dependence at the age of twenty-six. Young men who attended these schools were twice as likely to be diagnosed as other men. Luthar and her colleagues have argued that stress, anxiety, and depression, propelled by parental pressures to achieve, drive these kids to self-medicate.

When I hear all these numbers, my brain starts reeling. The question that streams like endless ticker tape through my brain is this: *How can I keep my kids safe?* Thankfully, science illuminates what parents can do, and some of it is surprising. Here's what you need to know.

Why Kids Use—and What Can Happen

First, I want to explain why teens often use alcohol and drugs, and why even experimenting can be dangerous. This isn't to say that all kids who dabble will go on to develop problems, by any means—but there are complicating factors all parents should know.

As you know if you've ever encountered one, tweens and teens are unique and wonderful creatures. And they are often getting themselves into trouble. Teens are more likely than adults over twenty-five to binge drink, smoke cigarettes, have casual and unprotected sex, and get into car crashes. That's in large part because of changes their brains undergo during adolescence, which prime them to take risks. But despite what you may have heard, teens don't take more risks because they think about risk in fundamentally different ways than adults do, because they think they are immortal, or because they are incapable of rational thinking. Instead, their attraction to risk stems from biochemical changes in the brain.

Researchers believe that teens value novel and risky experiences because of changes that occur around puberty that affect the brain's reward circuitry and make such experiences especially enjoyable. As for why these brain shifts occur, they may be an adaptive evolutionary relic—perhaps our adolescent ancestors who took more risks were more likely to survive. Maybe risk-takers were more likely to procure food. Researchers have also theorized that risk-taking, especially for young males, was linked in the past to social dominance, which may have made the trait especially attractive to women, ensuring that these men would reproduce and pass on those risk-taking genes. (We all know the trope that girls are attracted to "bad boys," and there is, in fact, research supporting this phenomenon. See also: action movie heroes, who always take insane risks and are, inevitably, heartthrobs.)

It's important to keep in mind that the teen proclivity toward risk-taking isn't all bad in today's world. Risks can have negative consequences, but they also have positive ones. The attraction to risk encourages teens to try new, hard, and potentially beneficial things, whether they're AP classes, school musical auditions, or peaceful protests.

But, of course, this penchant for risk-taking can lead teens down dangerous roads (sometimes quite literally), too. One thing we know is that teens take more risks when they're around their peers. Teens are much more likely to get into serious car accidents when other teens are in the car with them, and they are more likely to be sexually active when their peers are (and even when they just *think* their peers are). This trend has important implications for alcohol and drug use, because substances are often offered in social situations, where kids are primed to take the most chances.

Making matters worse, animal studies suggest that substances don't affect adolescents in the same ways they affect adults—and that these differences could prime adolescents to continue using. Alcohol's sedative effects seem to be more subdued in teens compared with adults, which means teens who drink feel less tired and are more likely to feel a pleasant and energetic "buzz." Adolescent hangovers also aren't as bad as adult hangovers, and they resolve more quickly, which means that teens are less likely to wake up in agony and promise themselves that they will never, ever drink again.

Teen brains are especially vulnerable to damage from substance use, too. A little bit of experimentation with, say, alcohol or marijuana likely won't do much harm, but research suggests that regular use can have devastating consequences. Alcohol damages cells in various parts of the brain, leading to long-term memory problems and impaired decision-making.

Marijuana is also not as innocuous as it used to be. "The cannabis of today is a totally different drug than it was just a couple of decades ago," said Danielle Dick, the director of the Rutgers Addiction Research Center. Back in 1980, pot typically contained about 3 percent THC, whereas today's pot can be as high as 30 percent THC—ten times stronger.

Yet research on marijuana hasn't caught up with these momentous shifts. Most scientists studying cannabis have been able to procure only low-THC samples for research purposes, Dick said, so there's a lot we don't yet know about today's pot and what it does to the adolescent brain. Still, the research we do have suggests that regular pot smoking can have profound effects on memory and motivation, and Dick said that kids who use cannabis regularly also become somewhat indifferent to its effects over time. "One of the symptoms of using too much is not caring about how it's harming your life," she said.

The other thing that's important to note is that there is some truth to the so-called gateway hypothesis—kids who dabble in cigarettes, marijuana, or alcohol early in adolescence are indeed more likely than other kids to use harder drugs later in adolescence. The good news, however, is that the trend does not seem to persist through adulthood—meaning that kids who use gateway drugs are not more likely than other kids to use illicit substances once they've become adults.

Fentanyl is another drug that can pose tremendous risks—and there are a lot of misconceptions about how teens get exposed to it. Fentanyl is a synthetic opioid drug that is about fifty times stronger than heroin and one hundred times stronger than morphine. It's often used in outpatient surgeries, because it works quickly and its effects rapidly wear off. But its extreme potency means that even slight dosage errors can cause the heart to stop.

"One grain of salt is the size of the actual active ingredient in a fentanyl pill. And if there's, like, two grains, it can kill you," explained Jonathan Pettigrew, a researcher at Arizona State University who studies the science of substance use prevention. Whereas heroin overdoses can take minutes to hours and thus can often be intercepted, lethal fentanyl overdoses can take seconds to minutes—and there's no undoing them.

Many parents assume that kids encounter fentanyl only if they're doing "hard" drugs like heroin or cocaine, but that's not true: Many kids die from fentanyl overdoses after taking what they thought were prescription drugs. The internet—and more specifically, social media—is teeming with drug dealers who sell teens what they claim are Xanax, Adderall, oxycodone, and Percocet, but which are actually fentanyl pills.

If fentanyl doesn't kill you, it can instead quickly lead to dependence. As Caleb Banta-Green, the director of the University of Washington Center for Community-Engaged Drug Education, Epidemiology and Research, told me when I interviewed him for a story I wrote for *The New York Times*, fentanyl "makes you feel really good. And then it goes away really quickly, and you have to use it again and again and again."

Protecting Our Kids from Substance Abuse

If this all feels terrifying, I get it—I think so, too. But it's less scary when you keep in mind that we do have power as parents when it comes to protecting our kids from substance use. Yes, it's true that teens are prone to risk-taking and that they often value the perspective of their peers more than their parents. But this doesn't mean that parents don't matter. The conversations we have with our kids, the limits and rules we set, and the behaviors we model really do make a difference.

"Parents maintain an influence over their kids all through their teenage years," Pettigrew told me. "And most teenagers, according to research, still look to their parents for advice and for guidance, and respect what they have to say about drugs."

Here are four key science-backed ways you can help keep your kids substance-free.

1. Have frequent and direct drug conversations with your kids from a young age.

Parents really don't like talking to kids about drugs. Perhaps it's because we don't think they're old enough or we believe that the topic will overwhelm or confuse them. Maybe we worry that discussing drugs will make them even *more* likely to use. Or, possibly, we think we don't know how to talk about drugs in an age-appropriate way.

I get it. I'd rather hear my kid drone on and on about his favorite YouTuber (a regular experience I do not, by the way, enjoy) than bring up the dangers of fentanyl. But the research clearly shows that conversations about drugs are crucial for preventing substance use in kids, and that certain kinds of conversations are more helpful than others.

When kids are young—we're talking toddlers, preschoolers, and those in early elementary school—we should start by having broad conversations around building healthy habits. We can explain that we do certain things—brush teeth, drink milk, and get enough sleep—so that our bodies stay happy and grow strong. We should connect our choices to potential outcomes by explaining that, for instance, we brush our teeth so that we don't develop cavities.

As kids get older—and certainly by early middle school—parents should also start having regular and explicit conversations about drugs and alcohol. The "explicit" part is important, because research finds that many parents make indirect comments to communicate their opinions about substance use without connecting the dots, and that kids don't benefit from such vague references.

Here's an example: You're watching a movie with your kid that shows a man drinking alcohol and getting into the driver's seat of his car. You say to your child: *That guy's an idiot*. Clearly your intention is to communicate to your child that you don't think drinking and driving is okay, but your child may not understand what you're referring to. It's far better to be more detailed and direct: *That man just drank a lot of alcohol, and now he's planning to drive. You can't drive safely after you've been drinking, so this is a dangerous choice, both for him and for the other drivers he could hurt. Drinking and driving is never okay.*

Also, the kinds of warnings parents provide really matter. While there's nothing wrong with talking about how drugs affect the brain or discussing the broad harms of drugs, experts told me it can be more effective to instead help kids understand how their daily lives would be affected by drugs. Consider the infamous school-based program known as Drug Abuse Resistance Education, or DARE, which was implemented in many US schools in the eighties and nineties. In this program, police officers lectured students about what various drugs were and what their effects were. Unfortunately, these programs largely didn't deter kids from using.

What seems to help more is to focus on kids' choices and their immediate consequences, creating what Pettigrew refers to as an "implication wheel." You might say something like: *If you drink alcohol, how might that affect your soccer playing? What might it do to your relationships with your friends? What about that guy you like? If I caught you drinking, what would happen then?*

Also, try not to think about drug conversations as "one and done" lectures. "This isn't something where you can just say, *Okay, we're going to sit down when you're fourteen, and we're going to talk about the harms of alcohol*, and then you never speak about it again. Eliciting an ongoing conversation is important," said Melissa Cox, a behavioral scientist who studies teen alcohol use at the University of North Carolina Gillings School of Global Public Health. And make it a two-way conversation rather than a lecture. Ask your kids questions about what they've seen or heard and explain that you're always happy to answer questions, no matter what they are.

Fearmongering—saying things like *Even if you smoke pot only once, your brain will forever be damaged*, or *If you drive drunk, you'll get in a car crash and die* isn't particularly useful, either, Cox said. Among other things, kids may be able to tell you're exaggerating and then be less likely to trust whatever else you say. It's far better to convey risks accurately—which, to be fair, for something like fentanyl, can sound a whole lot like fearmongering. Everyone I talked to said that it's totally fine to be honest with kids about the very serious risks of prescription pills that aren't procured directly from a reputable pharmacy—that one pill could kill you in seconds and that you should never, ever accept pills from friends or strangers. But with other, less immediately dangerous drugs, stick to the facts rather than trying to stoke fear.

It's also extremely helpful to teach kids refusal skills. "Talk about potential excuses that they could use," Pettigrew said. With his kids, he has talked through various things they could say to their peers after being offered drugs or alcohol. Like: *No, I can't do that, because I'm running cross-country this semester*, or *Oh gosh, my dad would kill me.*

2. Be warm and nurturing, but set rules and limits.

Although it's important to directly and explicitly talk to kids about drugs and alcohol, how we broadly engage with our kids matters, too. Parenting style—the emotional climate parents create that shapes their attitudes toward, expectations of, and interactions with their children—has been repeatedly linked to kids' propensity toward substance use.

The researcher who popularized the concept of parenting style and conducted some of its most seminal research is Diana Baumrind, a clinical and developmental psychologist at the University of California, Berkeley. She, and others after her, spent decades observing parents and determined that most parents fall into one of four broad categories:

1. **Authoritarian parents** believe in a strong family hierarchy. They are typically strict and not very warm or respectful with their kids. They are often coercive and quick to punish and may shame their kids in order to control them. These are the parents who bark *Because I said so!* when their kid asks why they have to do their homework before checking TikTok.

2. **Permissive parents** are essentially the opposite of authoritarian: They consider kids and parents to be close to equals. They let their children make most of their own decisions without setting many expectations or limits.

3. **Authoritative parents** (the similarity of the word to "authoritarian" drives me bananas!) are a somewhat in-between, Goldilocks category. These parents treat their kids with warmth and respect but also set limits and rules.

4. **Neglectful parents** are precisely what you think they are: parents who are barely involved in their children's lives and only accommodate basic needs.

Research has shown that children of authoritative (not authoritarian!) parents tend to fare the best on many fronts: Compared to kids raised under the other parenting styles, they perform better in school, are more mentally healthy, take fewer risks, and are the most compassionate. (It's important to note, though, that much of the research on parenting style was conducted among white families from Westernized countries, so the effects of parenting styles may vary in different cultures and contexts.)

Baumrind also studied which parenting styles specifically protect against substance use, and again, authoritative parenting came out on top. In a 1991 paper, she observed and interviewed 139 middle-class kids and their parents over the course of eleven years, starting when they were four and until they were fifteen. Based on what she observed, she concluded that authoritative parents are "remarkably successful in protecting their adolescents from problem drug use."

Other, more recent research has supported Baumrind's findings.

In 2014, researchers evaluated teen substance use among nearly eight thousand white European adolescents as well as their parents' parenting styles. They found that teens who had authoritative and permissive parents were less likely to use alcohol, tobacco, and illegal drugs than kids with authoritarian or neglectful parents. In a separate review of forty-four published research studies on the topic, researchers concluded that "the authoritative style is the most protective."

The point here is that it's helpful to set limits and expectations with your kids—more on how to do that in a minute—while also treating them with warmth and respect.

3. Communicate rules and expectations—yet don't be overly controlling.

Let's dig into the "limits and expectations" part a little bit more. Researchers have teased out some of the key aspects of authoritative parenting that seem to matter for substance use, and one key takehome is that it's important to set clear rules and expectations.

For instance, a 2020 study found that adolescents were less likely to consume alcohol in the future when their parents had set strict rules about drinking—and that those teens were also less likely to use tobacco and marijuana. Another study found that, in the Netherlands, overall teen alcohol use dropped precipitously after about 2003, which coincided with a series of mass media campaigns encouraging parents to set strict rules with their kids surrounding alcohol use.

I want to address a common parental misconception, which is that making alcohol less of a forbidden fruit at home can keep kids healthier. Many parents believe—and understandably so—that letting kids try sips or glasses of wine or beer at home will help them learn how to drink responsibly, reducing the risk that they will drink to excess with friends. The idea is that if alcohol becomes less of a "forbidden fruit," kids might not over-imbibe, and it's rooted in the notion that kids in Europe, where drinking at home is sanctioned, develop healthier relationships with alcohol than American kids do.

Unfortunately, this approach is not supported by the science. "The research does not at all support the idea that letting kids try alcohol, or making it less forbidden, reduces the likelihood that they're going to use or they're going to use in risky ways," Dick said. "In fact, it supports the opposite."

The truth is, European kids do have serious problems with alcohol—more so in many countries than kids in the US. Moreover, studies have found that the more teens drink with their parents, the more they drink with their friends—and the earlier kids drink, the more likely they are to develop problems with alcohol. One study conducted by Kristina Jackson and her colleagues at Brown University's Center for Alcohol and Addiction Studies found that kids who admitted to having had sips of alcohol—but not even a full drink—by the sixth grade were, compared to non-sippers, nearly 5 times as likely to have gotten drunk and 2.6 times as likely to have used other drugs by the time they were in the ninth grade.

"I have yet to see a paper that has said that parental allowance of early drinking, even at a sip, is protective," Cox said.

What substance use prevention researchers advocate for instead are "no tolerance" rules—telling kids that they are not allowed to drink or use drugs until they are legally sanctioned. And keep in mind that you can set clear expectations and *also* tell your kids that if they ever make a mistake with substances and need help, they can and should call you.

"No tolerance" rules are useful for cannabis, too, by the way. To be clear, a bit of marijuana probably isn't going to hurt your teen. But when parents allow kids to use marijuana at home—some parents even smoke *with* their teens—they often send a message of permissiveness that could ultimately set kids up for problems.

As Dick explained to me, two key factors shape whether kids will develop issues with substances: how accepted the substances are, and how available they are. The legalization of marijuana around the country, combined with increasing permissiveness at home, check off both of these boxes and have led to an escalation of regular cannabis use among teens. Recent data suggest that one in fifteen high school seniors smokes pot daily—a worrying statistic considering that marijuana is much stronger than it used to be and that regular use of even the mild stuff can affect young people's brains.

This all said, research suggests that being overly controlling with kids can backfire, too. There's a fine line between enforcing age-appropriate rules, like *It's not okay to drink before you're twenty-one*, and giving kids very little autonomy overall, which can actually make them more likely to drink and use drugs. In other words, both not having rules and having too many rules are associated with bad outcomes. Did I mention parenting is hard?

The kinds of rules that cause problems, researchers find, are the ones that prevent kids from doing age-appropriate things. In a 2013 study, Dutch researchers followed 2,230 teens over a period of six years, asking them questions about their substance use and how their parents treated them at home. The parenting behavior that was most strongly tied to regular alcohol use in those teens was overprotectiveness, in that adolescents who reported that their parents wouldn't let them to do things that their classmates were allowed to do were more likely to drink in the future than teens whose parents granted them autonomy and independence.

Here's a more specific example of this phenomenon in action. In a study published in 2018, researchers at Brown, Dartmouth, and East Carolina University surveyed nearly one thousand American kids between the ages of eleven and fifteen about whether their parents let them watch PG, PG-13, or R-rated movies. Then, one and two years later, they asked the same kids whether they had started using alcohol or marijuana.

Perhaps unsurprisingly, the researchers found that teens whose parents successfully restricted R-rated movies were less likely to use alcohol and marijuana a year later than kids who were allowed to watch R-rated movies. (This makes sense because drugs and alcohol are often portrayed positively in R-rated movies.) Here's the fascinating part, though: The researchers found that kids whose parents restricted PG-13 movies as well as R movies were *more* likely, a year later, to use marijuana than teens whose parents restricted R movies but allowed their kids to watch PG-13 movies.

Why? We can't say for certain. But the researchers have a hunch: Adolescents may perceive the restriction of PG-13 films to be excessive control, which they respond to with rebellious acts such as using marijuana. In other words, while some rules and limits are protective, having too many can backfire, causing kids to want to rebel in various ways—including, possibly, by using drugs.

How can we find the appropriate middle ground? We should absolutely set age-appropriate limits to keep our kids safe—such as by saying *No alcohol until you're twenty-one*—while also explaining the rationale behind them so that our kids can understand that our rules are in the service of keeping them safe and healthy. "It helps them to feel like, *Oh, they're doing this because they want the best for me, they love me,*" Cox said.

We should also give our kids the freedom to think and act

independently in areas where the stakes are lower. We should let them take ownership of their schoolwork (and make mistakes). We should give autonomy in terms of their friendships and how they spend their free time (within reason). If we don't give kids the autonomy they crave, they will find ways to take it for themselves—perhaps by rebelling in ways that put them at risk.

4. Model healthy habits and be open about substance-use issues that run in the family.

Kids learn a lot from what they see us do, not merely from what we say. If we want to minimize the chance that our kids will use substances, we have to consider the messages that our own substance use sends our kids. If we drink or smoke a lot, especially in front of our children, they may assume that drinking and smoking are perfectly okay for them to do, too.

This doesn't mean you have to be a teetotaler. Although the research conflicts on this issue, some studies suggest that when parents drink in moderation, and especially when they talk to their kids about drinking and set alcohol-related rules, their kids are no more likely to drink than kids whose parents don't drink at all. Other research has found that moderate parental drinking in and of itself isn't a huge risk factor for kids' substance use but that risks go up when parents regularly drink in front of their kids or when they ask their kids to bring or make them drinks. And, as I already mentioned, teens are more likely to become problem drinkers when their parents allow them to drink at home with them. (There is less research on how parental cannabis use affects teen cannabis use, but some research does find that when parents use marijuana, their kids are more likely to use marijuana, too.)

What if your kids ask you if you drank or used drugs when you were young and you did? You have several options. "You can certainly say to your child, *You know what? We're talking about you, we're not talking about me,*" Dick said. Or you can be honest but include some caveats. If you used drugs or alcohol in your youth, you can tell your kids the truth—but add that we now know a lot more about how substances harm kids' brains, and if you'd had that knowledge then, you might have done things differently. Point out, too, that due to the internet and social media, it's a lot easier today for kids' bad choices to be documented and used against them. And that drugs are much more dangerous now because of fentanyl.

What if they ask you if you smoke marijuana now and you do? Again, there is no one "right" answer, and what you say may depend on various factors, such as how much you use, whether pot is legal where you live, and how old your kids are. If you decide to be honest, be sure to explain that there's a body of research showing that occasional use among adults—unlike among kids and teens—doesn't cause harm and that you use marijuana only when you know and trust the source. Then reiterate your expectations for your kids and why they exist.

If you or someone else in your extended family has had a substance-use disorder, "absolutely, you should share that information with your kids," Dick advised. Since 40 to 60 percent of a person's risk for addiction is shaped by their genetic makeup, this information directly impacts children. If you had heart disease, you'd want your kids to know because they might want to make lifestyle changes to minimize their risk. The same is true for addiction.

One thing to keep in mind about the genes that confer an increased risk for addiction is that they don't always shape how a person *responds* to drugs. Some of these genes increase risk in more indirect ways: They may influence how strongly teens are drawn to risk-taking or sensation-seeking behaviors, or they may increase the chance that teens will develop anxiety or depression, both of which increase the risk for substance use later in adolescence and in early adulthood, Dick said.

How should you broach the subject? You could say something like this: *Aunt Ida struggled with alcohol. Part of what causes people to develop problems with substances is rooted in the genes they have inherited. This means you could also be at increased risk, so you are going to need to be extra careful about how you use substances. This is information that's important for you to have so you can make the best choices for yourself.* Be careful with your language so as not to imply that substance use is a moral failing. As one therapist suggested to me, it can help to talk about the fact that people may struggle with addiction in part because they are trying to cope with big feelings or problems but aren't able to do it in the most constructive way.

There's so much unfair stigma attached to substance-use disorders, and we also don't want to scare our kids—so it's understandable to want to omit or hide potentially worrisome information. But consider that the more you share, the more your kids will know about the potential harms of substance use and the more control they will have over their future. Knowledge, as they say, is power.

KEY POINTS

1. Know that kids use fewer substances than they used to, but the risks associated with many drugs are now higher.
2. Parents should have regular, explicit conversations with kids about drugs and alcohol. Discuss how substance use could affect their current lives. Teach refusal skills.
3. Be a warm and respectful parent but set rules and expectations surrounding substance use. Grant your kids age-appropriate autonomy in other areas.
4. Don't let kids drink or use drugs at home.
5. Share details about substance-use challenges that run in the family.

4

"I Have Too Much to Do!"

Helping Kids Recognize When to Rest, Relax, Have Fun—and Quit

When I was a teenager, my life was a how-to manual for how *not* to cultivate a healthy work/life balance. From ninth through the twelfth grade, I attended a boarding school in New Hampshire, and because I always got good grades and stayed out of trouble, I avoided the watchful eye of teachers and dormitory families.

None of them, as far as I know, understood the exhausting schedule I kept: I practiced the piano during every minute of free time I had during the day and evening until I had to check into my dorm at 10:00 p.m., at which point I finally started my homework, typically finishing around 2:00 a.m.

Then, I'd set my alarm for 5:00 a.m. so that I could get in a few hours of piano practice before 8:00 a.m. chapel. Yes, you read that right: I typically got about three hours of sleep a night—even on the weekends, because we also had Saturday classes.

I was also in the school orchestra, the school chorus, and two other singing groups, performed in plays, and regularly competed in state and regional piano competitions. I was under an enormous amount of self-induced pressure and stress, and I was chronically exhausted. My friends today laugh at me because I never "get" cultural references from the late 1990s—I never watched TV or went to movies during my boarding school years and rarely, if ever, listened to music unless it was classical. And, of course, maintaining a schedule like that, I had a pretty nonexistent social life.

As an adult, I've eased up on myself, but I still have workaholic, antisocial tendencies. Recently, I've spent a lot of time reflecting on why I did—and sometimes still do—hold myself to such unhealthy standards. To be honest, I'm still not entirely sure. But what I do know is that I do not want this kind of life for my kids. I do not want them to equate their self-worth with how much they accomplish. I want them to embrace leisure, fun, and rest, and to cultivate a healthy work/life balance.

This is, of course, easier said than done. During the 2018–2019 school year, Challenge Success, a nonprofit organization associated with Stanford University's Graduate School of Education, surveyed more than twenty-one thousand US students attending high-performing high schools. More than half said that a major stressor in their lives was a lack of time to play, relax, or be with friends and family, and nearly 60 percent lamented their lack of sleep. When Challenge Success resurveyed similar high school students two years later, in 2020, 56 percent said that their school-related stress had gotten even worse.

For kids from affluent families, many of whom grow up in achievement-oriented communities, this stress can be suffocating. As Jennifer Breheny Wallace, the author of the book *Never Enough*, told me when we once spoke over the phone: "For too many kids today, they feel like their childhood, their high school years, are just a means to an end."

For her book, Wallace interviewed teens and their families, discovering that the adolescents who truly thrived were those whose parents emphasized the importance of rest and recuperation. They did this by encouraging kids to pull back when they could, to be strategic about their efforts—sometimes it's wiser to put in 90 percent effort rather than 110 percent—and to find and cultivate healthy ways to relax in their downtime. She quoted the psychologist Lisa Damour, who describes the energy kids have available to expend during a week of school as a single tank of gas: "If you're flooring it on everything, you'll be running on fumes by Thursday."

Wallace also discovered through her interviews that when parents *fail* to cultivate this balance—when they push their kids to work ever harder and rarely encourage rest and relaxation—kids sometimes end up abusing substances. They may drink to the point of blackout because they don't know how to rest. Research conducted by psychologist Suniya Luthar has found that kids who attend what she called "high-achieving" schools—schools with high test scores and many extracurricular offerings—are more than six times as likely as other kids to be depressed and anxious and to use alcohol, marijuana, and other drugs. (For more on raising kids who make healthy choices regarding substances, see chapter 3.) That's because, according to Luthar, these kids are under what she has referred to as "unrelenting pressures to accomplish ever more."

Teaching Our Kids to Relax

So aren't leisure and rest things we should value, seek to understand—and ensure that our kids come to embrace? The answer to that is clearly yes. The answer to the follow-up question—how exactly do we do that?—is more complicated, but there are simple steps parents can take to help children adopt a wholesome, joyous approach to life.

1. Let your kids play—without adults—and find other families who do the same.

Plenty has been said in recent decades about the importance of play for kids. Heck, I wrote a feature about it for *Scientific American Mind* magazine back in 2009 titled "The Serious Need for Play," and I've already mentioned the value of play in earlier chapters. We know from research that play helps kids develop social skills, learn to problem-solve, and relieve stress, among other things. (For more on how play builds resilience, see chapter 2.)

But what I didn't know until recently is that play—and especially unstructured play without adult supervision—likely also helps kids grow into human beings who can embrace exploration and leisure throughout their lives.

When kids have ample time to play, they discover and develop a repertoire of activities they find enjoyable and rewarding, said Heather Gibson, a leisure researcher at the University of Florida. They might find they love singing or drawing or exploring in the woods. As they grow into adults, they draw from this library they established in childhood. Adults who had ample play experiences as kids, in other words, have an easier time figuring out how to enjoy their free time. "That foundation from early childhood is actually very, very important," Gibson said. In a 2014 study, adults who reported having more opportunities for free and adventurous play during childhood were psychologically and physically healthier than adults who didn't play as much as kids.

It's important for children to continue to have playful experiences throughout their adolescence and young adulthood, too. "Curiosity, imagination, and creativity are like muscles: If you don't use them, you lose them," Tufts University child development expert David Elkind told me when I spoke to him for my article for *Scientific American Mind*. These changes can be observed within the brain: During adolescence, neuronal connections that aren't used get eliminated or "pruned." As one academic paper put it, "adolescent brains are primed to become hardwired for developing leisure activity preferences, setting the stage for continued participation throughout adulthood."

When kids *do* play these days, that play is often structured and organized—which is not always ideal. Kids play soccer, video games, and the saxophone, all of which are oriented around rules and structures determined by adults. These experiences are very different from unstructured free play. In a documentary filmed in 1975, Cornell child development expert Edward Devereux contrasted an organized Little League baseball game that took place in Auburn, New York, with a pickup baseball game that happened in Ithaca, New York. What is striking about the video is how much less engaged the Little League players were than the kids playing the pickup game, who, among other things, had to improvise and problem-solve throughout. They were in charge, which made the experience that much more engaging and fun.

Because many families prioritize structured play over free play (and academics and extracurriculars over rest), it may also help, as mentioned in chapter 2, to connect with families that share your values and consider rest and leisure a priority. Plus, then your kids will have other friends to play *with*.

2. Don't pressure kids to achieve.

If we reflect on why kids today often feel the need to do more and more and more, it makes sense to ask whether it's because they perceive that this is precisely what we want.

Consider all the ways in which we communicate to kids that their accomplishments matter. We hire tutors when their grades aren't high enough. We enroll them in SAT prep classes. We take them for ice cream after their games, but only if they scored. (My son had a school soccer coach who, he said, explicitly told them they would stop for dinner on the ride home only if they won.) We encourage kids to continue the extracurriculars they excel at and to drop the ones they don't.

In a 2014 Harvard University survey, researchers interviewed more than ten thousand middle and high school students from thirty-three diverse schools around the country. The students were asked which of the following was most important to them: achieving at a high level, happiness, or caring for others. Nearly half of the students chose "achievement." When asked what they thought *their parents* prioritized most, more than half of the students, again, chose "achievement." The students were also three times more likely to agree than disagree with the statement "My parents are prouder if I get good grades in my classes than if I'm a caring community member in class and school." As Amherst College sociologist Pawan Dhingra put it in his book *Hyper Education*, "Children are not simply too busy; their development is increasingly measured through their degree of skill accumulation."

When kids perceive that their parents care predominantly about achievement and skills, they tend to fare worse in a number of ways. In a 2017 study, researchers interviewed more than five hundred middle school students from affluent communities, giving them tests to evaluate their self-esteem, mental health, and behavior. They also asked the students to rank their parents' goals for them, giving them a range of options: being respectful to others, being kind, helping others in need, excelling academically, attending a good college, and having a successful career.

The kids who felt their parents valued achievement over caring for others had lower self-esteem and more psychological problems, and, ironically, performed worse in school than kids who felt their parents were less achievement-oriented. In a follow-up study published in 2020, researchers published findings suggesting that fathers' achievement-oriented expectations for kids are particularly harmful. (So, dads: Please ease up.)

Why do kids suffer under this kind of pressure? I'm sure there are many reasons. Kids end up exhausted and stressed, both of which undermine mental health. But beyond that, these kids may internalize dangerous messages about their self-worth. They may come to believe that their self-worth is a direct reflection of what they do, rather than who they are. They may start to measure themselves against external checklists rather than listening to and honoring their authentic selves. This, over time, can make them feel unhappy and unfulfilled.

Okay, but, you might be thinking, *I don't explicitly tell my kids that their grades, test scores, or achievements matter more than anything else, so none of this applies to me*. But here's the thing: The parents evaluated in these studies probably didn't explicitly say these things, either. Nevertheless, kids pick up on our priorities based on the subtle (and not so subtle) clues we give them.

When the first thing we ask our kids after arriving home from school is *How did your math test go?*, when we pay them for good grades, or when we email their science teachers to ask them to bump up their project grade, we inadvertently communicate to our kids that academics matter most. When we celebrate them more when they win the game, get the lead in the play, or win the award, and celebrate them less when they don't, we teach them that accomplishments matter most—and that their value stems from what they achieve.

How can we be sure to send our kids healthier messages? We can explicitly tell our kids that grades matter less to us than learning and engagement. We can comment on their sportsmanship rather than their performance. When they arrive home from school, we can say *Tell me something fun that happened today* rather than *Tell me how your social studies test went.*

We can also encourage our kids to enjoy themselves and to relax and commend them when they do. I'll admit, this one is tough for me: My teenage son is quite adept at relaxing. On Saturdays, he'll sometimes spend the entire day in his pajamas, reading or playing video games. I know his ability to chill is something I should appreciate—I sure wish I'd been more like him at thirteen!—but sometimes I find myself wanting to needle him to get up and do something productive, to tell him not to be lazy. *Get out of bed already, dude!* I have to remind myself the notions of rest and leisure as "lazy" are inaccurate and harmful—and that those same notions are what turned me into an overworked and exhausted teen myself.

3. Model healthy relaxation habits.

Perhaps the best way to encourage our kids to rest is by showing them that we make the time and effort to rest, too. On Sunday mornings, my kids' dad used to sit down to read the paper for several hours, and they would often join him with their copies of *The Week Junior.* I used to feel mild resentment toward him for taking this time for himself—I was almost always tidying up or doing laundry while he lounged—and then I realized that perhaps I should be more like him, rather than the other way around. He did plenty around the house at other times; it was actually a gift that he gave himself time to relax, and, moreover, wonderful that he did it in front of the kids, who were learning these values with him.

In a 2016 study, researchers surveyed South African eighth- to eleventh-grade students twice a year over the course of two to four years. They found that kids who spent more time in healthy leisure activities were less likely to use substances. The researchers argued that modeling from other adults in their lives likely played an important role on setting these kids down a healthy trajectory.

When we think about modeling rest and leisure, though, we need to be careful that we're not being performative (for our kids, for others, or even for ourselves). In her book *Real Self-Care*, psychiatrist Pooja Lakshmin discusses the concept of "faux self-care," which are the superficial choices we make to check off the boxes of self-care without actually tending to our needs. Going to a spin class because you feel like you should, or taking a bubble bath so you can feel like you did something for yourself, are two examples. Faux self-care often involves consumerism and consumption (classes, healthy foods, fancy bath salts), whereas real self-care is a product of reflection and meaningful change.

"Faux self-care is a method—in the moment, going for a run might improve your mood, but it does nothing to change the circumstances in your life that led you to feel drained, energy-less, or down," Lakshmin wrote. "On the other hand, the work of real self-care is about going deeper and identifying the core principles to guide decision-making."

So as you lean into leisure, reflect on and consider your values, needs, and wants. Taking care of yourself is not another checklist to complete but a process that requires recognizing and listening to your deepest needs and desires. (The desires part is crucial. So often, we attend only to our *needs* and dismiss our desires as superficial. But our kids are always watching, and we don't want them to internalize our sacrifices as sacrifices they need to make, too.)

As you engage in this process, it can also be helpful to talk to your kids about it. Explain that you are going to sit down to read the paper because you want to recuperate and do something relaxing. Before leaving for a walk, tell your kids you're going out because you want to enjoy the fresh air and need some alone time. If you ever take a weekend away with friends, explain that you're spending the weekend with friends because you want to have fun. (Every year, six friends of mine from graduate school meet at a different spot in North America for a long weekend, where we talk, read, and giggle more than I do the entire rest of the year.)

Put more simply, make deliberate choices about your time and consider how those choices reflect your values—and make those connections explicit to your kids.

4. Teach your kids it's okay to quit.

Another powerful—and pernicious—narrative in our culture is that quitting represents weakness and failure. Think about all the clichés: "Winners never quit," "Quitters never win," "If at first you don't succeed, try, try again." Many of the stories and books we share with our kids, too, are about the value of perseverance: *The Tortoise and the Hare*; *The Little Engine That Could*; *Rosie Revere, Engineer.*

Then there are our misconceptions about "grit." A term made famous by University of Pennsylvania psychologist Angela Duckworth in her book with the same name, grit is a commitment to work over long stretches of time, often in the service of challenging goals. We might assume that a person who exhibits grit is a person who never quits. But when I interviewed Duckworth years ago, she quickly disavowed me of this notion and emphasized that quitting is crucial—especially for kids.

Children, Duckworth explained to me, need to be able to explore a variety of activities. They need to try them out to see if they enjoy them—often they won't like them, and that's valuable knowledge. Consider that when kids make the decision to try new things, they typically don't know much about those activities. When they agree to take horseback riding lessons, for instance, they may not even yet know what horseback riding *is*. As your kid takes those first few lessons, they uncover lots of new information about what the activity entails and whether they enjoy it—information they could not have gotten without giving it a go. But they might very quickly—or, eventually, after a year or two of lessons—realize that riding is not really their jam. Quitting gives kids the opportunity to make an informed decision and clear space for something else.

Put another way, quitting is only counterproductive when kids quit something they *should* continue doing. If they're doing something that isn't a good fit, then quitting is actually essential so that they can make room in their life for things that will be more fulfilling. In her aptly titled book *Quit*, champion poker player and decision scientist Annie Duke wrote that "success does not lie in sticking to things. It lies in picking the *right* thing to stick to and quitting the rest."

Often, though, our biases get in the way of letting our kids quit. There's the sunk-cost effect, which is a cognitive error in which we take into account the money, time, effort, and other resources we have already put into an endeavor when deciding whether to continue and spend more. If we've spent $500 on our kids' hockey gear, we are going to be extra annoyed when they tell us six months later that they want to take swimming lessons instead. Our frustration is, of course, totally understandable, but it is more rational to focus on *future* costs and benefits.

Parents often struggle to let kids quit things for another big reason, too: college. We want our kids to have stellar applications, and perseverance—not to mention awards and accolades, which often come with perseverance—looks good to admissions committees. We may also hope our child can get a scholarship or be recruited by an athletic director. In one small study published in 2017, researchers surveyed more than two hundred parents and found that half had encouraged their child to specialize in a sport and that parents of specialized athletes were more likely to expect that their kid could play collegiately or professionally.

The sad truth is, though, that only about 6 percent of high school athletes participate in NCAA sports, a mere 2 percent of high school athletes receive college athletic scholarships—and fewer than 2 percent of *those* college athletes continue to play professionally after college. Also, successful athletes often do not specialize as kids. When researchers surveyed 309 US Olympic athletes in a study published in 2014, they found that these exceptional athletes had not specialized early—instead, they typically played between two and four different sports when they were kids and teens (undoubtedly quitting some along the way!), and only specialized later, when they were in their late teens. LeBron James and Abby Wambach are among the many professional athletes who did not specialize early.

Still—if your kid has been enjoying an activity and suddenly decides to quit, it can be hard to know whether to let them. Maybe they just had a few tough practices, or a friend of theirs wants to quit and they can't imagine continuing without them. In other words: Are they asking to quit for valid reasons, or are they just being impulsive or feeling anxious? It can be hard to tell.

Duckworth told me that with her kids, she's made a "hard-thing rule": She expects them to do a fun and hard activity each year that requires deliberate practice. They *can* quit, but not in the middle of the season or school year—they have to stick it out for a predetermined amount of time. So if your kid announces in the middle of October that they want to quit soccer, by all means, have a conversation about it then—but it's perfectly reasonable to tell them that they can't quit mid-season. Encourage them to think about the long-term costs and benefits of sticking with the activity or quitting, too—to not merely consider what they are feeling right now.

Even better, communicate your expectations about quitting in advance, before your kid embarks on a new activity. And, while you're at it, help them come up with what Duke calls "kill criteria." Kill criteria are the signals they might see in the future that would tell them it's time to quit. Maybe one criterion is that they discover they don't like the activity—but they can quit only if they feel that way for at least three months. Have them think about the signs that would tell them that they enjoy the activity and the signs that would tell them they don't.

When I went to college, I was certain I wanted to be a concert pianist. I'd spent my childhood and teen years practicing hours upon hours each day, and I won several statewide piano competitions. Playing the piano had become an integral part of my identity—I defined myself primarily as a musician.

But two years into my piano-performance degree in college, I realized that I wasn't nearly good enough to make a living as a performer, that I didn't particularly want to earn a living as a piano teacher (which is what I'd likely have to do instead), and that keeping up with the demands of the performance degree was making me miserable. I reflected long and hard on what to do and eventually realized that the benefits of quitting—I still had two years of college left and could, potentially, uncover other passions—far outweighed the benefits of sticking with my degree. Even though I wasn't sure who I even was if I wasn't sitting on a piano bench, I recognized that quitting was the wiser option. And I'm so glad I did, because otherwise I wouldn't have discovered my love for science and writing and you likely wouldn't be reading this book.

5. Communicate that girls deserve the same access to rest and fulfillment as boys.

Because I have a daughter and a son, and because I'm fascinated by the ways boys and girls get socialized, I've noticed—with sadness and frustration—that my daughter takes on a lot more household labor than my son does. All things being equal, I'd expect the trend to go in the opposite direction, because she is three years younger. Yet she's typically the one offering to help cook, clean the house, and fold clothes. I make sure to solicit my son's help, too, but her eagerness means she spends more time overall doing household tasks.

Our family situation is not unique. Research suggests that girls are often more likely than boys to help around the house, and that, as a result, they are also less likely than boys to relax and take time for themselves. This is because kids learn a lot about domestic expectations from observing their parents—and because parents sometimes unwittingly communicate different expectations for girls than for boys.

In one study, researchers in Canada analyzed data from a large study that tracked how more than two thousand adolescents in grades seven through twelve spent their time and how busy they felt. They found that girls spent more time on household tasks than boys did on school days, and that on Sundays, that difference skyrocketed—twelve- to fourteen-year-old girls spent, on average, thirty-five minutes longer on household tasks on Sundays than boys. The researchers also found that girls had less free time than boys, especially on Sundays, and that girls felt more time pressure—meaning that they often felt they had more things to do than what they had time for and wished for more hours in a day.

The researchers theorized that boys tend to feel a sense of entitlement to leisure, whereas "for girls, there is a notion that leisure is residual, or something that happens after other obligations have been met." Another study found that when teen girls actually did relax and do "fun" things, they said they often did them not because they wanted to but because they were trying to please other people. How sad is that? When girls actually rest, they do it out of a sense of duty.

Girls conform to these gender-stereotypical expectations for many reasons. They internalize them based on what they read in books, see in movies and TV shows, and observe around them—including, if not especially, at home. If they notice that Mom is constantly running around—tidying, cooking, doing things for others—while Dad watches TV, they might assume that this is just what girls versus boys do in the world. Kids notice household inequality, even from a young age, and they often assume that it's normal and fair. Since parents are also shaped by social pressures and gender stereotypes, we might ask our daughters to do more around the house than we ask of our sons, even if we don't realize we're doing it.

I'm not sharing this research to depress you; I'm sharing it because awareness is a crucial first step toward change. When we're aware of these tendencies, we will be more likely to notice and challenge them. I now pay more attention to the things I ask my kids to do around the house and try to ensure that they are fair. I make more of a concerted effort to relax in front of them. I also interpret my daughter's inclinations differently than I used to. I used to assume that my daughter's propensity to cook and clean was merely a reflection of her personality or temperament (and these factors certainly do play a role!). Now, however, I consider that her choices may also reflect the messages she's getting from me and her dad and society at large about how girls should act at home and in the world.

Experts told me that one of the best ways parents can combat these nefarious influences is by talking about them with their children. If we can make kids aware of gendered expectations and stereotypes, we can help them become more intentional in the choices they make. When I see my daughter offering to clean up her brother's mess, I tell her that it's wonderful that she feels so generous, and I point out that this dynamic may also be a reflection of the many messages society sends to girls versus boys about what they are and aren't entitled to.

We should also explain to our kids that kindness and generosity should ideally be reciprocated, because girls are just as entitled to rest and relaxation (and having kind things done for them) as boys are. We can point out patterns of unfairness that we observe in boy-girl sibling dynamics, too, and help our daughters stand up for themselves around boys.

A few months ago, on vacation, we all went shopping together for groceries and I let my kids pick out their cereal and their yogurt. Of course, they fought over the choices: My daughter wanted strawberry yogurt, whereas my son wanted cherry. My daughter wanted Crispix, while my son wanted Cheerios. I stood back and let them duke it out, only to observe that in both situations, my son "won" because my daughter capitulated first. At that point, I spoke up and pointed this dynamic out to them, adding that it would be fairer if he got to make one choice and she got to make the other. They agreed, and my daughter got her yogurt.

In separate conversations, I've talked to my kids about this broader dynamic—the fact that girls and women often accommodate more than boys and men do due to gender norms—so that they can more easily notice their tendencies and, hopefully, resist them. The more visible we can make these gendered expectations and stereotypes, the more easily we can, collectively, work to change them—and ensure that all our kids feel entitled to spend time doing things that give them joy.

KEY POINTS

1. Let kids engage in free, independent play.
2. Don't pressure kids to achieve.
3. Model healthy relaxation and leisure habits yourself.
4. Teach your kids it's okay to quit.
5. Tell and show girls that they deserve the same access to rest, relaxation, and fun as boys.

PART II
Connect

5

"That's Her Problem, Not Mine."

Building Empathy and Compassion

Let's face it: Empathy and compassion are skills that come easier to some kids than others. I have seen the full spectrum, over the years, as I've observed my kids on playdates. Some of my kids' friends keenly decipher moods and are quick to offer support, encouragement, and help. Others seem a bit more . . . well, let's say *oblivious*.

The fact that kids differ in these ways is normal and expected, because compassion is a complex social skill. A compassionate person has to be able to notice other people's feelings or goals based on subtle cues like facial expressions or body language, which requires emotional literacy. They must recognize that those feelings can be different from their own, which requires a cognitive skill known as theory of mind. Next they have to figure out appropriate ways to respond to make their friend feel better, which draws in part from their own past emotional experiences. And they have to do all of this while denying or delaying their own immediate wants and needs, which requires impulse control and emotional regulation.

It's like an intricate Rube Goldberg machine: If one tiny part of the process goes awry, the whole thing gets derailed. And then you have two kids smacking each other with Squishmallows.

Given its complexity, it's perhaps not surprising that compassionate behavior typically doesn't arise until the preschool years or even later. Babies and toddlers sometimes do things that *seem* compassionate and helpful, but researchers believe that their motivations mostly stem from wanting to be social. If an eleven-month-old helps their dad clean up toys, it's probably not that they actually want to do a good deed—it's that they want to continue their playful interaction, and Dad is putting away toys, so they'll do it, too.

At around the first birthday, some kids do start to develop a propensity to be generous. But they often do it only when it comes at no cost to them—when it doesn't involve giving away a cookie they want or a toy they love. With each passing month, though, toddlers tend to get more kind and generous; researchers have found noticeable differences between how helpful thirty-month-olds are on average versus eighteen-month-olds. Then, between ages two and three, kids also start to weigh, based on social norms, whether people *deserve* kindness and help, which complicates matters further. Kids at this age are less likely to help people if they got hurt while stealing, for instance.

All of these skills develop over time in line with brain development—though, of course, older kids aren't exactly bastions of self-sacrifice, either. Every Mother's Day, I'm blown away anew by how difficult it is for my kids to center my interests and needs for just one day of the year. But the good news is that compassion and empathy are skills that can be strengthened—so we, as parents, can absolutely shape how empathetic and compassionate our kids become. And it's a skill that can benefit them in many ways. Research finds that kinder, more compassionate people are happier and even more successful.

But What If Empathy Actually Hurts Others?

In recent years, there's been a bit of a backlash against empathy. In his book *Against Empathy*, Yale psychologist Paul Bloom argues that certain kinds of empathy can actually incite people to make immoral, biased choices. We tend to feel more empathy for people who are close to us, seem like us, or remind us of people we love—so empathy can indirectly, in certain contexts, fuel discrimination.

In one study, researchers recruited soccer fans and had them witness shocks being given to a stranger who was posing as either a fan of the subject's favorite team or a fan of their rival team. As the subjects observed the shocks, the researchers measured their brains' empathic responses, finding that people felt much more empathy for the other person if that person was a fan of their favorite team versus the rival team. The researchers also offered the subjects an opportunity to help the other person by taking a shock on their behalf. Subjects were more likely to offer to take the other person's shock if that person was a fan of their team.

As parents, empathy can also bias us in ways that benefit our own children at the expense of others. When you hear about parents of teen boys lamenting how unfair it is for allegations of sexual assault to "ruin" boys' lives, empathy could be at play: These parents may be imagining what their own sons would experience in this situation and therefore feel more empathy for potential rapists than for rape victims. The problem with empathy, in other words, is that we focus it toward some people more than others.

"Whether or not you feel empathy depends on prior decisions about who to worry about, who counts, who matters," Bloom explained in his book. Because of this, he wrote, "Empathy distorts our moral judgments in pretty much the same way that prejudice does."

Interestingly, too, our own empathy as parents can cause us to make decisions that don't serve our kids very well. In chapter 2, I discuss the importance of letting children experience discomfort and failure. If we are steeped in empathy and feeling our children's pain, it can be very hard to do this. Empathy makes us want to solve our kids' problems and resolve their suffering, even when we know deep down that challenges are good for them. As Bloom explained, "Making children suffer temporarily for their own good is made possible by love, intelligence, and compassion, but yet again, it can be impaired by empathy."

At this point you're probably wondering why I have written an entire chapter about promoting empathy if empathy is terrible. Here's the thing: Bloom's arguments against empathy are much more nuanced than they first seem. His concerns are directed at one specific kind of empathy, known as affective empathy or emotional empathy. Emotional empathy is the act of experiencing another person's feelings. When someone else feels sad or frustrated, and you feel sad or frustrated, too, you are experiencing emotional empathy.

This form of empathy is different from the kind of empathy I encourage parents to teach kids, which is known as cognitive empathy. Cognitive empathy is the act of perceiving and understanding other people's feelings, but not necessarily feeling those emotions yourself. Cognitive empathy is involved when you see another person's facial expressions or body language and judge from them how they feel. Cognitive empathy is what helps you figure out how best to comfort or help someone. It allows you to understand another's distress without experiencing that distress firsthand yourself.

It might seem silly to distinguish between these seemingly very similar experiences—don't academic psychologists have more pressing things to argue about?—but research does show these two forms of empathy are distinct. Studies have found, for instance, that emotional empathy and cognitive empathy involve separate parts of the brain.

Teaching Our Kids Cognitive Empathy

Throughout this chapter, then, I will be focusing on what parents can do to foster compassion and cognitive empathy in kids. These characteristics are what lead to thoughtful and generous behavior, and they also avoid the potential discriminatory downsides associated with emotional empathy—a win-win.

1. Be a sensitive and compassionate parent.

One of the hardest things about trying to be a "good" parent is that it often feels pointless. When your kid screams because you served lunch on the "wrong" plate and you take a deep breath and validate their frustration and then they just keep screaming, it can feel like the kindness you've gone to great lengths to muster is useless. Like it's just been sucked into a giant black hole along with the grilled cheese your kid angrily threw on the floor.

But research suggests that our day-to-day parenting choices can actually be incredibly meaningful. They often work in invisible ways but can have powerful ripple effects, even generations down the line.

In a 2024 study published in the journal *Child Development*, researchers at the University of Virginia followed 184 adolescents from the age of thirteen until they were in their mid-thirties (quite a feat!). They observed how the mothers interacted with their teens, how the teens interacted with their friends, and then, many years later, how these teens eventually interacted with their own children.

What the researchers found was fascinating and powerful: The more empathetic mothers were with their teens, the more compassion those teens showed for their close friends throughout adolescence. The supportiveness they showed in their adolescent friendships also predicted how supportive those teens would become, as adults, with their own kids, *and* it predicted how empathetic they thought their young kids were. "If we want to raise empathic kids, we need to give them firsthand experiences of being understood and supported," said study coauthor Jessica Stern, a psychologist at the University of Virginia, in a Q and A published by the Society for Research in Child Development.

When we connect emotionally with our kids and provide them with warmth and support, then, we are literally shaping our future society.

How does our compassion shape their compassion? There are many possible pathways. According to research on attachment theory, when parents are consistently warm and responsive to their kids, children develop what are called "secure" attachments to their parents, which give them a deep sense of safety and security. Compared with other, less securely attached kids, those with secure caregiver attachments develop better emotional regulation skills, which, researchers have found, help them show more compassion for others. It makes sense: Kids have to feel calm themselves before they can focus on other people's feelings and needs.

Studies find that one of the strongest predictors of secure attachment is when parents sensitively respond to their children's distress—for instance, by emotionally connecting with their upset kid and acknowledging, labeling, validating, and trying to understand their feelings. Secure attachments are also thought to help kids develop healthy ideas about relationships, because they consider themselves and others worthy of love and care and feel confident that they can trust their loved ones.

A number of studies have pointed to a robust link between sensitive, compassionate caregiving and the degree to which kids show compassion to others. In 1979, researchers conducted a landmark study in which they assessed the attachment relationships of thirty-two kids when they were fifteen months old. They then observed these kids at the age of three and a half in their preschool classroom over the course of five weeks. Kids who were securely attached with their caregivers demonstrated better social skills than kids who were not securely attached. In another study, researchers watched how preschoolers reacted in situations in which a peer became distressed. Compared with kids with "avoidant" attachments—which develop when caregivers do not respond well to kids' needs—the securely attached kids had more concerned facial expressions and expressed more care for their peers. "Because their own emotional needs are presumably satisfied, they develop the capacity to respond emotionally, sensitively, and empathically toward others," the researchers concluded.

More recent studies have come to similar conclusions. In a 2019 study, researchers found that when mothers made an effort to help their toddlers manage stressful situations, those kids, one year later, were more likely than others to comfort, seek help for, or ask after a researcher who acted like they had been hurt. When parents respond warmly and kindly to their kids, kids can then recognize—and respond to—needs they observe in others.

Being a kind and compassionate grown-up can make kids kind for another reason, too: Kids love to imitate adults, and they learn what kind of behavior is appropriate based on what they observe. Studies have found that kids—even young ones—imitate adults in terms of their propensity to help and be generous. In an experimental study published in 2019, researchers found that sixteen-month-olds who'd recently observed helpful adults became more helpful themselves. Research has found similar patterns among older kids, too.

The next time you feel like your thoughtful caregiving isn't making an iota of a difference to anyone, remember that kids absorb much more from our actions than we realize. Warm and compassionate parenting is like a manifestation of the butterfly effect: Our daily kindnesses are like the flap of a butterfly's wings, shaping our children's lives—and the other lives they go on to touch—in powerful and unexpected ways.

2. Talk to your kids about feelings—and let them express their own.

When one of my kids is having a tantrum, validating their feelings seems like an express route to *more* selfishness, not less. And yet, research consistently shows that talking to kids about feelings, and letting them express their feelings in appropriate ways, actually makes them more empathetic—not more self-centered.

In one fascinating study, Celia Brownell, a psychologist at the University of Pittsburgh, and her colleagues invited toddlers and their caregivers—mostly mothers—into the lab for a study. First, they asked the moms to read a book to their kids, and they recorded how many times the moms stopped reading to discuss the characters' feelings. The assumption was that the moms who did this more in the lab probably also did this more at home. Then they invited each toddler into another room to play with a researcher. As they played, the researcher pretended to need help, for instance by saying they felt cold and wished someone would bring them a nearby blanket.

Brownell and her colleagues found that the more the moms encouraged their kids to talk about and label feelings during the reading portion of the study, the more likely the toddlers were to help the researcher as they played. Scientists have also found that kids whose parents let them express their emotions become more tuned in to other people's emotions. Researchers found in one study that two-year-olds whose mothers had encouraged them to express their feelings six months earlier scored higher on tests of empathy than other kids did.

Why does this happen? When parents educate kids about the different emotions and give kids license to experience them, they help kids become more emotionally literate in ways that set the foundation for compassion. In order for a child to recognize that someone else is suffering and take appropriate steps to make them feel better, they first need to be able to recognize that the person is experiencing something difficult. Then they have to do the tricky detective work of deciphering which emotion that person is feeling, because you'd comfort an angry friend differently than an embarrassed one or a terrified one. To do this, they need to have a working knowledge of what different feelings feel like and what kinds of comfort people want when they are experiencing different feelings.

This is all much easier to do if adults have regularly talked to kids about feelings, helped them identify which ones are which, and given them license to experience the full spectrum of emotions throughout their day-to-day lives.

It helps to encourage kids to consider other people's perspectives, too, and the fact that those perspectives might differ from theirs. One day, my son came home from school upset that the bus driver had told him and his friends they were being too loud. I asked him why he thought the driver might have said that, and his answer was along the lines of *He was just trying to be mean!* I then asked my son to consider what the driver's job was—to get kids home safely—and whether too much noise might interfere with his ability to focus on the road and do that. Although his response was partially hidden behind a scowl, a little light bulb went off in my son's head when he considered this.

As I mentioned earlier, the ability for a child to put themselves in another person's shoes, and to recognize that other people can have different thoughts and feelings than they do, is an important skill known as theory of mind, and it improves with practice. Research has linked theory-of-mind skills to kindness and generosity—because again, kids must recognize that other people have different needs and feelings than they do in order to show them compassion.

None of this means that we should pander to our kids' feelings or let them express them however they like. It's okay if your kid is feeling ragey because you told them they can't wear their underwear on their head to school—but you shouldn't look the other way when they then angrily throw their Stanley cup at their sister. You can validate their feelings and set limits by saying something like, *I know it's frustrating that you can't wear your underwear that way. But you still can't throw obscenely large water bottles at people's heads.*

Recently, among certain circles, there's been a bit of a backlash against parent-child emotion talk, and I want to address that briefly. In her book *Bad Therapy*, and an excerpt that was published in *The Wall Street Journal*, journalist Abigail Shrier argued that parents harm their kids by asking them how they feel and encouraging them to talk about their feelings. Among other things, Shrier claimed that parents ask after their kids' feelings because they always want their kids to be happy, and she argued that focusing myopically on kids' happiness can backfire, making kids more distressed rather than less.

I agree that our job as parents isn't to ensure that our kids are always happy—kids learn how to cope with hard feelings and challenges by experiencing them, so they really need that practice. But I disagree with Shrier's negative assessment of emotion talk. Noticing and labeling feelings helps kids develop emotional literacy, which makes them more compassionate people. And it can achieve the opposite of what she argued: Learning how to talk about emotions (good and bad) can help kids better cope with a variety of situations and feelings, making them more resilient and mentally healthy.

When I interviewed Christopher Willard, a psychologist at Harvard Medical School, he explained to me that naming feelings helps to settle down the nervous system. In one brain-imaging study, for instance, researchers at UCLA found that putting feelings into words reduces activity in the amygdala and other limbic brain regions associated with emotional reactions. So the act of noticing and naming feelings not only quells kids' emotions but also likely helps them tolerate challenging things more easily.

I want to mention one other emotion-related strategy parents can use that can make kids more compassionate. Called "induction," or "inductive discipline," the approach was developed and studied by psychologists Martin Hoffman and Herbert Saltzstein in the 1960s. Induction involves referencing emotions when we make requests of children and explaining the impact of their actions. Hoffman and Saltzstein found that when parents talk to kids about how their choices affect others, kids more easily grasp the broader impact of their actions and then make more compassionate choices.

Parents use induction when they say things like: *Can you please sit down and eat your muffin over your plate, because otherwise you get crumbs all over the floor and someone has to clean them up*, as well as: *Please turn your music down until I'm done with this work call, because otherwise I can't hear my boss and it's embarrassing.* These examples focus on the negative impacts of our kids' choices, but we can also use it to focus on the positive by saying things like *Sharing your new toy truck with your brother for a few minutes would make him really happy.*

The easiest way to use induction is to always provide the *why* behind your requests, especially when the *why* involves other people's feelings. So the next time you're barking an order at your child, like *No hitting!* or *Don't interrupt, please!* try tacking on a bit about why, even if it feels obvious: *No hitting, because hitting hurts*, or *Please don't interrupt, because it's very frustrating when you talk over me.* You can even turn the situation around to help kids who struggle with perspective-taking skills by saying something like *How do you feel when I interrupt you?*

Induction works for multiple reasons. Kids are more interested in complying when they understand the rationale behind our asks, and they are also more likely to act compassionately when they recognize that their actions and choices have impacts beyond themselves. In one study, researchers surveyed mothers of middle schoolers about how they disciplined them, also interviewing the children's teachers about how helpful and kind the students were at school. They measured the kids' propensity for generosity and other prosocial behavior, too, by giving them the option to donate money to a charity. The kids whose parents used induction were more generous and empathetic than kids whose parents relied on other forms of discipline, such as harsh punishments.

Induction can have immediate and specific impacts: In one

study, third- and fourth-grade kids were given money and encouraged to donate it to kids in need of food and toys. Some were told that sharing would help the other children and make them happy. Others were simply told that sharing "is the right thing to do." The kids who'd been encouraged to share because it would make kids happy were more likely to be generous.

3. Encourage kids to help from a very young age.

There is nothing cuter—and, if I'm honest, more frustrating—than little kids who "help" around the house. As a toddler and preschooler, my daughter begged to help make pancakes with her dad every weekend, and the collaboration made breakfast four times more work than it otherwise would have been. As developmental psychologists aptly noted in a 2015 paper: "Unfortunately for adults, toddlers' 'help' is not always very helpful. Young children fold, but also unfold, laundry. They load both dirty and clean dishes into the dishwasher."

Perhaps this is why researchers have observed that parents often choose to do household tasks while their children are napping.

Here's the worst part of it, though: Once kids have developed passable fine and gross motor skills and could actually *truly* be helpful, they often seem to lose interest in pitching in. Research suggests that this could be in part because of how parents and other adults responded to their desire to help when they were younger.

This may sound obvious, but kids are more likely to help when they have been encouraged to do it. In a 2017 study, researchers split infants into two groups. The babies in the first group were repeatedly encouraged to help and praised when they did, while those in the second group were not. Then, all the infants watched an adult accidentally drop something on the floor and act as if they were unable to reach it. The babies who'd been encouraged and praised to help were twice as likely to hand the coveted item back.

Researchers have also found that when adults scaffold kids' help—meaning that they transform tasks that are beyond a child's current abilities into activities that they can understand and master and also provide verbal cues and instructions—kids become more interested in offering their help, too. To scaffold my daughter's pancake making, her dad used to premeasure ingredients the night before so she could dump ingredients into a bowl without having to worry about measurements (that said, the cup of mix did not always end up in the bowl; thank goodness for our dustbuster). Scaffolding can also involve giving kids simplified and specific tasks, such as sorting cups rather than trying to put all the dishes away.

When parents provide scaffolding in one situation, kids often offer their help in other situations, too. In one study, kids of moms who scaffolded during a cleanup task "tended to have children who were more likely and better able to help an experimenter who encountered a variety of unique problems," researchers observed.

This doesn't mean, of course, that parents *always* have to say yes when kids want to help out. If we did, none of us would probably ever be able to put down the dustbuster. And, of course, we sometimes need to say no for safety reasons. My kids' dad rented a skid steer to do some yard work recently, and he wisely wouldn't let my kids within two hundred feet of him when he was using it. But when opportunities for kids' help arise and we have time, energy, and safety on our side, we might want to consider inviting them to participate.

Research involving children in other cultures illustrates that when kids feel truly useful, they keep wanting to help, and they often start doing it without prompting. In one fascinating study, researchers from ITESO University in Mexico and the University of California, Santa Cruz, interviewed mothers in Mexico with Indigenous heritage about what their six- to eight-year-old children did around the house and compared this to what parents reported from what they called a "cosmopolitan" Mexican community with more Western values. They found stark differences: Children in the Indigenous communities frequently helped around the house, including doing complex tasks such as cooking. Few of the other kids helped to the same degree, and none helped with complex tasks.

Moreover, 74 percent of the children from Indigenous communities took initiative in doing this work rather than waiting to be asked or directed. None of the kids from the Western families did. As one Indigenous mother reported of her daughter: "There are days when she comes home and says: 'Mom, I'm going to help you do everything.'" Researchers have noticed that kids from more Westernized families often help only "under adult management and control, in contractual arrangements."

What might explain these stark differences? The authors speculate that toddlers from all cultures are interested in helping, but that Western kids lose interest over time because they are regularly discouraged from helping by their parents, who consider them to be in the way. "Perhaps these children learn that they are both obliged and allowed to stay out of the 'adult world,'" the authors wrote. "This contrasts with the Indigenous-heritage families, where children are included as an integral part of family and community activities from infancy and encouraged to help with initiative, as an honorable way of belonging and showing maturity."

Kids from Indigenous communities enjoy helping in part because they experience it as a collaborative effort. As researchers explained: "Sharing in and accomplishing this work with others can be highly engaging." Put another way, if we make helping a social experience for kids, they will be much more interested in doing it again in the future, because they are social creatures. In a 2014 study, researchers interviewed nine- and ten-year-old Mexican children about how they viewed their participation in household work. Kids from Indigenous-heritage communities often emphasized their collaboration with other members of the family as a key reason for their participation.

This all rings true when I think about my daughter and her pancake making. Despite the fact that her "help" often created more work for him, her dad regularly encouraged her forays into cooking, and it was always a collaborative effort, with her making pancakes while he made eggs and bacon. By the time she was eight, she stopped needing any assistance at all—she now gets out the ingredients, measures everything, pours the pancakes, and takes them off the griddle herself. She wouldn't have it any other way, and I'm actually truly grateful for her help.

If you have older kids, all is not lost—you can still get your seemingly lazy tween or teen to pitch in around the house. First, talk about the *why*. Your child will probably want to know why you suddenly want them to do things you used to do for them, so give them your rationale, even if it's something as simple as *I realized the other day that you're old enough to do some of the household things I used to do for you, and that's great—the family could really use your help!* Make it clear that their labor has value. Ideally, offer them choices—maybe they can either unload the dishwasher every morning or walk the dog each evening—because choices make kids feel less controlled, which will make them more motivated. Emphasize the collaborative nature of the work, too—that every family member has tasks they do to support everyone else. The more we support the people we love, the more they can support us back, and the stronger we become as a family.

KEY POINTS

1. Know that kids vary in their propensity for compassion and generosity, and that's normal.
2. Try your best to warmly and sensitively respond to your children's needs.
3. Talk about feelings, and let your kids experience the full range of emotions without dismissing or chastising them.
4. Provide the why behind your requests so that kids understand that their actions affect others.
5. Encourage kids to help starting in toddlerhood, and emphasize collaboration.

6

"I Am So Lonely!"

Setting Kids Up for Healthy Friendships

When my friend Chloe's daughter Reya turned nine, her friendships suddenly became very complicated. Like clockwork, every night, five minutes after they had said good night, Reya would call out to Chloe, in tears. Chloe would come back into her daughter's room, sit at the foot of her bed, and listen as Reya regaled her latest friend-related dramas—sometimes wanting reassurance, sometimes wanting advice.

Chloe was floored at just how complicated a nine-year-old girl's social life could be—not least because she'd never gone through anything like this with her fifteen-year-old son. He had never opened up to Chloe about his friendships, and she had assumed that was because they were easier and more straightforward—but Chloe confessed to me that she wondered if it's because her son didn't know how to talk about his friends or his feelings, or because he is much more disconnected from his peers.

When it comes to what we can do as parents to help our kids lead healthy, happy lives, ensuring that they know how to build and maintain strong relationships should be a key priority. Much research shows that feeling connected is a major predictor of future happiness and success. In 1939, researchers at Harvard began tracking the lives of 268 white male college sophomores. The goal of the study (which is still ongoing) has been to understand the factors that shape well-being and overall physical health throughout life. Over the years, the researchers expanded the study to include the children of these men and many of their spouses as well as more than 450 inner-city Boston residents.

The study certainly has its limitations, having included only white men for years. Still, its findings have been noteworthy. It found that close, deep relationships are strongly linked with happiness throughout life, and that they seem to shape people's well-being more than money, fame, social class, genes, or IQ. As two of the scientists involved in the study wrote in *The Atlantic* in 2023: "It's brought us to a simple and profound conclusion: Good relationships lead to health and happiness."

Friendship seems to have similar protective effects on kids and teens. Youth who felt lonely during the pandemic, for instance, were more likely than other kids to report having mental health problems. Kids who feel more connected with others visit the doctor less frequently, are less likely to use drugs, and have better general health. One longitudinal study found that the quality of a child's friendships at age thirteen—and especially their ability to respectfully engage with friends during disagreements—predicted their academic attainment years later.

It's worrying, then, that research conducted before and during the pandemic has suggested that adolescents are lonelier, on average, than they used to be. The factors shaping this trend are likely complex and could include the explosion in the use of digital technology and social media (see chapter 10). Yet despite all the hand-wringing over online bullying and the other unsavory effects of social media, research suggests that the strength of kids' in-person, real-life friendships matters more than anything else for their happiness. Studies find that when teens feel lonely, it's often due to problems they are experiencing within their in-person relationships, rather than a direct result of online activity. Overall, the research suggests we should spend a lot more time focusing on kids' real-life social networks and helping kids strengthen those friendships.

Boys and men, especially, are suffering as a result of their loneliness. In the 2023 State of American Men survey conducted by the nonprofit organization Equimundo, two-thirds of men aged eighteen to twenty-three said they felt that "no one really knows me." Fifteen percent of men have said they have no close friendships, a fivefold increase since 1990. Perhaps this helps to explain why suicide is worryingly common among men: In the Equimundo survey, a whopping 44 percent of men reported having had thoughts of suicide over the past two weeks. Eighty percent of deaths by suicide happen among men, and adolescent boys are 2.5 times more likely to die by suicide than adolescent girls.

Why do so many kids struggle with friendship, and what can we do as parents to help our children build strong, stable relationships? It's a complex question with complex answers—not least because, as my friend Chloe noticed with her own kids, the issues that plague youth relationships can differ dramatically by gender.

The Crisis of Connection Among Boys

Over the course of two years, Stanford scientist Judy Y. Chu observed a group of boys and how they engaged with each other at school. When they first arrived in pre-K, the boys connected with each other, both physically and emotionally, engaging in displays of tenderness and affection. They would, for instance, hug each other and tousle each other's hair, as Chu wrote in her 2014 book *When Boys Become Boys*.

But about halfway through that pre-K year, Chu saw the dynamics of these friendships dramatically shift. The boys became more emotionally guarded and "began to shield the qualities that had marked their full presence and genuine engagement in relationships," she wrote. "They began to look more like stereotypical 'boys,' or how boys are often said to be."

What Chu observed in those classrooms has now been documented many times over. If you're raising a boy, you may have noticed it yourself. Starting in childhood, boys tend to pull away from their friends and family members as they internalize unhealthy expectations surrounding masculinity. Through messages they get from the media and the adults around them, they come to believe that they should avoid expressing emotions and not be open and vulnerable with their friends.

These shifts intensify through late childhood and adolescence. Not too long ago, I had a brief conversation with my kids about their friendships. My nine-year-old daughter said that she had a small number of friends, and several she felt close enough to share secrets with. My twelve-year-old son said that he had lots of friends, but none that he felt close enough to confide in. I remember being shocked. My son had what I considered to be very close friends—

including one we podded with throughout the pandemic—and I'd always assumed they shared some level of emotional intimacy. When I asked him why he felt he couldn't trust his friends enough to confide in them, he corrected me: It wasn't that he didn't trust his friends; it was just that they never talked about feelings, asked each other for advice, or shared much about themselves.

My son also made it clear he didn't really *want* to confide in his friends. The implication was that intimacy wasn't something he craved or needed. But research suggests that while boys (and men) may think they don't need close relationships, they often suffer without them.

Soon after my son confided in me, I called up the psychologist Michael C. Reichert, the founding director of the Center for the Study of Boys' and Girls' Lives at the University of Pennsylvania and the author of the book *How to Raise a Boy*. When I told him what my son had said, Reichert replied: "He's just trying to be included in the world of boys, not be marginalized or relegated to a subordinate status. Kudos to him. It's just tragic that it comes with a cost—a sacrifice."

Niobe Way, an applied psychologist and the director of the Science of Human Connection Lab at NYU Steinhardt, has chronicled what she refers to as the "crisis of connection" among boys, noticing that it often worsens in adolescence. One adolescent boy who was interviewed as part of her research, and who had comfortably described his close friendships only a year earlier in another interview, all but refused to talk about his friends. "Why are you asking me so many questions about my friendships? I am not gay!" he said. (For some boys, it's not that they don't have a closest friend—it's that they feel they shouldn't *admit* to having one.)

The net result of all of this: Boys often become emotionally starved and lonely. "By middle to late adolescence, the boys and young men in my studies seemed to face a crisis of connection in which they found it increasingly difficult to find or maintain 'deep depth' male friendships," Way wrote in her 2024 book *Rebels with a Cause*. "Not only was their crisis evident in their struggle to find friendships but also in their depressed affect and their attempts to sound like they didn't care when they clearly did."

When boys reject these interpersonal needs, they end up, according to Way, "lonely, depressed, anxious, suicidal, and, in some cases, homicidal." Research suggests that the more strongly boys and young men adhere to the expectations of masculinity, the more depression symptoms they suffer, the lower their self-esteem becomes, the lower their academic achievement is, and the less they enjoy school.

Girls Struggle, Too—but for Different Reasons

At this point you might be assuming that the crisis of connection affects only boys—but it does not. Girls are also socialized in ways that ultimately harm their connections with others and with themselves, although the details typically differ. Whereas boys are socialized to sacrifice relationships in order to seem "tough" and self-sufficient, girls are socialized to sacrifice their authentic selves in order to better serve their relationships.

In the late 1980s, developmental psychologist Lyn Mikel Brown was working on her PhD at Harvard. Her adviser was Carol Gilligan, a psychologist whose work focused on girls' and women's moral development. Brown and Gilligan conducted extensive interviews over time with nearly one hundred girls between the ages of seven and eighteen who were students at the Laurel School in Cleveland, Ohio.

Tween girls, they observed and described in their 1992 book *Meeting at the Crossroads*, tended to be emotionally perceptive and able to clearly see the complexities of social situations. They also understood their values and priorities and could typically stand up for themselves and their needs. Psychologist Annie Rogers called this "ordinary courage," or the ability to "speak one's mind by telling all one's heart."

Brown and Gilligan shared, for instance, the story of a girl named Neeti. Her voice, they wrote, "carries the sound of a candid, confident, psychologically astute and shrewd twelve-year-old." At overnight camp with her seven-year-old homesick cousin, Neeti stood up to the dismissive camp director who told her that her cousin could not call home. She talked candidly about her relationship with her cousin and her response to his distress.

But a year later, when Brown and Gilligan interviewed Neeti again at age thirteen, they noticed a profound shift. Neeti talked a lot about being caught in unwanted friendships that she felt compelled to continue because she didn't want to hurt her peers' feelings. "What she wants to say now is, to her, unspeakable," they wrote. Brown and Gilligan continued to follow and interview Neeti for several more years, and the transformation intensified. When she was fifteen, Neeti was asked to write an essay for school called "Who Am I?," and Neeti said she realized that she didn't know.

This was something the researchers observed in many girls: As they progressed through adolescence, girls would start saying "I don't know" and contradicting themselves, as if they really didn't know what they knew, who they were, or what they stood for. As Neeti told Brown and Gilligan, "The voice that stands up for what I believe in has been buried deep inside of me."

Neeti's shifting experience was common, Brown and Gilligan learned, as they interviewed more and more girls for their study.

"Over and over again in their interviews, we hear these girls struggle as their strong feelings come up against a relational impasse that shuts out their experience or shuts down their loud voices." I'll point out that this did not happen with *all* the girls they interviewed; some were able to hold on to their voices, but those girls were often labeled by peers and adults as "troublemakers" or "bossy know-it-alls." (Cases in point: "know-it-all" Hermione from *Harry Potter* and "troublemaker" Elphaba from *Wicked*.)

So both girls and boys experience crises during adolescence: Boys get disconnected from others, while girls become disconnected from themselves. With girls, "what happens is you lose a lot of who you really are," Brown, now a professor emerita at Colby College, told me. Eventually, some of these girls find themselves in friendships and romantic relationships in which they prioritize the needs and desires of others over their own.

How do we square these depictions with the fact that girls are sometimes very mean to each other, especially during adolescence? We can all conjure up scenes of girls talking behind each other's backs, taunting each other, and policing one another's fashion choices and body sizes—what researchers call "relational" or "indirect" aggression. For her book *Girlfighting*, Brown interviewed 421 girls in order to address this apparent contradiction, which she ended up not seeing as a contradiction at all.

First, Brown explained, we set girls up to be mean to each other. In our misogynistic society, it's safer for girls to channel their anger against other girls than against boys, adults, or the broader culture. "It is a protective strategy and an avenue to power learned and nurtured in early childhood and perfected over time," Brown wrote.

It's also a direct reflection of the way society has always treated girls. Girls internalize that being disrespected is a fundamental part of girlhood, so it's hardly surprising that they give it right back to other girls. They may also see power as a precious and limited resource, feeling like players in a zero-sum game in which to claim power for themselves requires taking it from the other girls around them. Who's surprised, too, that girls' aggression is often passive and subversive, given that society has told girls over and over again that overt anger is not feminine? "We set them up completely for this, because we don't make it appropriate for them to be direct and honest," Brown explained to me.

In her book *On Our Best Behavior*, writer Elise Loehnen explained it this way: "Because we cultivate no appropriate channels, this aggression finds its way out sideways." If girls are direct or openly express their anger, they are punished by being called emotional or hysterical. But, of course, girls who engage in more passive aggression are denigrated, too, when their behavior is described as animalistic ("catty"). They just can't win.

Of course, I am oversimplifying, too. There are many other gendered—and often contradictory and confusing—expectations for girls today. They are captured beautifully in the heart-wrenching speech delivered by America Ferrera's character Gloria in the movie *Barbie*: "You have to never get old, never be rude, never show off, never be selfish, never fall down, never fail, never show fear, never get out of line. It's too hard. It's too contradictory, and nobody gives you a medal or says thank you. And it turns out, in fact, that not only are you doing everything wrong, but also everything is your fault. I'm just so tired of watching myself and every single other woman tie herself into knots so that people will like us."

With all these conflicting and demoralizing pressures, it's not surprising that adolescent girls are not doing very well. More than half of all girls report symptoms of depression, compared with fewer than one in three boys. Although a higher proportion of boys and men kill themselves, a whopping one in three teen girls considers it.

And as they grow up, women are nearly twice as likely as men to experience anxiety.

What About Trans and Nonbinary Kids?

Of course, not all boys and girls follow these gendered patterns. Though the bulk of research to date has focused on the "average" boy or girl, each child is unique, and many kids have different gender identities. As you read on, I'll describe strategies to strengthen friendships that are broadly applicable to just about everyone—even most adults. But I do also want to take a minute to highlight several of the unique friendship-related issues nonbinary and trans kids can face. And in the second half of the chapter, I'll provide a few suggestions that might be especially helpful for gender-nonconforming kids.

Two key foundations of friendship are safety and authenticity. With close friends, we know we can safely be ourselves. But for trans and nonbinary kids, the fear of rejection and judgment can be so profound that it can be hard for them to establish feelings of trust with their peers. "There's a real, real fear for a lot of young people about showing their true selves, whether that's talking about who they are and how they identify, or just showing who they are through their clothing, their hair, their preferences of activities, of hobbies, of art, of music," explained family therapist Jean Malpas, the founder and director of the Ackerman Institute's Gender & Family Project.

It's no wonder trans and nonbinary kids feel this way; their peers do often outwardly question their gender identities and taunt them for not conforming to gender stereotypes. This is the case for my friend Eunice's nonbinary twelve-year-old, Alex. "The gender expectation that Boys Do Sports has probably caused the most trouble,"

Eunice told me. One neighbor boy that Alex had been friends with—they podded together during the pandemic—has posed an especially big problem. "This kid's skepticism about Alex's identity and resentment of new pronouns and bafflement that Alex didn't like dodgeball did get under Alex's skin and made them feel uncertain about being welcomed in the world at times," Eunice said.

Malpas told me these are issues many nonbinary and trans kids face regularly. "The pushback is constant, with lots of bullying—and when it's not straight-up bullying, it's like, 'Huh, how come? Who are you? Are you a boy or a girl?' It's a lot of constant questioning," Malpas said. "It can be really exhausting." The fear of judgment can make it difficult for gender-nonconforming kids to connect in authentic ways with their peers and establish deep friendships. What they experience is, in some ways, a combination of what cis boys and cis girls often do—they may understandably fear opening up and being emotionally vulnerable, just as many boys do, and they may also be nervous about the repercussions of being their authentic selves, as cis girls often are. Importantly, these social struggles are not rooted in their gender identities but are instead direct consequences of the fact that they live in a world that doesn't always understand them, accept them, or treat them well.

Teaching Our Kids to Build Healthy Relationships

How can we, as parents, address the complicated social issues and pressures our kids will face? How do we help kids connect deeply with others while also helping them stay true to themselves within their relationships? Here are several essential strategies.

1. Model high-quality listening skills.

Relationships are, in large part, rooted in good communication—but many people misunderstand what good communication entails. Recently, Guy Itzchakov, the director of the Interpersonal Listening and Social Influence lab at the University of Haifa in Israel, explained to me that listening (not speaking!) is the foundation of good communication—and many people never learn how to do it well. It's not, as many people believe, a passive behavior; it's not about smiling and nodding and keeping quiet. "The listener has a very active role in shaping the conversation through verbal and nonverbal behaviors," Itzchakov explained.

Thankfully, listening is a skill that can be taught and learned—though it is a complex process that can't easily be broken down into specific "ingredients." When you think about a conversation in which you felt like you were being deeply listened to, you probably can't point to the specific things the listener did to make you feel that way. Feeling heard and understood is a holistic experience. And yet, Itzchakov said, the research suggests that there *are* specific things that good listeners tend to do.

- **The first thing that most high-quality listeners do is that they give the speaker their undivided attention.** They make near-constant eye contact and avoid getting distracted by noises or movements around them. When people talk, they often move their eyes around the room, but every few minutes they do look back at the listener to make sure they're paying attention—and if, at that moment, the listener is looking elsewhere, the speaker feels as if they are not being heard. Maintaining eye contact "sends them the meta message that *You're important to me, you're worthy* *of my attention*," Itzchakov explained. The sense of having the listener's undivided attention is, he said, "very, very crucial."

- **The second thing good listeners do is to communicate that they understand what the speaker is saying**—because feeling understood is deeply powerful and is in fact one of the most important predictors of intrapersonal chemistry. A good listener communicates their understanding—and their desire to understand—by asking follow-up questions or summarizing what the speaker just said. *So let me make sure I understand: You think X, Y and Z?* Itzchakov emphasized that good listeners don't necessarily ask questions to satisfy their own curiosity—they ask questions to ensure that they understand what the speaker has been saying.
- **The third—and often overlooked—component of high-quality listening is called "positive intention."** As Itzchakov explained to me, a police officer running an interrogation might maintain constant eye contact and ask good follow-up questions, but the interviewee is probably not going to feel like they are being heard and understood. That's because the officer has a hidden or explicit agenda. When people listen with positive intention, they are conveying to the speaker that the speaker is free to express their views without having to worry about negative repercussions. Importantly, positive intention is not the same thing as agreement. You can listen to someone you staunchly disagree with on an issue and yet still convey positive intention by saying things like *Thank you for sharing that with me; that must have been hard*, or *That really helped me understand where you're coming from*.

Itzchakov emphasized to me that even if you know what high-quality listening entails, you can't just magically perfect it—it takes practice. And we can and should practice on our kids for a number of reasons. Although we need more research on the issue, Itzchakov suspects that kids who regularly experience being listened to and understood will be more likely to do the same for others, and therefore be able to build stronger relationships.

Of course, we can't attentively listen to our kids *all the time*. My son will sometimes go on twenty-minute monologues about TikTok while I'm cooking, and I simply cannot give him my full attention without losing my mind and delaying dinner. But we can at least schedule times in which we give our kids our undivided attention. "Create these times when you have no distractions when you are with your child," Itzchakov suggested. Maybe it's in the car on the way to piano lessons, after dinner, or in the half hour before bedtime. Maybe it's not even every day, but once every few days. Just make sure it happens at least occasionally.

Also, we need to be extra attentive to the *positive intention* part when we listen to our kids. Often we enter into conversations with our kids focused on what they might have done wrong or what life lessons we want to teach them. This, however, is an agenda (albeit one that we think is good for them!)—and when we jump in with our ideas or advice, it can make our kids feel like they're being belittled or corrected. In these moments we are not modeling high-quality listening skills, and we are also increasing the chance that our kids will think twice before opening up to us in the future.

What should we do when our kids struggle with some of the aspects of high-quality listening? Look, it's inevitable, because good listening is not an innate skill. Whenever I visit my parents, I notice (and am horrified) that my son rarely makes eye contact when they are talking with him. I think it's because he feels shy—he's not trying to be disrespectful—but when I see it happen, I pull him aside later and remind him that people like to be looked at when they're talking. In my experience, it can be helpful to not just model the listening skills you want to see but also explicitly talk about them and explain why they are important. Encouraging perspective-taking can help: *How do you feel when you're telling me a story about your day and I'm looking at my phone? Probably not great, right?* We can also set our kids up for listening success by removing distractions from potential conversations (no phones at the dinner table) and setting ground rules (no interrupting).

2. Encourage kids to be curious and emotionally vulnerable.

Building on the idea that listening is the foundation of communication, the next step toward forging deep bonds is to encourage dialogue that is open-minded, curious, and vulnerable. I witnessed middle schoolers learn to do this firsthand in 2023.

I was standing in the back of a seventh-grade classroom at the University Neighborhood Middle School in New York City's Lower East Side, watching a transformation take place. I was there to observe the Listening Project, an educational intervention cofounded by NYU's Way and Swarthmore sociologist Joseph D. Nelson. The project is designed to help students tap into their natural capacities to listen and engage with each other in ways that transcend stereotypes and build deep relationships. Its powerful approach is one that all teachers—and parents—can use to help kids connect with others.

The project grew out of Way's training as a qualitative researcher, in which she was taught how to conduct semi-structured interviews with adolescents to learn more about them, their desires, and their beliefs. When she started teaching these interview skills to doctoral students, she heard from them that the technique transformed their own personal relationships. "I realized it was more than just a research method," she explained in her book *Rebels with a Cause*. "It was a way to build human connection."

Since 2014, the Listening Project has been implemented and tested at a handful of middle and high schools, including boys' schools, in New York City. Over the course of twenty-six sessions, the project teaches students how to engage in transformational interviewing, which involves tapping into their curiosity and empathy to interview other people in ways that encourage open, honest, and vulnerable responses. The students start by interviewing each other with open-ended, probing, personal questions such as *Tell me about a time in which you felt listened to* or *Who do you trust the most and why?*, with the goal of reminding the students of their natural curiosity about each other—what Way calls their "relational intelligence."

The Listening Project teaches kids that it's okay—even good—to be curious and vulnerable, because both those traits can reap rewards in the form of building deep, meaningful connections with others. It helps kids nurture their natural capacities for connection and push back against cultural messages that tell them to do the opposite.

University Neighborhood Middle School, where I was observing the Listening Project on a chilly February morning in 2023, was ranked in 2019 as being in the bottom 10 percent of schools in New York. Sixty percent of the students in the school were Hispanic, 26 percent were Black, and most of the students qualified for free or reduced lunch, indicating that many families served live below the poverty line.

On that particular day, the students were, as a class, interviewing a school staff member: Mr. Engelbert, the new restorative justice coordinator. Before he arrived, the class's teachers reminded the students of the core tenets of transformational interviewing—to ask nonleading, open-ended questions (no "what" questions!) and to let his answers guide where they went next.

"If one particular question is very effective, if it leads to a story that we want to know more about, we might stop asking those other questions we have planned, we might shift to asking follow-up questions so that we can go deeper," explained one teacher, a lanky man in his thirties with a shaved head and a gentle demeanor.

Mr. Engelbert walked in and sat in a chair front of the class. He wore long dreadlocks pulled back from his face by a color-blocked scarf and a gray sweater that matched his salt-and-pepper goatee. He seemed laid-back, but exuded a bright intensity that was accentuated by his matching neon-green glasses, iPhone, and sneakers.

"Please feel free to be curious and ask whatever you guys want," he said.

When the students started asking questions, they were quiet and meek. They defaulted to the "what" questions they were told not to ask—what he did in his job, what he liked about it, and what he did in his previous job. At one point, I caught a student snoozing.

But then the students started asking deeper, emotionally probing questions. One girl asked him to describe his favorite memory, and he told a story about his mother's reaction when he told her, as a teenager, that he wanted to be a musician. Another student asked him why he had wanted to be a musician, and another wanted to know if a particular person had inspired him. (At that point, he let drop that he'd once toured with Bob Marley and the Wailers, and the adults in the room let out a collective gasp.)

Next, a student asked him if he had liked school when he was younger, and why or why not. Mr. Engelbert's response: "Ooh, wow. Okay." He paused to consider his answer.

The students, at that point, seemed rapt. He explained to them that he'd been a good student, but that he'd also been rebellious, because the teachers and principal at his school hadn't supported him in the ways he needed.

"I believe that rules without relationships are a call for rebellion," he said.

At that point, I observed a change move through the class. The students' mindsets seemed to collectively shift as they started to warm to Mr. Engelbert. One student asked him how he went from being a rebel to a leader; another asked him to describe specific ways he'd rebelled. He said he had once dropped a sodium tablet from the science lab into a school toilet and caused a huge explosion that destroyed the school's pipes, at which everyone giggled. It was like the students couldn't believe that a staff member at their school, someone they'd likely assumed was going to be boring and straitlaced, had such a fascinating and complicated backstory. I could sense them envisioning their own futures, considering whether they could one day sit in front of a seventh-grade class telling students about their childhood and the mistakes they'd made that somehow didn't preclude them from having a rich and successful life. The process seemed to help both Mr. Englebert and his student interviewees connect with the various parts of themselves and with each other.

In 2024, Way asked me if I would be willing to be interviewed by two college students of hers who were learning this interview technique. I agreed and spent an hour in conversation with two international students—initially, total strangers—who asked me deep, probing questions about my life, my values, my relationships, and my fears. I was extremely nervous going in, and I wasn't sure if I'd be able to open up to people I didn't even know. But I did, and the experience really was transformative: Afterward, I felt like I more deeply understood myself and felt strongly connected with my interviewees, even though they had shared very little about themselves. I could imagine how meaningful this experience would be for disconnected middle schoolers, especially boys.

It may seem surprising that kids in middle school are willing to ask complete strangers probing personal questions, but Way finds that they are usually more than happy to once they are given permission. "Children and teenagers—including twelve-year-old boys—are teeming with thick questions, and they can easily follow their curiosity and become more emotionally vulnerable if given the permission by the adults in the room," she wrote in *Rebels with a Cause*.

As an example, Way once asked a group of middle school boys to read a passage from her book *Deep Secrets* in which a fourteen-year-old boy talked about how much he loves his close friends. Immediately, the boys reading the excerpt started laughing. When Way asked them why, they demurred. She pressed them.

Finally, one boy said, "The dude sounds gay."

"Let me tell you," Way replied, "eighty-five percent of all the boys I've ever interviewed over thirty years sound like that when they're teenagers. That's what teenage boys sound like."

The room went silent. One boy said: "For real?"

Way replied: "Oh, yes, that's what teenage boys sound like."

All of a sudden, the tenor of the room shifted. The boys opened up and started talking about their own searches for close friendship. One boy even used the phrase "broken up" to describe a friendship with another boy that had ended.

"All I had done is normalize it," Way told me. "All I had done is normalize it—and then they were willing to talk."

Emerging findings suggest that this is precisely what the Listening Project does: It helps students change how they see themselves and others and helps them feel more connected to peers, teachers, staff, and family members. It has also helped students see that expressions of vulnerability draw people closer together. The students who have participated in the project have reported feeling more interested in relationships and feelings and more confident in their ability to nurture friendships. Listening with curiosity, Way explained, "allows you to see someone's full humanity."

We, as parents, can do the same at home. We can be curious about our kids, especially our boys, and encourage them to be curious about and vulnerable with others. "Being vulnerable is a skill that can be practiced," explained health educator Christopher Pepper, the coauthor of the book *Talk to Your Boys*. Even if they have already internalized masculine norms, boys can be freed of them—at least for short periods of time—when they are made to feel that their emotions and stories are welcome and that they are safe.

This means that when our kids do open up to us, we should try to be as welcoming as possible and resist the urge to chide or question them. Sometimes, at the dinner table, my son shares stories about things that he did with his friends after school, and more often than not, they involve questionable choices—like jumping in large groups on trampolines or swimming in the Hudson River. *You did what now?* is what I always want to say. But researchers who study parent-child relationships—and the circumstances that help them share and be vulnerable—have warned me to bite my tongue. "You have to sort of take a breath, which is really hard in the moment," said Judith Smetana, a psychologist who studies adolescent-parent relationships at the University of Rochester, and try to respond positively rather than negatively. For me, this usually involves swallowing, forcing a smile, and saying something like *Well, that sounds fun*. If you have legitimate concerns, it's okay to bring them up—but calmly, later, at a neutral time, so that your kid doesn't feel punished for opening up to you.

If your kid is not a natural sharer, you can develop trust by first getting them to talk about other people's experiences and feelings. My son loves to do this with characters in books, movies, and TV shows. The show *Ted Lasso*, which openly explores issues around masculinity, friendships, and feelings, was an especially great source of fodder. After watching an episode with him, I would often start a conversation with an open-ended question like *How do you think Ted felt when his friend did that?* Often my son had plenty to say. (It probably helped that we watched the show in the evening and our conversations would sometimes delay his bedtime.)

When our kids take emotional risks, we can show them that we appreciate it by saying things like *That was a really brave thing to do.* "When we see boys being good friends to one another and providing support—really praise that in the same way, with the same enthusiasm, that we praise them for making a great three-pointer on the basketball court," Pepper said.

What if your child doesn't feel safe opening up to friends or challenging social norms? For nonbinary and trans kids especially, these kinds of emotional risks can feel extremely scary—not least because kids may be punished by peers for their nonconforming identities and perspectives. Malpas encourages parents to stay curious and not make assumptions or jump to conclusions. We may feel inclined to encourage our kids to dress the way they want or to talk back to unkind peers, but it's often more helpful to first ask our kids what they are anxious about, how they feel when they dress or act in certain ways, and what we can do to best support them, Malpas said. If the peers your child typically engages with aren't kind and supportive, consider widening their social net by helping them safely connect with like-minded peers online (many websites exist for this exact purpose!) or in person through school- or community-based or gender and sexuality alliances or LGBTQ clubs. You can contact the Trevor Project, a nonprofit organization focused on LGBTQ suicide prevention, and ask for suggestions for local resources.

We can also encourage kids to take emotional risks by getting them to envision what they want and having them consider potential outcomes. Counselor and educational consultant Phyllis Fagell suggested to me that parents can say something like *If you could wave a magic wand, what would your friendships look like? What do you wish you could talk about with your friends?* Some kids, especially boys, may not be willing or able to admit that they want more than they have, but for those who do, you could then say something like: *Have you ever tried having that conversation? What do you think would happen?* Fagell often tells kids that if they do for their friends what it is that *they* want, they might find their efforts reciprocated.

This is where I get to share some good news. Research suggests that some boys *do* successfully resist the norms of masculinity, at least in part, and that they are better off when they do. In one study, Way and her colleagues repeatedly interviewed a group of boys from when they were in the sixth grade through when they were in the eleventh grade. They found that most boys increased their adherence to masculinity norms as they progressed through their teen years. But 29 percent of the boys nevertheless continued, throughout high school, to express their feelings with friends and family members, to talk about their desire for close relationships, and to have close friends.

Way and her colleagues noted that these boys were more likely to be Latino than white, Black, or Chinese American, and they surmised that Latino boys were less strongly influenced by macho American values and more entrenched in what they call "Latino values," which include being emotionally expressive and family-oriented. But the masculinity resisters were not all Latino, and culture was not the only factor that shaped whether the boys were able to continue rejecting masculinity norms. Importantly, the boys who resisted traditional masculinity norms had stronger, deeper friendships, and they also reported having at least one parent who remained emotionally engaged with them and offered a safe space for them to talk about their feelings. So even if weeks have gone by and you feel like you haven't gotten a word out of your tween or teen, remember that it takes only one adult, providing an emotionally safe space, to teach kids the value of connecting deeply with others.

3. Be compassionate and affectionate with your kids—including (if not especially) your boys.

One thing that is clear from the research is that parents engage with boys very differently than they engage with girls, especially when it comes to affection and emotion. Studies have shown that parents talk about emotions less with their sons than with their daughters. When mothers reminisce about the past, they elaborate less on their feelings with boys than with girls. When mothers actually *do* talk about feelings with their boys, they tend to focus more on anger with them than they do with their daughters.

I certainly found this to be true of myself. I spent many years believing that my kids' vulnerable emotions—and especially my son's—were bad. When he was sad, scared, frustrated, or even "too excited," I worried that other people would judge him as being too soft or un-resilient, and my instinct was to tell him that he was over-reacting. I think I believed, deep down, that he needed to be stoic to make it as a boy in this world. Seeing him openly display his emotions somehow felt . . . wrong.

We tend to expect—and appreciate—different emotion-based behaviors from girls versus boys. One study found that fathers of preschoolers tend to reward daughters for being compliant, while they reward boys for assertiveness. As Boston University psychologist Leslie Brody concluded in her book *Gender, Emotion, and the Family*, "American parents and caregivers strongly, and sometimes unknowingly, reinforce boys' aggressiveness." Is it any wonder, then, that so many men turn their sadness into anger, the much more appropriately masculine emotion?

Parents tend to be less affectionate with boys than with girls, too. Moms smile less at their infant sons than at their infant daughters, and when reading to boys, they sit farther away, engage in less physical contact, and use a less pleasant tone of voice. When she interviewed mothers for her book *The Mama's Boy Myth*, journalist Kate Stone Lombardi discovered that mothers who felt emotionally close with their sons often worried that they would be judged for it. "There seem to be no words, no examples, no context whatsoever to describe a close bond between mother and son that doesn't in some way raise eyebrows and invite strict censure," she wrote. The fear is that close bonds will "create effeminate 'mama's boys' who will invite contempt from their peers and be forever maladjusted."

Another reason parents are more distant with—and tough on—boys versus girls is that they perceive boys to need less care and connection than girls do. Yet research actually suggests the opposite. Compared with females, male babies cry more often and have a harder time calming down. In one study, researchers at Harvard Medical School and the University of Pittsburgh observed that six-month-old boys expressed more frequent emotions than six-month-old girls did in various situations. This is in part because the part of the brain responsible for emotional regulation develops more slowly in boys than it does in girls.

I have certainly seen this sensitivity in my son. From a young age, he has been incredibly emotionally perceptive—keenly aware of others' moods and feelings, and very sensitive to them. This is why I'm especially floored that he doesn't seem to see the value in close friendships. Way said she's observed this in the boys she has studied: "I was always struck with the boys in my studies—but also, of course, my own son, and my brothers, I have a lot of boys and men in my family—with their emotional acuity. The ability to read things," she said. "It's not just that they're emotional. It's that they're emotionally intelligent."

As they get older, though, boys start to shift. Compared with younger boys, for instance, older boys show less sadness when watching sad movies. This could be because boys start to recognize and internalize the signals they are getting from the world about masculinity. Their behavior reflects, in Chu's words, "an adaptation to cultures that require boys to be emotionally stoic, aggressive, and competitive if they are to be perceived and accepted as 'real boys.'"

So the idea that boys don't need or want nurturing and connection is woefully incorrect—if anything, boys may need or want *more* of these things than girls do. As parents, this means we need to work to overcome our gendered biases and offer our boys regular emotional support and affection. They really do want it; recently, while saying goodbye to my teenage son before a short weekend trip, he came back to me for an extra hug.

We also need to be careful about the nonverbal signals we send our kids through facial expressions and body language. "We don't necessarily have to say 'man up' or 'suck it up' to a boy for him to perceive that he's outside of an adult's comfort zone," Reichert explained to me. "We withdraw, we stiffen, we get uncomfortable. We find ourselves feeling conflicted in our hearts, and it causes us to be somewhat distant or somewhat tense." Reichert suggested that when our kids are being affectionate, vulnerable, or emotionally expressive, we should pay attention to how we're feeling (both physically and emotionally) and, if we notice tension, acknowledge it and try to work through it, maybe take a few deep breaths.

When we treat our kids with empathy and acceptance, we also help them learn how to treat others compassionately—which will strengthen their future relationships. In a 2024 study, researchers at the University of Virginia found that the more compassionate and emotionally supportive mothers were with their teens, the more compassionate these teens then were with their friends in the future.

4. Encourage healthy conflict within relationships.

One evening, not too long ago, my nine-year-old daughter lost her temper.

We were all eating dinner. She asked her twelve-year-old brother a question—some kind of follow-up related to the conversation we were having—and he didn't answer her. He just shrugged, which he sometimes does even when a shrug is not appropriate. He probably did it just to annoy her.

Well, annoy her it did. In fact, she started crying. And yelling. She told him that it wasn't okay for him to be rude, that he does things like this all the time, and that she was sick and tired of it.

My inclination was to briefly validate her feelings but to mostly try to help her calm down. I wanted to work to reclaim some semblance of civility for the rest of dinner, try to smooth things over so everyone would get along.

But that day, I didn't. That day, I said something like: *I hear you. And I think you are making a very valid point.*

Her dad peered at me curiously, like he was trying to figure out if

I had lost my mind. Was I actually egging her on? What her brother had done wasn't that big of a deal. He was being a tween. He was not always responsive in the ways we wanted him to be.

But the fact was, his slight had upset her. She was entitled to her feelings. And her reaction, while more outsize than usual, was something I realized I wanted to defend rather than quell.

One of the reasons many kids, especially girls, struggle in relationships as they go through adolescence is because they have been socialized to suppress their anger—which is harmful on multiple levels. Anger has been nicknamed the "political emotion," because it can be a source of power and social change. Anger can also reflect a sense of self-worth and self-respect; if you're angry, it's often because you feel wronged, which you can feel only if you recognize that you are worthy of being treated right.

Some people might counter that girls simply don't experience as much anger as boys do—that there are gender differences in the propensity for rage. But the research says otherwise. Women are just as likely to get angry as men are, but they are less likely to express it.

One clever study illustrated this phenomenon. In it, researchers at the University of Amsterdam and Cardiff University invited college students into a lab and told them they would be participating in two unrelated experiments (although in fact, the two experiments were related, as you shall see). In the first experiment, the researchers asked the students to write an essay about the death penalty, telling them that their essays would be shown to another participant as an independent evaluator and that they would be given a meager cash reward at the end depending on how good their essays were.

The researchers rigged the results. Regardless of how good the essays actually were, the evaluators rated some of the students' essays as excellent and some as poor—and the ones rated as poor included a caustic comment that the writer was "naive and had an immature point of view." The students were then given their essays back and allowed to fume for a minute. The goal was to ensure that those who got the poor ratings were feeling angry as they went into the second part of the experiment.

In this second part, all students were told that they would be partnered up with a stranger for a study about taste preferences. The students were given tortilla chips and hot salsa and asked to decide how much their new partner should eat. Then they were told that, by random luck, they had just been paired with the person who had judged their essays. Some of the students were told that they would meet their partner at the end of the experiment, and others were told they would not.

The researchers observed what the students did next and how their gender and feelings impacted their choices. As you might guess, the subjects who'd been given poor grades on their essays, compared with those who'd gotten good grades, wanted their partners to consume more of the hot sauce (ostensibly as a form of punishment). But—although the men and the women in the study who'd gotten poor grades had become equally angry—women were less likely to give their partners tons of hot sauce if they thought they would have to meet that partner later. The angry men didn't care whether they would meet their partner; they gave their partners lots of hot sauce no matter what.

The authors concluded that women, compared with men, are more concerned about the negative social consequences of showing anger—supporting the notion that women are likely punished more than men are when they express their displeasure. In her 1985 book *The Dance of Anger*, therapist Harriet Lerner highlighted the unfeminine, unflattering labels that society uses for angry women, which include "bitch," "hag," "shrew," and "man-hater." There are far fewer denigrating labels for angry men, but two that stand out are "son of a bitch" and "bastard," both of which actually *blame the man's mother.*

When girls discover that their anger isn't welcome, they may internalize the idea that their voices, opinions, and feelings don't matter as much as other people's do. We can't shield our daughters from these omnipresent social messages, but we can at least provide a counterpoint at home. We "need to take what girls say seriously and start to think about sharing power with them," Brown advised when I asked her what parents can do to help girls find—and hold on to—their voices.

This can be as simple as tuning in and listening when our daughters share their opinions. This doesn't mean that we always need to agree with them, that we should allow them to do whatever they want, or that we should give in to all their requests and demands. But before we voice our own opinions or set the limits we know we need to set, we should at least ensure that our girls feel heard and respected. In her book *Girls on the Brink*, science journalist Donna Jackson Nakazawa explained that because of what happens to the brain during adolescence, tween and teen girls are often hyperfocused on what other people think of them and are especially sensitive to criticism. So when our girls come to us with ideas, problems, or difficult feelings, we should be careful to listen, validate them, and encourage their assertiveness.

This can be hard to do because it can involve challenging our own socialized beliefs or expectations. Recently, my good friend's seven-year-old daughter attended a birthday party, and the boy she had a big crush on was there. Repeatedly, at the party, the boy asked her to play tag with him, but my friend's daughter politely declined, explaining later to her mom that "I just don't really like tag." My friend felt a strong urge to chide her daughter—to say something like, *You know, if you want him to like you more, you should really accept his invitations to play.* Just in time, however, she caught herself. "I was like, *WTF am I doing*?" she told me. "I pivoted to *It's great that you know yourself well enough to say no to a thing you don't like even though the person asking is a boy you have a crush on.*"

Sometimes we may need to do a bit more to help our kids find their voice. In our house, we have only one television, in our basement, yet both my kids have screen time at the same time. My son has always watched on the TV and my daughter has always watched on her iPad, and I've never questioned why—I just assumed that she preferred the iPad and he preferred the TV. But one day, my daughter came to me and complained, saying it felt unfair that he got the TV every day and that they never took turns.

She admitted that she hadn't wanted to bring it up before for fear of making her brother mad, and I admit, I felt the same way: I knew he'd likely throw a fit. But I realized, too, that the status quo wasn't fair—and that I didn't want my daughter to not demand fairness simply because she was afraid of what other people might do. So I said, "You know what, you're right, this isn't okay. It should never have become the status quo that your brother always gets the TV." That night, as a family, we sat down and planned out a fair TV-watching schedule—and yes, my son was upset, but he adjusted.

I was lucky in this situation, because my daughter came to me to complain. If she hadn't, I never would have known she was unhappy. But I did follow up with her and encouraged her to speak up if she found herself in similar situations in the future. All kids, but especially the ones who are less inclined to speak their minds, benefit from this kind of encouragement—from being reminded that they deserve to voice their wants and desires just as much as everyone else. And when they do speak up or speak out, we should praise them for their courage.

We can also help kids learn how to respond to their anger and engage in healthy conflict. Remember that study I mentioned that found that kids' ability to respectfully engage with their friends during disagreements predicted their future academic success? That is a teachable skill, thank goodness. When boys get angry, it is often explosive—it may involve punching a wall or throwing things across a room. In these moments, it can be hard for parents to stay calm, but it's in our best interest to try, because responding with anger or with an overbearing attempt to control the situation is like "pouring gasoline on a fire," Reichert wrote in his book *How to Raise a Boy*. Often, Reichert explained, anger is the emotion boys feel first, but there are other emotional layers underneath. If a parent stays calm and communicates that all feelings are welcome (though of course it's okay to set limits on bad behavior!), they make it easier for boys to access the deeper layers of emotional pain, process them, and talk about them.

As for the girls, it may help them to think about different ways they could choose to behave when they feel angry. In her book *Under Pressure*, the psychologist Lisa Damour described three unhealthy ways girls often deal with conflict. There is the "bulldozer," who runs people over with her anger; the "doormat," who allows herself to be run over; and the "doormat with spikes," who uses passive-aggressive approaches like talking behind people's backs. A much healthier approach, Damour wrote, is to be a "pillar," who stands up for herself without stepping on or disrespecting anyone else.

When helping kids decide what approach to take, Damour often asks them to imagine and describe what each of the unhealthy reactions might look like. Then she asks them to come up with a more pillar-like plan: a way in which they can stand up for themselves without hurting others.

5. Help kids cultivate supportive friendships and recognize worrisome patterns.

I'm going to wrap up this chapter with an anecdote that brings together many of the strategies outlined above and gets into the reality of the complex social situations kids often face. A few years ago, a good friend of mine, Alexis, came to me feeling stuck as she tried to help her tween daughter, Emma, navigate a complicated relationship. For many years, Emma had been close friends with a girl named Tessa who lived down the street, but Alexis had mixed feelings about the relationship. She would often overhear Tessa saying mean things to Emma during playdates, such as criticizing her dance skills or telling her that she talked funny. With increasing frequency, her daughter would come home from school in tears, almost always because of something hurtful Tessa had said to her.

Yet despite these unkindnesses, Emma continued to want to be friends with Tessa—a choice Alexis found concerning and heartbreaking. She worried about the impact Tessa was having on her daughter's self-esteem, and she worried that Emma's tolerance of the cruelty was already a sign of confidence issues. (Alexis was certainly picking up on the tendency for girls to lose touch with themselves to serve relationships.) Alexis tried to talk to Emma about Tessa's unkind choices, but her daughter would often dismiss them, saying things like *Yes, Tessa can be mean to me, but she can be really nice, too.* Alexis also tried to help Emma brainstorm ways to respond to the cruel comments with boundary-setting responses like *I don't like it when you say things like that to me. Can you please stop?*

Often, as parents, we see—or choose to see—only small slices of our kids' relationships. Because our job is to keep our kids safe, our observations are sometimes incomplete—we tune in to the worrying aspects of our kids' friendships at the expense of the full picture. We always need to keep in mind that kids can have different kinds of friends, for different kinds of reasons, said psychologist Eileen Kennedy-Moore, the author of the book *Growing Friendships*. My friend's daughter was clearly being hurt by Tessa's words, but she may have been getting something good out of the friendship, too.

Still, Alexis couldn't shake that notion that the relationship was doing her daughter more harm than good—especially since her daughter reported that setting boundaries didn't seem to be working. So I advised Alexis to talk to her daughter about Tessa—and about friendship in general—and to lead with curiosity, rather than with an opinion. If she started a conversation with *I think you should stop being friends with Tessa,* her daughter would likely spring into defensive mode and argue back. Nobody—especially not a tween girl—likes being told what to do. On the other hand, employing some of those listening strategies I described above—being curious, asking open-ended questions, trying to listen without an agenda, and validating—could perhaps further the conversation and even more deeply connect Alexis and her daughter.

When I spoke with child and adolescent psychotherapist Katie Hurley, the author of *No More Mean Girls,* she suggested that parents who are concerned about their kids' friendships should start with open-ended questions. "One thing I always encourage parents to do is to say to their kids, *Tell me, what do you love about that friend?*" Hurley said. "Meeting our kids with curiosity keeps us out of the judgment zone, which is important." You can ask other, more thought-provoking questions, too: *What do you admire about your friend? What does she do to show you that she cares about you? How do you usually feel when you're hanging out with her?* If you want to talk about friendship more generally, without zeroing in on this particular friend, you could say: *What do you think are the qualities of a good friend?* Questions like these can help prompt kids to think about the benefits and drawbacks of their relationships.

When Alexis asked these questions of Emma, she learned that her daughter enjoyed Tessa's humor and the fact that they enjoy the same activities—dance and softball. Emma also said she believed that friends should always be supportive and want the best for each other—statements that seemed to contradict her daughter's experience with Tessa. When Alexis asked Emma if she felt Tessa did these things for her, Emma demurred, saying that she didn't know.

It soon became clear, though, that Alexis's questions sparked ongoing reflection. A few weeks later, Emma told her that she wasn't sure that she wanted to be close friends with Tessa anymore, but that she didn't know how to create some distance. She didn't want to completely sever the relationship and cut off all ties with her friend; but she recognized that she wanted to spend less time with her, at least for a little while.

In these kinds of situations, experts say, it can help to brainstorm with your kids to see if there are ways to keep the good parts of the friendship and avoid the bad parts. With a little probing, Alexis learned that much of the mean behavior happened on the school bus in the afternoons, so she suggested that Emma tell Tessa that she wanted more space on the bus ride home. Emma seemed to feel conflicted and worried that creating space would be unkind, but my friend told her daughter that it's okay—even important—to set healthy boundaries. She explained that it's crucial to tend to your own needs as long as you do it in a way that's respectful to others. "Encourage girls to speak directly about what they need and want from their friends and to know their boundaries and what they are unwilling to give up for the sake of a particular relationship," Brown wrote in *Girlfighting*.

It's also important to remember that we shouldn't assume that kids who are "mean" to our children are bad people. Their behavior may well be rooted in pain or fear, either from what they are experiencing in their families or their schools, or from the broader cultural messages they are internalizing. As I already mentioned, girls are somewhat conditioned to be mean to each other, and boys often aren't given much practice at emotional and relationship skills. It's always important to encourage our kids to be empathetic and respectful, including of peers who do not always treat them well. (We should also be careful that we aren't falling prey to gender stereotypes by expecting girls to always be sweet and demonizing those who aren't.) When my kids come to me to talk about a peer being unkind, I often encourage them to consider what the other child might be going through—not to excuse, but at least help understand, their choices.

When I checked back in with Alexis a few months later, she said that things had very much improved on the Tessa front. The girls still sometimes played together at recess, but their difficult school bus interactions had become rare. Alexis felt relieved that her daughter had eventually recognized, on her own, that she deserved to have her needs met and her boundaries respected—and had taken the necessary steps to make that happen. Her daughter had successfully become a "pillar" in this situation—standing up for herself without treading on anyone else.

KEY POINTS

1. Know that boys, girls, trans kids, and nonbinary kids often struggle in different ways with relationships because of gender stereotypes and expectations. In general, boys are socialized to sacrifice relationships in order to appear tough, while girls are socialized to sacrifice their authentic selves in order to better serve their relationships—but friendship-strengthening strategies can help all kids across the board.
2. Listen to your kids, and teach them how to listen well, too.
3. Foster kids' interpersonal curiosity and vulnerability.
4. Support your kids emotionally and be affectionate with them.
5. Encourage your kids' voices and perspectives and teach them how to engage in healthy conflict.
6. Teach your children to recognize and cultivate respectful friendships and recognize unhealthy patterns.

7

"Those People Are Dumb."

Promoting Curiosity and Inclusion—and Preventing Bias and Polarization

One winter day when she was in the fourth grade, my friend's daughter, Olivia, came home from school absolutely distraught. Earlier that day, she'd learned that a good friend of hers, Clara, supported Donald Trump in the 2024 election. This, to Olivia, meant Clara was "evil" and that they could no longer be friends. Clara, it seemed, had come to a similar conclusion about Olivia. Their friendship quickly dissolved.

When I heard this story from my friend, I couldn't help but contrast it to my own fourth-grade political experiences. My friends and I certainly had some (I'm sure very uninformed) conversations and disagreements about the merits of Bush versus Dukakis, but nobody judged a friend's character based on which candidate they supported—and political differences certainly didn't end any friendships.

Our kids are growing up in a much more polarized world than we did, and one in which people have become more willing to openly condone beliefs and behaviors rooted in sexism and racism. I've long worried about the impact of these shifts on kids—it's why I wrote my first book, *How to Raise Kids Who Aren't Assholes*—because we know from the science that kids tend to look to the adults around them and those in power to determine what kind of behavior is acceptable.

Thankfully, though, kids also look up to *us*—parents and other caregivers—to understand more about social norms and how to think about the world. And there's lots we can do to nudge them in the direction of open-mindedness and inclusivity. These traits don't merely benefit others—they directly benefit our kids, too. Research suggests that open-minded, curious people are happier, feel more satisfied with their lives, and are more academically successful than their closed-minded peers.

The Road to Polarization

First, it's important to understand why and how bias and polarization form. Kids are like little social detectives—they are constantly observing the people around them and deciphering what they can about them, including who has power and prestige, who does not, and why. "Kids' minds are always searching for explanations for what they experience, for what other people experience," explained Laura Elenbaas, a developmental psychologist at Purdue University. Kids are also trying to figure out with whom to align themselves to maximize their social prospects. They're not being jerks; they're just being human.

Our ability to lump things into categories has long been an extremely useful shortcut for understanding and making predictions about the world. But categorizing *people* can have drawbacks—especially when kids make unfortunate and inaccurate inferences about social categories, which often happens. One problem is that kids often engage in "essentialist thinking": They believe that observable differences between people—such as skin color, gender, or religion—reflect deeper, innate biological differences. This causes them to think that members of a social group are similar to one another in numerous, deep-seated ways.

Sometimes essentialist thinking can be a good thing: If I encounter a tiger in the wild, I don't need to ponder whether it might come after me—I will run, because I believe tigers all share an inherent aggressive nature. But with people, essentialism can lead to stereotyping, prejudice, discrimination, dehumanization, even genocide. In a 2015 study, researchers found that kids who developed essentialist ideas about an imaginary social group were less likely to share resources with individuals in that group compared with kids who had not developed these essentialist ideas. Another study found that kids who have essentialist ideas about race are more likely to believe negative racial stereotypes, such as that African Americans steal and that Asian Americans are submissive.

Kids engage in essentialist thinking at the same time that they make unfortunate inferences based on what they see in the world around them. They'll notice, for instance, that there's never been a woman president, and they'll try to understand why. If kids don't know about gender discrimination, they'll try to come up with their own reasons—and the simplest one is that women aren't smart or capable. They'll see, too, that white people tend to have more power and money than people of color, and they might assume, if they don't know about the structural causes of the power hierarchy, that people of color are less smart, less hardworking, or inherently less deserving of power than white people are.

"For kids, it's pretty cognitively easy to make that leap from thinking, *Well, if hard work and smarts lead to success, then it must be that rich people and white people and men, boy, they really put in the effort,*" Elenbaas explained to me. "And poor people, people of color, girls, nonbinary people—they must not be putting in the effort. Maybe they're just not smart enough to really succeed." Essentialist thinking is often used to rationalize and even endorse existing social hierarchies, making people believe that discrimination doesn't exist and that power hierarchies are simply a reflection of innate differences. They come to believe that the inequalities that exist in the world reflect natural, inherent hierarchies rather than flawed, biased beliefs and policies.

When kids are trying to figure out the world, they may not only develop concerning beliefs about groups of people, but also about ideas. And research suggests that children today are more politically polarized than they used to be. Before about 1980, kids tended to view political leaders positively regardless of their party affiliation and didn't equate political beliefs with moral identity. But boy, have things changed. In a 2023 paper, Stanford political scientists Matthew Tyler and Shanto Iyengar compared adolescents' responses on political surveys conducted in 1980 and 2019 that were designed to assess kids' trust in the major political parties. They found that adolescents have become much more polarized with regard to their political beliefs since 1980 and are now just as polarized as adults. They also compared levels of parent-child political agreement, finding that in 1980, only 56 percent of teens favored the same political party as their parents, whereas in 2019, 81 percent did. The findings suggest that parents today have a strong political influence on their kids—much stronger than in the past.

Why does polarization develop? It's a complex question; there have been entire books written about it. But part of it is rooted in the desire for social belongingness as well as the need to make an uncertain, complex world easier to understand.

If you spend any time on social media, you've probably noticed that there is now an expectation to voice moralized opinions about . . . well, just about everything. These incentives are often baked into the algorithms themselves, because more strongly worded posts typically get more eyes and traction, explained Eric Torres, a researcher at Harvard University who studies polarization. Research has found that social media posts that include expressions of moral outrage are more likely to go viral. These incentives, Torres explained, not only affect how kids and teens (and adults) behave online but also likely shape how they engage with the ideas of the world. Kids may come to believe that it's better to make strong snap judgments than to reflect on or analyze issues before forming and expressing an opinion.

Unfortunately, in some ways, they are right. In a 2022 study, Ike Silver, now a marketing researcher at the University of Southern California's Marshall School of Business, and Alex Shaw, a psychologist at the University of Chicago, conducted a series of experiments involving more than four thousand adults. They found that, across a variety of workplace contexts, people were more suspicious and less trusting of people who declined to take sides on an issue compared with people who had shared strong opinions—even if that opinion was one they disagreed with. In other words, we tend to value people with strong opinions, even bad ones, more than people who take the time to self-educate and consider nuances. It's a worrying finding, and it helps to explain our collective propensity to broadcast black-and-white beliefs. No matter what we say, we are, on balance, rewarded for having said it.

It doesn't help that the internet and social media tend to keep us safely housed in bubbles that reinforce these assumptions and beliefs. Studies show that most angry, polarizing social media posts are shared only among like-minded others. And the problem goes beyond online media—people typically only tune in to radio shows that reflect their political affiliations, subscribe to newspapers and magazines that reinforce their existing beliefs, and so on. Frankly, it's no wonder that kids today harbor such strong and extreme views: They are getting the message from so many sources that it's the right thing to do.

Teaching Kids to Avoid Bias

All hope is not lost, however. Research suggests that there are steps parents can take to interrupt the development of bias in kids and nudge them toward curiosity and nuance. Here's what the science says.

1. Model and encourage curiosity and uncertainty.

Primatologist Jane Goodall, one of the world's foremost experts on chimpanzees, has lived a life full of adventure and curiosity—and she credits her mother for nurturing her open-mindedness and love for exploration. When she was four, Goodall's mother took her on vacation to a farm, where Goodall was tasked with collecting eggs from the henhouse. Goodall realized she also wanted to know how chickens laid eggs, so one day, she hid in an empty henhouse for four hours, watching and waiting as the chickens went about their business. Her family had no idea where she was, and her mother called for her, but Goodall ignored her, staying put in the hopes of watching an egg get laid.

When Goodall eventually emerged, she was excited to tell her mother what she'd observed. Instead of berating her, her mother calmly listened to her tell the story of how the hen laid its egg. As Goodall has said, "A different kind of mother might have crushed that spirit of scientific curiosity. And I might not be standing here talking to you now." In that brief encounter, her mother taught Goodall that curiosity was something to be celebrated rather than punished.

As was the case with Goodall's choice to ignore her mom, curiosity and exploration in kids can sometimes look more like inattention, distractibility, or even bad behavior. When you ask your child to clean their room, then find them thirty minutes later studying a spider in the bathroom while their room still looks like an abandoned junkyard, it's easy to dismiss their behavior as disobedience. But the underlying reasons for their distraction may be biological, benevolent, and even evolutionarily adaptive.

As I already mentioned, kids are like young scientists. One of their most important jobs is to make sense of the world around them. To achieve this, kids need to take in all kinds of data from their surroundings. They need to pay attention to the things they encounter throughout the day, like weird spiders in the bathroom. As a kid, "what you want to be able to do is have the machinery that allows you to adapt to a wide range of experiences," explained Daniel Berry, a developmental psychologist who studies the development of self-regulation and attention at the University of Minnesota. You "want to have some freedom to make sense of your world." If kids' brains shut out all distractions, they won't be able to accomplish that.

Alison Gopnik, a developmental psychologist at the University of

California, Berkeley, has said much the same. "Grown-up brains and children's brains are really designed for different purposes," she told me when I interviewed her for a piece I wrote for *The New York Times*. Kids' brains are a lot better at exploring and being curious, she explained, while adults' brains are very good at getting things done (well . . . some more than others), and not as good at learning new things. (Related: Can someone please tell me how to use TikTok?)

I'm not saying that we should throw all rules out the window in support of our kids' curiosity and never make them clean their rooms—but I do think it's useful to understand that the behavior we sometimes find irritating can reflect skills and proclivities we want to nourish rather than stamp out. So instead of jumping down their throats upon discovering that they forgot to feed the dog because they were reading *The Week Junior*, perhaps we should respond with support and empathy. *I love that you are learning about what's going on in the world! But the dog looks hungry—please take a quick break to feed him.*

We can encourage curiosity in our kids in other ways, too. One is by asking our children questions—even when we already know the answer—rather than simply explaining how things work. In a 2018 study, researchers invited four- and five-year-olds into a classroom and introduced them to a new toy that featured various buttons and knobs that could be manipulated to produce different results. Some kids learned about the toy when an adult explained how it worked, saying things like *I'm telling you: You push this button.* Other kids were taught about the toy by an adult who instead asked the child questions like *I'm asking you to think about: What does this button do?*

Then the researchers left each child alone with the toy to play with it. The kids who'd been encouraged through questions spent more time exploring the toy and discovered more of its hidden attributes than the kids who were simply told how it worked.

These kinds of "pedagogical questions," as they are called, can be used in lots of everyday situations, explained Emily Liquin, a psychologist at the University of New Hampshire who studies children's curiosity. If you're reading a picture book with your child, you could point to an illustration and say, *What's happening here?* Or you can ask follow-ups about the story itself, like *Why do you think the kitten has a stomachache?* When walking down the street, pedagogical questions can be as simple as pointing to things and saying, *Hey, what's that?* With older kids, pedagogical questions might involve asking your kid why they think certain things happen the way they do—*Why do we have elections?* Or why they see certain things in the world—*Why do you think those people have that sign in their yard?*

Encouraging kids to ask their *own* questions can also foster curiosity. In one study, researchers invited five- to seven-year-olds to participate in a series of online science lessons. Kids were either encouraged to ask questions or told to "listen carefully." At the end of the lessons, the kids who were encouraged to ask questions learned more and were more interested in discovering other new things compared with the kids who'd been told only to listen. The same has been found to be true for teens—they also become more curious when they are encouraged to ask questions. It makes sense, right?

We should try to model open-mindedness and curiosity in front of our kids, too. I can't tell you how many times my kids have asked me questions about current events, and I've answered something along the lines of *That's a great question, and I don't know the answer. Let's do some research together to see what we can find out.* We can encourage thoughtful consideration of others, too: Instead of judging people's intent and character based on their personal choices, we can think aloud in front of our kids about the various possible rationales—concluding, perhaps, that we don't have enough information to come to a solid conclusion.

We should also communicate to our kids that it's okay to be wrong and to change our minds. As Torres explained to me, a common belief that fans the flames of polarization is that wrongness is morally bad—we often believe that it is shameful to be incorrect, to admit our errors, and to revise our thinking. We all saw this play out a hundred different ways during the pandemic, when safety guidelines changed in light of new information and some people characterized these revisions as evidence of scientific ineptitude, instead of as evidence that science was working the way it should (it's a process, not an outcome).

What if our kids still seem unwilling to consider new perspectives? Although our instinct may be to try to convince them with data and statistics, that approach typically doesn't help. "Just throwing facts at each other really doesn't shift people's willingness and openness to hearing the other side," explained Jamie Amemiya, a developmental psychologist at Occidental College who studies how children think about and respond to societal problems. Research suggests that a far better approach is to share stories that illustrate why individuals have a particular point of view—and that these stories are especially powerful when they are personal and involve perceived harm or suffering. Perhaps my friend's daughter Olivia could have better understood Clara's support for Trump if she heard that Clara's father recently lost his job and that Clara believed that Trump's policies would help him find a new one.

We should also model taking responsibility for our mistakes, including apologizing and trying to make amends. Research suggests that while most mothers *say* that they apologize to their kids, their apologies tend to miss key components. This is unfortunate, given that proper apologies can strengthen parent-child relationships and help kids learn to apologize more thoughtfully themselves. In my opinion, a complete apology involves five components: (1) an expression of remorse or regret—*I'm sorry for yelling at you*; (2) an admission of responsibility—*I made a mistake*; (3) an acknowledgment of the other person's emotions or suffering—*I can see that you're upset and that I hurt your feelings*; (4) a plan to do better in the future—*I promise I'll work on this by taking deep breaths next time I feel upset*; and (5) an offer of repair—*What can I do right now to make you feel better?*

2. Listen to your kids with curiosity—rather than judging or correcting.

A while back, I watched the Guardians of the Galaxy movies with my son. In a scene that at first tugged at my heartstrings, Drax the Destroyer, a heavily muscled but rather dim-witted male character, admitted to the three other misfits he had been working with—Quill, Groot, and the lone female, Gamora—that he considered them to be his friends.

"You, Quill, are my friend," Drax said. "This dumb tree, he is my friend. And this green whore—" he started, referring to Gamora. He wasn't able to finish, because she interrupted him to scream at him, but it was clear that the scene was meant to be funny rather than infuriating.

I, however, instantly got angry. Not because the scene didn't reflect reality—guys often do feel the need to degrade women when paying them compliments—but because I knew that millions of kids would watch that scene and learn from it that it's okay—even funny—to call women "whores."

After the movie, I mentioned the scene to my son and told him that I thought it was sexist. He flat out disagreed, telling me the various reasons he thought it wasn't. It was all I could do not to start yelling—but I took some deep breaths and tried to listen to him. In the end, instead of my lecturing him, we had an actual conversation in which I agreed with some of what he said, and he eventually agreed with some of what I said—including that calling a woman a "whore," even in so-called jest, is totally unacceptable.

When we engage with and listen to our kids instead of lecturing them, we do many good things. We communicate to our kids that we think their perspective matters, which is important for their self-concept and self-esteem. We model having a curious, rather than judgmental, mindset, a precursor to humility and open-mindedness. It's also helpful for fostering thoughtful information literacy—the ability to evaluate and use information effectively (for more on helping kids develop this skill, see chapter 9). Seth Ashley, a communications and media literacy researcher at Boise State University, recently explained to me that it's important for kids to have the opportunity to work through their thoughts and ideas on their own, rather than always being provided with the "correct" answer. This approach helps them to become more comfortable with uncertainty, which is an important aspect of information literacy.

More broadly, research has shown that when parents treat kids with respect and autonomy, listening to what they have to say and giving them voice in family decisions, kids develop more support for democratic values, including the notion that people can have different perspectives and that conflict should be resolved with negotiation and compromise.

There are other reasons not to cut off, yell at, or try to silence our kids when they say things we disagree with—especially, perhaps, with our boys. In a 2024 essay for *The Cut*, columnist Kathryn Jezer-Morton admitted that she, too, finds it very hard not to jump down her son's throat when he expresses distasteful opinions—especially when they relate to gender and power dynamics. "I think many of us adults are so entrenched in social media political discourse that it feels dangerously transgressive to allow a teen to articulate beliefs we disagree with at our dinner tables," she wrote. "But coming down too hard risks playing right into the paranoid hands of masculinist discourses of male disempowerment."

What Jezer-Morton is referring to is the notion that many young men today—and the influencers who appeal to them, such as Andrew Tate—have latched onto what she calls a "grievance-based identity." They feel the need to position themselves as wronged or disadvantaged so they can blame others for their failures and challenges—and so their own narrative can be one of vindication and emancipation.

We as parents, then, may not want to offer ourselves as potential oppressors. If we immediately correct or chastise our kids when they say things we dislike, we will only make them feel defensive, which could make them less willing to hear what we have to say. And we may give them reason to feel more aggrieved, which could encourage them to blame others for any challenges they face.

I'm not saying we should let our kids say offensive things and shrug them off. I am saying that we can often make more headway with our kids when we approach their perspectives with curiosity rather than judgment. If we ask questions to explore where their opinions or attitudes are coming from, it can help us put their ideas in perspective and give us insight into how best to engage in them.

Listening to our kids with openness and curiosity may reduce their propensity for judgment and polarization for another reason, too. Guy Itzchakov, a psychologist who directs the University of Haifa's Interpersonal Listening and Social Influence lab and whom I introduced in chapter 6, has conducted research showing that when people feel heard—even by people who don't necessarily agree with them—they become more self-reflective and open-minded.

In one of Itzchakov's studies, published in 2023, college students had a conversation with someone who held an opposing political opinion. Some of their conversation partners listened well, providing consistent eye contact and responsive and open body language, and gave verbal responses that indicated their interest in and understanding of the subject's perspective. For instance, they said things like *I just want to make sure I understand* and summarized what they had just heard. Other subjects were paired with conversation partners who listened only moderately well, providing little verbal feedback.

Afterward, the subjects who'd been paired with good listeners said their conversation helped them think more deeply about the topic—and by the end, those participants held less extreme views on the issue they had discussed. It's important to note, too, that this kind of high-quality listening does not require the listener to *agree with* the speaker. It simply involves acknowledging the speaker's right to speak their mind without being censored.

Itzchakov's work has also found that the feeling of being listened to makes people more humble and willing to consider their weaknesses. In another of his studies, business school students were asked to consider how they felt about becoming managers in the future. Some of these students then engaged in conversation on a totally different topic with a partner who listened well to them, while other students talked with a more distracted and uninvested listener. Those who felt they'd been heard were later more likely to acknowledge their potential limitations as future managers.

Why does feeling heard and understood make people less polarized and more open to self-reflection? People adopt extreme views and opinions when they feel anxious and threatened, Itzchakov explained. This response is evolutionarily adaptive; if you suspect an intruder is in your home, for example, it's important for your brain to weed out unnecessary considerations and nuances so you can focus on keeping your family safe. On the flip side, when we feel listened to, we then feel safer and calmer and are better able to pay attention to peripheral details—in other words, we become more open-minded.

With our own kids, it can be really hard to listen without judgment. Again, I only *barely* bit my tongue after I talked with my son about that Guardians of the Galaxy scene. Itzchakov, who has three daughters, openly admitted that he also struggles to listen to them in a nonjudgmental way when they say things he disagrees with. But he strives to do it nonetheless, knowing that doing so strengthens his relationship with them and helps them grow into more thoughtful, curious humans.

3. Avoid using generic group labels to describe people.

I don't know about your social media feed, but mine is full of people using broad labels to pit groups of people against each other. It's men versus women; boomers versus millennials; Jews versus Palestinians; Democrats versus Republicans.

We frequently use labels to describe people even when we're making innocent observations—because, let's face it, it can be easy to refer to people based on the groups they belong to. It's why we say things like *Those ladies over there look sad* and *Black people have a lot of rhythm*. The problem is, this kind of group labeling can fuel the development of prejudice, even when we don't mean for it to. When we refer to people by the groups they are members of—"boys" versus "girls," for instance—we send a message to our children that these group distinctions really matter. Then, kids start to wonder what makes girls "girls" and what makes boys "boys," which can lead them to assume there are more—and deeper and more innate—differences between groups of people than there really are.

This comes back to the concept (and dangers) of essentialism, which is the tendency we all have to assume that people who are members of a group share predictable, stable, and innate qualities. Research finds that the words people use to describe groups shape how likely kids are to develop essentialist ideas—and, ultimately, how likely they are to develop prejudice.

In a 2014 study, researchers at Bar-Ilan University in Israel invited seventy-six five-year-old Jewish Israeli children and their parents (mostly mothers) to participate in a study to understand how children develop essentialist ideas about ethnicity. One thing we know about essentialism is that although the tendency to do it is likely universal, the ways in which it's done are powerfully shaped by culture. Kids in the United States, for instance, tend to develop essentialist beliefs about race and gender, believing that boys and white people are smarter than girls and people of color. In Israel, kids tend to develop essentialist ideas about ethnicity (Jews versus Arabs); in Chile, they essentialize social status; in India, they essentialize caste.

For the study, the researchers visited the families' homes and gave the families a book they had created titled *What Different People Do,* asking the parents to read it aloud with their child and talk about the different kinds of people in the book. Each page portrayed either Arab or Jewish characters, identifiable by visual cues such as yarmulkes and head shawls, doing various things, some of which were stereotypical for their ethnicities and some of which were not. The researchers recorded the conversations the parents had with their kids about the book, taking note of how often the parents referred to groups as if they were homogenous—such as *Arabs don't do this* or *Jews are smart*. They also recorded other information, including how many times the parents used ethnic labels and how often the parents made statements that accentuated differences versus similarities between the groups.

Separately, the researchers gave the children and parents tests to assess their beliefs about the two social groups, such as how similar and different they felt Jews and Arabs are. They also asked them questions to determine how much the parents and kids engaged in essentialist thinking.

The researchers found that the more the parents used broad labels like "Arab" and referred to Arab individuals as if they were members of a homogenous group, the more strongly their kids' essentialist tendencies were—those kids believed stereotypes about Arab people and assumed that Arabs were all pretty much the same. Interestingly, the parents' own beliefs had less of an impact on their kids' beliefs than their word choices did. As the researchers concluded, "social essentialism is not transmitted by parents to their children via explicit and systematic communication of intergroup values, beliefs, or attitudes"—but, rather, by how they talk.

Other research confirms that language makes a big difference in terms of how kids think about group members—even when those groups aren't real. In one study, researchers at NYU and Princeton told four-year-olds about an imaginary group of people they called "Zarpies." Some kids learned about Zarpies from adults who spoke about them using generic language, saying things like *Zarpies are scared of ladybugs*, which implies that all Zarpies share a common essence. (We do this all the time when we say things like *Girls like Taylor Swift* or *Boys like sports*.) Other four-year-olds learned about Zarpies from adults who were careful to attribute characteristics only to individuals; they said things like *This Zarpie is scared of ladybugs*.

Kids who heard adults talking about Zarpies as a generic group, as if they shared certain properties—e.g., *Zarpies are afraid of ladybugs*—were more likely to believe essentialist things about Zarpies. They believed that their characteristics were shared, innate, and inevitable—in other words, all Zarpies are the same. The study, the researchers argued, provides "strong evidence that generic language is a mechanism by which social essentialist beliefs can be transmitted from parents to children."

This research suggests that there is a simple way, then, to reduce the kids' propensity for prejudice: Don't talk about—or passively refer to—groups of people in generic ways, as if they are all uniform and share similar characteristics. We should avoid saying things like *Teenagers are always on their phones* or *Girls love dancing*. Even if we are making what we think of as a positive comment about another group, like *Black people are good athletes* or *Asian kids are smart*, we are still encouraging our kids to assume that all Black or Asian people are similar, which is a dangerous road to walk down. (If nothing else, when you find yourself saying something about a group, insert the word "some"—like *Some teenagers are always on their phones*. Nobody could argue with that!)

We can also gently insert nuance when we hear others—including our kids—say essentialist things. If your kid points out that girls don't like soccer, or that the eighth graders are mean, ask follow-up questions. *Do you think all girls don't like soccer—what about Celia down the street?* or *Well, Jesse is in eighth grade, and he's pretty nice, right?*

4. Talk to kids about isms (racism, sexism, feminism, ageism, ableism, et cetera) and their structural causes. Discuss other forms of bias, too, like homophobia and transphobia.

As I mentioned before, children are constantly trying to make sense of the world. Among other things, they notice hierarchies and inequalities at a young age: Kids as young as three and a half believe that boys have higher status than girls and that white people are wealthier than Black people. Their next job is to try to decipher what causes these status differences—and the simple answers, which kids tend to gravitate to, are often the most biased. Kids may start to believe that people with more power in society, such as men and white people, have power because they are inherently smarter, better, or more deserving. These beliefs lead to prejudice and discrimination.

Indeed, multiple studies have found that kids are more likely to perpetuate inequalities when they believe that those inequalities are caused by differences in ability or deservedness compared with when they believe the inequalities have structural causes. Kids are especially likely to perpetuate inequalities when they benefit from them. (For more on talking to kids about inequality, see chapter 8.)

It makes sense, then, for parents to introduce the notions of racism, sexism, and other isms when kids are young (such as in preschool), because doing so helps kids understand that power hierarchies are often driven by structural issues rather than differences in character or ability. We should also talk about homophobia, transphobia, and other forms of sexual and identity-based discrimination, once kids are old enough to understand them.

How do we do this? It can certainly be uncomfortable, but I've found that the conversations get easier the more you have them. I often look to examples of isms I see playing out in the real world or in the media (in books, movies, or TV shows) and then start a conversation about them with my kids. For instance, when we watched the summer Olympics a few years ago, I noticed that the announcer kept referring to male kayakers on the US kayaking team as "men" and the female kayakers as "girls." I paused the TV and asked my kids: *Did you notice the way he was referring to the men as men and the women as girls? Why do you think he did that?*

Often, questions are the best place to start, because they give you the chance to see where your kids are and what they understand before you add your two cents. But almost always, the conversations I've had with my kids on these topics have resulted in brief forays into history and how social norms, stereotypes, the desire for power, and discriminatory laws and policies have shaped ongoing prejudice and discrimination. That said, the conversations don't have to be long and they don't have to touch upon everything—it's better to have brief but regular talks about these issues than, say, one or two long talks per year. And it's totally fine to make mistakes—it's hard not to!—because mistakes are opportunities to bring the topic back up and to model to your kids that everyone is a lifelong learner.

Research finds that educating kids about discrimination does indeed reduce prejudice. One study, for instance, found that kids who believe that racial inequality has structural causes are less racist than kids who believe this inequality is the result of intrinsic differences between Black and white individuals. In another small study, researchers presented elementary-aged white children with short biographies of famous white and Black individuals over the course of six days. Half of the kids heard about the racist experiences the Black individuals had endured throughout their lives, while half did not. Then the researchers gave the kids tests to evaluate their levels of racial prejudice, finding that the kids who'd learned about racism had more positive attitudes toward Black people than the kids who hadn't. In a follow-up study, they repeated the study but with Black kids, to determine whether the racism-based lessons were difficult for the Black students to hear. On the contrary, they found that students were more satisfied with lessons that acknowledged racism than those that didn't.

This brings me to another point: Yes, white parents need to explicitly talk to kids about race and skin color. (I single out white parents because white parents tend to go out of their way to avoid the topic; parents of color, and parents of kids of color, tend to have frequent conversations about race and racism because they have to.) There's a common misconception among white parents that it's best to act "color-blind": to never mention skin color differences or bring attention to race. In fact, research suggests that approaches that foster color-blindness cause kids to become *more* racist, not less, for the reasons I've already outlined: Kids nevertheless notice the racial hierarchy in society, and if we don't explain that racism is the cause of it, they will come up with their own explanations, which are likely to be racist.

If you worry that talking about race and racism could make your kids uncomfortable, consider that children of color typically *experience* racism on a daily basis—which is far, far more troubling. "Parents who benefit from the way that society is structured today [should] step up and help the next generation understand how we got here," Elenbaas said. Although there's concern as to whether discussions of racism could make white kids feel some shame, this isn't the case with my own kids. They've told me that, instead, it's made them feel inspired to work to change the status quo.

5. Expose your kids to diversity and encourage (and model) diverse friendships.

Talking, of course, goes only so far. If we want to raise inclusive kids, we should normalize and celebrate diversity in our lives, in part by encouraging diverse friendships. "We have known for a long time that a huge positive predictor of not having stereotypes and prejudice is having friends from a group that you might perceive to be different," Elenbaas said.

This isn't to say that you can just throw your kids into a situation with kids of other races, gender identities, or abilities and everything will be peachy. In 1954, psychologist Gordon Allport proposed a now well-supported theory known as the contact hypothesis. He argued that one of the best ways to prevent and overcome prejudice was through contact with others—but he stipulated that the interactions should be cooperative, with individuals working toward a shared goal; that everyone should have equal standing; and that ideally, the contact should be endorsed by some sort of authority figure. In competitive situations, when some people have higher status than others, or when the contact is not encouraged by someone in charge, these kinds of interactions can actually worsen prejudice rather than alleviate it.

One powerful illustration of the importance of these conditions arose in Austin, Texas, in 1971, when public schools had just been desegregated. Suddenly, Black, white, and Mexican American kids were all learning together for the first time. Yet all was not well: Fights were regularly breaking out in classrooms, and prejudice was rampant.

The assistant superintendent of the Austin school system asked social psychologist Elliot Aronson if he would be willing to observe the classrooms and make suggestions. Aronson immediately noticed that the classrooms were highly competitive, with students regularly being pitted against one another. So he suggested that the schools try to create a culture of cooperation instead. To do this, teachers instituted a group project in some classrooms in which five or six kids from different races and genders had to work together to write a biography. Each student was assigned to research an essential part of the biography and to recite it to the other group members, so the groups could complete the project only if they listened attentively to each student's input. "It was like a well-functioning basketball team with each kid having a particular skill, a particular piece of the action," Aronson explained in an interview.

After the "jigsaw" classrooms, as Aronson called them, were implemented, kids in those classrooms had higher self-esteem, liked school better, and were more empathetic than the kids in regular classrooms—and the students in the jigsaw classrooms stopped fighting with each other, too. When Aronson climbed to the roof of the school building and took photos of the students at recess, he found the students from the jigsaw classes intermingling, having become friends.

Similar things happen when people with different political backgrounds spend time together in noncompetitive situations. In a 2023 study, University of Notre Dame political scientist Erin Rossiter randomly assigned Republican adults and Democrat adults, who did not know each other, to chat online with each other one-on-one. As a control, she assigned other adults to write something alone about the meaning of life.

Compared with those who'd completed the writing exercise, the adults who'd engaged in the short online chats—regardless of what they talked about—felt more positive toward people in their opposing political party afterward compared with before. Those who chatted were also less likely to describe opposing political party members as closed-minded, hypocritical, mean, and selfish, and more likely to describe them as honest, intelligent, and patriotic.

What can parents do to encourage interactions that will bring their kids closer to others, rather than driving them further apart? It's tricky, because you don't want to tokenize children who are different from your own—you don't want to encourage your kids to befriend, say, Black or Republican children *just because* they are Black or Republican. At the same time, it may be helpful to encourage kids to spend time with other kids and adults with different backgrounds, interests, beliefs, and abilities.

Our encouragement is important because sometimes, even when we do not say so, our kids infer that we value certain people and friendships more than others. When my daughter was in preschool, she was invited to participate in an online study led by NYU developmental psychologist Marjorie Rhodes. I got her set up for the experiment on her iPad and then sat back and watched as the study started. In one part, my daughter was shown side-by-side photos of kids of different races and was asked: *When you're at school and it's time to play outside, which of these kids would your parents want you to play with the most?* The question was repeated multiple times, with different arrays of photos. Every single time, my daughter chose a photo of a white child. I was horrified: I'd never told her that I wanted her to play only with white kids, but somehow she had come to the conclusion that this is what I wanted—perhaps because I'd never explicitly told her otherwise.

A similar study conducted by Rhodes and her colleagues has since been published, and it found that kids who believe their parents don't value interracial friendships harbor more racial biases than other kids do. In other words, it's crucial for us to show our kids that we value interracial friendships ourselves and to encourage our kids to befriend people different from them—and we should also try to scaffold these interactions so that they are cooperative and kids are on equal standing.

Perhaps, when your child has a playdate, you can encourage the kids to work together on a fun task that they are equally adept at doing: building a fort, organizing a short performance, making a collaborative art project, or hosting a lemonade stand. Sports teams can be a powerful way to bring kids of different backgrounds together to work toward a shared goal, too, assuming that players do not have vast differences in ability. In a 2021 study, University of British Columbia economist Matt Lowe assigned Indian men to play on cricket teams together for a month. Some teams included men from the same castes and some included men from different castes. Compared with those who played on the same-caste teams, the men who played on mixed-caste teams had lower levels of prejudice at the end of the experiment.

Researchers have even looked at what happens in the brains of kids who are assigned to mixed-race teams, finding that the parts of their brains associated with group identity and affiliation become more active when they see other team members' faces—regardless of their gender, race, or ethnicity. When kids are primed to work cooperatively with others, the importance of other, potentially divisive social identities fall by the wayside—and everyone wins.

KEY POINTS

1. Kids develop biases because of how their brains work and because they observe hierarchies and misunderstand their causes.
2. Polarization is a growing problem among kids and teens, in part because they are rewarded for expressing strong, moralizing opinions.
3. Parents should encourage kids' curiosity and open-mindedness.
4. Listen to your kids even when they express ideas or thoughts you find distasteful. Don't jump down their throats.
5. Avoid using generic labels to describe groups of people.
6. Talk about isms—racism, sexism, ageism, and more.
7. Encourage your kids to befriend people who differ from them.

PART III

Cultivate

8

"Are We Rich?"

Fostering Financial Literacy and Accurate Perceptions of Inequality

One year for Christmas my son asked Santa for candy—and also a hotel.

"A toy hotel?" I clarified as I watched him carefully pen his letter to the North Pole.

"No, a real one," he said. "A really big one, like the one we stayed at when we went to Bermuda."

If I could ask an omnipotent being for whatever I wanted, I'd probably ask for a hotel, too. And a vacation home in Italy, a Mercedes convertible, and world peace.

In all seriousness, though, that moment made me realize just how little kids often understand about money—including, if not especially, how much things cost. I imagined him as a guest on *The Price Is Right* guessing that laundry detergent costs more than a vacation to Hawaii, while millions of people at home shook their heads in disbelief.

In many ways, this all makes sense. Money is extraordinarily complicated, and prices and costs aren't often intuitive. (Why does it cost $4,000 to fix a car dent? Asking for a friend.) Plenty of adults have trouble predicting costs and managing their finances, so it's no surprise that kids would, too.

Financial literacy is arguably one of the most important life skills. According to a 2023 Pew Research Center survey, parents say one of their top priorities is ensuring that their children become financially independent. Research shows that kids do actually have the capacity to understand complex financial concepts and that parent-child discussions about money can have lasting positive impacts on kids. Studies have found that when parents regularly talk to and mentor kids about money, those kids are less likely as adults to incur credit card debt and more likely to have healthy financial habits, including keeping track of their expenses, paying their bills on time, and saving money from each paycheck.

Yet surveys find that money is also a topic many parents steer clear of.

"It's kind of just avoided," said Ashley LeBaron-Black, a researcher who studies financial socialization at Brigham Young University. Sure, parents might point out prices at the grocery store from time to time and help kids recognize the difference between quarters and dimes—but parents rarely discuss with their kids how they make financial decisions, including how they manage their income, debt, and savings, even though these are important and complex skills kids need to learn.

Perhaps this helps to explain why many young adults these days struggle with their finances. A 2024 Pew survey found that young adults today, while more likely to be employed and earn higher wages, are also more likely to have outstanding debt than their 1990s counterparts. Only 45 percent of eighteen- to thirty-four-year-olds described themselves in the survey as completely financially independent from their parents, and 25 percent indicated that they weren't sure they'd *ever* be. (Not that their debt struggles are their fault: Among other things, college tuition has skyrocketed over the past few decades.)

Parents rarely talk with their kids about wealth, poverty, and inequality, too, which is worrisome—because "whether or not [parents are] talking about it, kids are picking up on it," said Nadia Chernyak, a psychologist who studies children's understanding of equity, justice, fairness, and equality at the University of California, Irvine. Kids notice inequality from a very young age—research suggests that even preschoolers can figure out who has money and who doesn't based on subtle visual cues—and they often make biased and inaccurate inferences based on what they observe.

These assumptions can incite kids to assume that inequality is not just fair, but *the way things should be*—and this can cause them to discriminate and be unwilling to help people in need. Research suggests that talking to kids about money and inequality in specific ways can help to thwart these biased tendencies, but how do we actually do that? And why does it feel so hard?

Why We Stay Quiet

There are, of course, many reasons we avoid the topic of money with our kids. For one, we often carry a lot of fear and shame around the topic. Having "enough money" is a cultural ideal—it is, after all, what underscores the American dream—so we may feel like failures if we don't have as much as we want.

There's another major reason we avoid the topic of money with our kids: We often think they are too young and innocent to learn about it. Money and inequality can feel like "grown-up" topics worth shielding our kids from for as long as possible.

Yet talking about money can actually help *ease* kids' anxieties. When my family was undertaking a home renovation a few years ago, my nine-year-old overheard her dad and me talking about the fact that our expenses were rapidly exceeding our budget. Later, she asked us if we were going to be able to buy enough food for dinner for the week.

That's the thing with kids: They are observant. They overhear the conversations we wish they didn't. (And then never seem to hear us when we ask them to put their clothes away. How?!) "When there is financial stress happening in the family, the kids are almost certainly going to be feeling that," LeBaron-Black told me. Because they're probably already aware of it, acknowledging the stress and talking explicitly to kids about how you're handling it often makes them feel better, not worse. Even if you are feeling hopeless or scared and you're not sure how things will financially shake out, talk about the steps you're taking to remedy the situation.

Also, when we avoid talking about money and inequality, our kids sometimes make worrisome inferences. Kids start taking in the world around them as soon as they're born, and among the things they desperately want to understand is: What makes people successful, and why do some people have more than others? (Even babies notice inequalities, such as when others have more toys than they do.) Kids very quickly figure out that money is key to success—so they start paying attention to how people use it and what kinds of people have lots of it. By age eight, kids can accurately rank jobs by income.

After noticing these inequalities, kids then try to figure out what causes them. Why, they wonder, do some people wind up with more or less money than others? Kids believe—often because we deliberately teach them this—that effort is tied to outcome. That the harder you try, the more likely you are to succeed. If they aren't given other explanations, kids may start to believe that people who have less deserve to have less because they didn't work as hard.

Studies have indeed shown that young kids tend to assume that people with less money are less competent, smart, and hardworking than people with more. These ideas ultimately cause kids (and many adults, for that matter) to accept inequality as fair, especially when they are on the privileged end of it—even though, of course, there are important structural factors, including racism and sexism, that make it harder for some people and groups to financially succeed than others. And because kids often confuse *how things are* with *how things should be*, they may then conclude that groups that tend to have less should always have less. When we teach kids the truth about inequalities, on the other hand, they are more likely to work to combat them—which can have broad benefits for them as well as everyone else. In societies in which there is less economic inequality, people tend to think more rationally, to be more trusting, and to be happier.

Teaching Kids About Money and Financial Differences

How do we raise kids who don't end up thinking this way—who don't accept or perpetuate inequality, and who also understand money and how to manage it? As it turns out, the kinds of conversations we have with our kids make a big difference—and we can also solidify important skills by letting our kids have hands-on experiences with money.

1. Talk to kids about money, budgeting, debt, and investing.

On a crisp spring morning in the quaint town of Bow, New Hampshire, I sat in the back of a classroom as second-grade students at Bow Elementary School learned about money. The lessons were developed by the nonprofit Jump$tart Coalition, which works around the country with schools to improve student financial literacy. The guest teacher was Kim Armstrong, a warm and effervescent business development manager at a Massachusetts credit union.

"Does anyone want to tell me what they think money is?" Armstrong asked.

A bunch of hands flew into the air. Armstrong called on a girl with long brown hair wearing teal fleece alpaca pajamas. (It was pajama day, though sadly, I didn't get the memo in time.)

"Money is something that you can spend to buy stuff like groceries and, like, clothes and stuff," the girl said.

"Wow, that's the best answer I've ever gotten!" Armstrong said.

Throughout her presentation, I was impressed by how much the kids instinctively already knew about money—and I was impressed by how much Armstrong covered. In just thirty minutes, she emphasized the difference between needs and wants and discussed the various reasons to spend, save, and share money. She even introduced the idea of interest and inflation. As we shuffled between classrooms later in the morning, I asked her about her decision to introduce these concepts: Weren't second graders too young to understand interest? She said no—she's been amazed at just how easily young kids can grasp these seemingly complex ideas.

Throughout the morning, I was surprised, over and over again, at how eager these young kids were to learn about money—and how comfortable they were talking (if not boasting) about it. One boy sporting a white button-down shirt and Crocs announced to the class that his grandparents once wrote him a check for $16,000 (unfortunately, this assertion cannot be fact-checked), and that the money was being kept safe in a bank account.

Despite kids' zeal for discussing money and finances, parents (and educators, for that matter) still seem loath to engage with kids about it. In a 2022 poll of over one thousand parents sponsored by CNBC and Acorns, a savings and investing app, 31 percent of parents said that they had never talked to their kids about finances, and another 24 percent said they had conversations about money with their kids less than once a month. And yet the researchers I spoke to all emphasized that when it comes to instilling financial literacy, parents are children's most crucial educators.

Indeed, research suggests that parent-child conversations about money can make a big difference. In a 2020 study, researchers including LeBaron-Black interviewed 437 young adults between the ages of eighteen and twenty-three as well as their parents. They asked questions to assess how often the parents had communicated with their kids about money when they were adolescents—such as whether the parents explicitly taught the kids about credit cards, debt, budgeting, and saving. The researchers also surveyed the young adults about their current financial habits: how often they paid bills on time, whether they kept records of monthly expenses, whether they paid off credit card balances each month, and whether they saved money from each paycheck.

Parental conversations about money during adolescence, they found, were tied to healthier financial habits during young adulthood. Kids whose parents taught them about finances were more likely to pay bills on time, to keep records of their expenses, and to pay off their credit card balances, and were less likely to have debt compared with kids whose parents avoided such conversations. The associations persisted even after the researchers controlled for differences in the young adults' incomes, ages, races, genders, and levels of materialism and impulsivity.

In another 2020 study, a different group of researchers found that young adults whose parents had taught their kids how to manage money, and who had also been open about their family finances, had less financial anxiety and were less impulsive in their purchases than other young adults were. The effects may even go well beyond influencing financial habits. Studies have found that kids whose parents talk about money grow up to have healthier romantic relationships than kids whose parents don't.

But when and how should we talk to kids about money? The devil is in the details.

The first thing to know is that it's almost never "too early" to educate kids about money. You can talk to little kids about what money is—that you use it to buy things—and give them the opportunity to ask questions. When you use your debit card, show it to your child and say, *Do you know what this is and why I'm using it?* When you run to the bank, bring your kid with you and talk to them about what banks are and how they work. When you're at the grocery store, show them the price tags and talk to them about coupons.

It's helpful to talk to kids about the many financial choices you make, too. "Let them see how you manage money and make decisions—and the kinds of struggles that you might have in making decisions," said Kenneth White, an associate professor of personal and family financial planning at the University of Arizona. This could be as mundane as explaining why you picked one brand of pickles over another, and it can include conversations about how you decided where to stay on vacation, why you don't go out to dinner more than once a week, and why you bought season passes rather than individual tickets.

What if your child asks how much money you make? The researchers I talked to said that this may not be information you need to share with, say, a five-year-old—they probably wouldn't know how to make sense of it—but that with tweens and teens, it absolutely makes sense to share that information and help kids understand where all that money goes.

"It's unfortunate when parents think, 'Oh, it's not appropriate for kids to know how much we make or what our budget is,'" LeBaron-Black said. "What a great example to use with kids to teach them about how expensive life is and how far a certain income can go."

But how do we keep our kids from blabbing about our finances to their friends? Financial educator Dana Miranda, the author of *You Don't Need a Budget*, suggested using the framework of consent to help kids understand that, just as it's not okay to touch people's bodies without their consent, it's not okay to share financial details about others unless they give their blessing—and that you'd rather they keep the details of your household finances to themselves.

That said, if your kids do let some details slip, it may not be a huge deal. When I spoke with Ron Lieber, a personal finance journalist and the author of *The Opposite of Spoiled*, he said: "Chances are, your family is running around with a group of people where the majority of them are roughly equal to you in terms of socioeconomic status—so they probably don't care all that much about what you have and what you do." As it is, we're often broadcasting our financial details to friends and acquaintances through what we share on social media: the clothes we wear, the cars we drive, the vacations we take.

White emphasized that parents should also talk about investing, which they almost never do. Explain to your kids what investing is and how and why you do it—if nothing else, the conversation will help them understand the importance of thinking about the future.

If you're not sure how to talk to kids about some of these topics—they are complicated!—feel free to lean on other resources. I love the Moneybunny book series by Cinders McLeod for teaching preschoolers basic money-related concepts; *One Grain of Rice* by Demi is a wonderful book that teaches kids about compounding and exponential growth.

Yet we should also strive for balance. Yes, we should talk to kids about the value of saving and investing, but we don't want them to equate spending with shame—nor do we want them to think that the only important goal involving money is to accrue more and more of it, Miranda said. If the messages we communicate to our kids are overwhelmingly focused on saving as much as possible and avoiding debt, then we aren't teaching them how to *spend* money in a healthy way, which is important as well. The goal is to help kids develop a holistic approach to money and spending, she said, rather than encouraging them to focus only on restriction.

It's crucial to talk to kids about money for another reason, too: It makes them more comfortable discussing the subject with others down the line. As White pointed out to me, when people feel money conversations are taboo, they are often hesitant to ask questions, share concerns with loved ones, or seek financial help from professionals. We want to raise kids who feel comfortable having money conversations throughout their lives—and the best way to do that is to normalize these discussions early on.

Especially with our girls. Studies find that parents typically start talking about money at a younger age with boys than with girls, and these differences have real ramifications: In a 2019 study involving nearly ten thousand high school students from eighteen countries, researchers found that boys had deeper levels of financial knowledge than girls did. It's likely that girls receive less financial education than boys do via other sources, too—teachers, other adults in their lives, and even their friends. Because of this, researchers argue that the conversations parents have with their daughters about money are especially important.

2. Give your kids hands-on experiences with money.

Of course, just talking isn't enough—kids should learn by doing, too.

One easy way to do this is to give kids an allowance. "Allowances are an easy, consistent way to get money into kids' hands to practice managing themselves and build good habits," LeBaron-Black told me.

There are, of course, many ways to manage allowances. My kids get half as many dollars per week as their age in years, but I know parents who give less than that and more than that—whatever works for your family is just fine.

There's lots of debate over whether to tie allowance to household tasks or not. (I'm not a big fan of the word "chores," because I think it frames domestic tasks as being unenjoyable by definition, and they don't have to be.) Should you give kids their allowance only if they've done certain tasks and frame the allowance as compensation? Or should allowance be given no matter what?

LeBaron-Black said the research doesn't point to one approach being better than another. But I like to keep allowance separate from tasks for several reasons.

For one, I think it's helpful to frame household tasks as work we do for the collective well-being of our families, rather than because we are compensated for it. We keep a tidy house because we care about one another and the space we call home. We feed the dog because we love him and want to keep him nourished. When we frame our choices in terms of their impact on others, we help to build empathy in our kids (for more on building empathy, see chapter 5). We also help our kids recognize that these kinds of tasks can be intrinsically satisfying: It feels good to do things for the people we love.

Separating allowances from household tasks may also give kids a greater sense of autonomy regarding the tasks, which could make them more motivated to do them. As I mentioned in chapter 5, research finds that compared with children from Westernized families, kids from Indigenous-heritage communities are typically much more involved in household tasks, often by their own initiative. In one small study, researchers found that parents in Mexican families, in contrast to European-American families, also tended to separate allowances from tasks. Researchers have theorized that children in such families contribute more in part because they feel they have more freedom regarding the household jobs they do. When kids are paid to do tasks, it is clear that the parents still "own" the tasks, which "may undermine children's initiative," researchers explained in a 2015 paper. Kids may feel they are being controlled, which can undermine their intrinsic motivation.

When we pay our kids for household jobs, we may inadvertently undermine those messages of collaboration, empathy, and care. Payments imply that the tasks don't have much if any intrinsic value; kids may think, *I unload the dishwasher only because I get money to do it*, and not consider how putting the dishes away actually benefits everyone.

Tying allowance to household tasks carries another risk, too, Lieber told me: Kids might assume they can stop whenever they want. "If we treat this like a job, the kids who are good savers are going to eventually collect enough money, and the smartasses are going to come to us and say, *Hey, I've got enough money for now and for the foreseeable future, so I'm going to quit!*" he said. And that's probably . . . not something we want.

Although our family doesn't tie our allowance to household

tasks, we do impose a structure. We have our kids split their money into three jars each week: "spend," "save," and "give." They can spend the money in their "spend" jar whenever they would like and on whatever they would like (though it's okay to create some rules around this if you want); their "save" jar contains money they are saving over time to make a larger purchase; and the money in their "give" jar is to be given away, either in the form of gifts or charitable donations. (After Ms. Armstrong's presentation, the students all received piggy banks with separate compartments for "spend," "save," and "share," too.)

We use these jars to help our kids understand that money can be used in different ways, and that how we use money reflects our values. We should take care of ourselves and enjoy ourselves (spend), but also understand the value of patience (save) and gratitude and generosity (give).

The idea of putting cash in jars may feel a little antiquated. There are, of course, other options, including allowance apps such as Greenlight, where kids and parents can keep track of money online and kids can spend their money with special debit cards. These apps may be easier to use, especially for tweens and teens—but LeBaron-Black noted that young kids often learn better when they can see and touch the concepts they are learning. "A kid handing dollar bills to a cashier can help solidify some of those lessons," she said.

As kids get older, they should also work with money in more abstract ways. They can benefit from kid-friendly bank accounts, debit and credit cards, and even opportunities to invest. They're going to make mistakes, of course, but that's how they learn—and far better for them to bounce checks when they're thirteen than when they're thirty-three.

We should encourage our kids to be entrepreneurial, too: to set up lemonade stands, babysit, or offer to shovel our neighbors' walkways. We should talk to our kids about how to value and price what they sell, too. When I used to hire high schoolers to babysit my kids, I would always ask them their hourly rate—and all too often, the teens would flounder and say something like, "Whatever you'd like to pay me is fine." We should explicitly teach kids how to name their price and negotiate—these are skills they will need throughout life, and if we don't teach them, they may never learn.

3. Talk to kids about inequality—and carefully frame its causes.

As I mentioned already, kids notice inequalities from a very young age—and they can start to make unfortunate inferences about them. Their thinking is rooted, in part, in how they perceive fairness.

Young kids—and you know this if you've ever had one—are preoccupied with fairness. When the chocolate chip cookies aren't divided evenly, they immediately and loudly protest. Young kids can take into consideration things like need or merit when they consider what's fair, but often, they just think everyone should get an equal share. Well, let's be honest: What they care most about is that *they* get an equal share.

Research suggests that as kids get older, during the elementary school years, they care more about what's fair for others, and they often start weighing merit more. (Interestingly, some research suggests that Western children consider merit more relevant than kids from non-Western cultures do, perhaps because our society focuses so much on productivity.) But this is also when other problems start to arise, because kids don't just believe that people who work harder deserve more—they also start to infer that people with more money and resources likely deserved their windfall, and that people with fewer deserved their plight. And yet, of course, many inequalities in our society are not a reflection of merit or value (what researchers sometimes call "intrinsic" reasons), nor are they justified—they are often instead a reflection of luck, laws, policies, and discrimination (these are called "extrinsic" or "structural" reasons).

The messages we give to kids about responsible spending can sometimes bolster this way of thinking. When Armstrong lectured the second graders about the benefits of saving over spending, her implication was that when people have the forethought and willpower to save, they can eventually afford anything. Although she didn't say as much, the flip side of her argument was that if you end up poor and in debt, it's probably your own damn fault.

Research has shown that young children tend to believe that economically disadvantaged people are less smart, hardworking, and competent than wealthier people are—and these inferences spill over into biased assumptions about entire groups of people. Kids tend to believe that girls are less intelligent than boys and that Black people perform less well in school than white people do. Kids who harbor these racist ideas are also less interested in playing with Black children.

Kids can even make such assumptions about imaginary groups. In a 2015 study, Larisa Hussak, then a psychologist at the University of Illinois, and NYU psychologist Andrei Cimpian told five- and eight-year-old kids a story about two kinds of aliens, the Orps and Blarks, explaining that Blarks had more money than Orps. The researchers offered the kids potential reasons for the disparity and asked which one they thought was true: either that the Blarks were smarter and better workers, or that something had happened in the world to make them richer (e.g., the Blarks won a war or found gold). The kids were more likely to choose the first option: that the Blarks had more money because they were smarter or better workers.

Why are kids (and adults, for that matter) attracted to these kinds of explanations? Research suggests that when we seek to explain things we observe, we often take heuristic shortcuts, and the information that is easiest for us to retrieve is "inherent" information—information about the group or person rather than contextual or historical information that might be relevant. Kids also make these unfortunate inferences because nobody is providing them with the information they need to properly understand the issue. "Families from more privileged backgrounds have the life circumstances to choose whether or not they are going to explicitly talk about social and economic inequalities with their kids—and the evidence suggests that many choose not to," said Laura Elenbaas, a psychologist at Purdue University who studies how kids think about people, groups, and society. These kinds of parent-child conversations are often a regular occurrence among families with less privilege, who may be trying to help their kids manage bias and discrimination on a daily basis.

In a separate arm of their study, Hussak and Cimpian provided kids with explanations about the Blark and Orp inequality themselves. Some kids were told the Blarks were wealthier because they were smarter and better workers, while others were told it was because the Blarks "live in a town with better jobs and a lot more banks." The researchers then asked the children whether they thought the wealth disparity between the Blarks and Orps was fair. The kids who were given the "smarter and better" explanation were more likely than other kids to believe it was, indeed, fair. The kids who were provided with structural causes for the inequality thought it wasn't.

When kids believe that inequalities are the result of intrinsic or effort-based differences between groups, they are also less likely to try to remedy them. In one study, children between the ages of three and eight learned about a peer who received fewer prizes than another peer. Some kids were told that the slighted peer had worked less hard, while others were told that the slighted peer got fewer prizes due to gender bias. Then the kids in the study were given the opportunity to give additional prizes to the peer who got more or the peer who got less. The kids who'd been told that the inequality reflected differences in effort were less likely to remedy it—those kids preferred to give their prizes to the peer who'd already received more. This study suggests that if kids believe inequalities are fair, they support the status quo. If they believe inequalities are unfair, they are likely to fight for change or to step up and help those in need.

We need, then, to talk to our kids about inequalities in ways that encourage them to consider their structural, extrinsic causes. Talk about how racism, sexism, and other biases hold certain groups of people back by giving people fewer opportunities. You can have these conversations with young kids, although researchers told me that kids are able to more deeply understand these complexities starting around the age of six or seven. And try not to oversimplify; the goal, ultimately, is to communicate to kids that a person's economic status has complex causes—it's not entirely determined by their effort or willpower, and it's not entirely determined by structural causes, either. When kids understand at least some of these nuances, they are less likely to pass judgment when they or others struggle with money (because they can recognize that structural causes could be playing a role), yet they are also able to feel hopeful that hard work or good money management can make a difference (because they know that individual factors do matter).

When I asked Elenbaas how to have conversations about inequality, she suggested that whenever parents observe inequalities or directly experience their negative effects in the presence of their kids, they should start a conversation driven by three key questions: (1) What is the issue? (2) Who is most affected? (3) Why is it like this?

Here's an example. Let's say you and your child just walked past an unhoused person on the street and they asked you why that person was there.

1. What is the issue? The issue is people experiencing homelessness, which you can explain to your child. Maybe there is a trend worth pointing out, too—like that there are more unhoused people in your town today than there used to be.
2. Who is most affected? Here you can explain that certain people and groups of people are more likely to be unhoused than others—people who have low-wage jobs, people of color, veterans, and people who don't have much family around to support them. Help your kids consider and understand the people who are most at risk.
3. Why is it like this? Perhaps you discuss changes in housing costs, a lack of employment opportunities, or low wages. Maybe a local hospital has closed, or your community lacks mental health treatment options. Maybe racism is playing a role. (Of course you don't have to—and perhaps shouldn't—cite *only* structural causes, and you probably shouldn't cite just one explanation, either. Often the causes are multifaceted and complex, and it's good for kids to know that.) Chances are, you won't have all the answers top of mind—and that's okay. You can talk about some potential causes, and then revisit the topic later. Or you can do research together.

To nurture a sense of hope, we also should go beyond merely describing the structural causes of inequality—we should explain to our kids that structural improvements can change outcomes and lead to equality. We can do this by citing examples from the past in which changes to policies, stereotypes, or social norms incited positive change—such as that when women or people of color have been given equal opportunities, inequalities have eased. And we shouldn't limit these to broad-reaching historical examples; we can point to recent examples from our own lives or communities that could give kids a more immediate sense of hope and agency, too.

One 2024 study illustrated the power of providing kids with these kinds of hopeful examples. In it, psychologists Jamie Amemiya and Lin Bian split kids into two experimental groups. Some kids were told that girls were less successful than boys in a robot-making competition because girls were given less instruction. Others were told that when girls were actually given as much instruction as boys, they did just as well. The researchers then asked all the kids to pick members of a team for the next robot-making competition, explaining that girls and boys would receive the same amount of instruction beforehand. Compared with the kids who'd merely learned about the structural impediments to success, those who'd learned that girls *could* do just as well as boys were more likely to choose girls for their team. This kind of framing fosters a sense of hope and agency, because kids start to recognize that they can, through activism and advocacy, nudge structures and policies in the right direction and change people's lives.

4. Remember that kids learn about inequality from what they observe at home, too.

While reporting this chapter, I reflected on the many different kinds of inequalities kids see. I realized that, every single day, many kids see huge social inequalities inside their own homes rooted in the unequal division of domestic labor—and I wondered what kinds of lessons these observations might be teaching them.

In a 2023 study, researchers surveyed three- to ten-year-old kids in the US and China, asking them which of their parents did most household tasks. Perhaps unsurprisingly, most kids reported that their mothers did more. When the researchers asked the kids whether they thought these domestic inequalities were fair, 95 percent of them said yes. "They're recognizing that their parents are doing this, and they think it's okay," explained study author Allegra Midgette, a psychologist at Texas A&M University.

It's long been documented in psychology that people, including kids, often confuse what *is* with what *should be*, which could help explain why children perceive the inequalities they observe at home as normal and fair. "Children are paying attention," said Kelly Kirkland, a research fellow at the University of Queensland in Australia who studies how kids learn about inequalities. "They're really, really paying attention and they're looking very early on at how people behave to inform how they *should* behave and the values that they *should* have."

Indeed, from a young age, girls help out around the house a lot more than boys do, perhaps because of what they observe at home. These patterns can persist. "Around the age of six or seven, young girls are already expecting themselves to do more of the chores and childcare when they grow up," Midgette explained.

The more work moms do around the house (and the less work dads do), the fewer career aspirations girls have, too. In a 2014 study, researchers at the University of British Columbia surveyed 326 children between the ages of seven and thirteen and at least one of their parents. They asked the kids and parents questions to assess their gender-role beliefs, interviewed the kids about their aspirations, and asked the parents how much paid work they did outside the home and how much unpaid domestic work they did. They found that girls were less likely to envision themselves as working outside the home when their fathers held less gender-egalitarian beliefs about domestic labor and when their mothers reported doing more domestic work.

Importantly, too, the researchers found that what the dads actually did—or didn't do—around the house mattered more than what they *said* to their kids. Daughters of dads who talked a good talk about gender equality, but who nevertheless didn't do as much as their partners in terms of domestic labor, had lower career aspirations than daughters of dads who pulled their weight around the house. As the researchers explained, "even when parents explicitly endorse gender equality at home, a traditional division of labor in daily life and implicitly held stereotypical attitudes can send a less egalitarian message to young girls."

When I asked experts whether kids' observations and acceptance of domestic inequality at home might make them more complacent about or supportive of other forms of social inequality, they said that research to answer this question has not yet been done—but they warned it was certainly possible. "The theory would be that yes, it would, because you're normalizing certain degrees of inequality," Chernyak said.

What's the solution to this problem? Well, in an ideal world, kids wouldn't grow up surrounded by blatant social inequalities—parents would pull close to equal weight at home, or at the very least, would sometimes make counter-stereotypical domestic choices (like having Dad stay home from work when the kids are sick rather than Mom). But, of course, this is not always within our control. Thankfully, we can make a difference in other ways, too—including by talking to our kids about the structural, historical, and familial causes of domestic inequality.

"Talk about why it's happening and what would be ideal," Midgette suggested. Explain how it came to be that women tend to do more around the house, how these expectations are slowly shifting over time, and what we and our kids can do to continue to fight against the unequal status quo, even if through baby steps.

KEY POINTS

1. Kids notice money—and who has more or less of it—from a very young age and seek to understand the patterns they see. But they often make inaccurate, biased inferences.
2. Parents should talk to kids about money and loop them into family financial decisions.
3. Let kids have hands-on experiences with money management through allowances, debit cards, investing opportunities, and jobs.
4. Talk to kids about the many causes of economic inequality—including the fact that many groups have more or less not because of how hard they work or how smart they are, but because of laws, policies, biases, and other structural causes.
5. Try to model domestic equality at home, or at least talk to kids about the causes of household inequality.

9

"I Learned It from YouTube."

Encouraging Media and Information Literacy

A few years ago, for a story I wrote for *Scientific American*, I connected with Amanda Gardner, an educator with more than two decades of experience. Gardner had recently started a new charter elementary and middle school outside Seattle. She was shocked when she started working with her new students and learned about the various conspiracy theories they believed: that the Holocaust didn't happen, that COVID was a hoax, that the 2020 presidential election was rigged. Both misinformation (which includes honest mistakes) and disinformation (which involves an intention to mislead) have had "a growing impact on students over the past ten to twenty years," Gardner said.

It makes sense. Kids now have unprecedented access to the internet and social media, which are rife with bad information—bias, conspiracy theories, fake news, and more. Research suggests that many kids now start believing in conspiracy theories by the age of fourteen, probably in part because they have trouble assessing the credibility of online information. I'm just waiting for my thirteen-year-old to tell me that the moon landing never happened.

In a 2016 study, Stanford University researchers analyzed 7,804 responses from middle school, high school, and college students who had been asked to evaluate the trustworthiness of online content. They found that 80 percent of middle schoolers believed that advertisements clearly labeled as sponsored content were actually news stories, and that more than 80 percent of high schoolers blithely believed spurious claims made on social media. Only 6 percent of Stanford college students—6 percent!—identified that a sleek website arguing against increasing the minimum wage was actually run by a PR firm that represented the restaurant industry.

Making matters worse, disinformation campaigns often directly go after young users, steering them toward misleading content. In 2022, researchers at the University of California, Davis, reported that YouTube's recommendation algorithm—the box that says "What's Next" when you're watching a video—often recommends videos promoting extremist ideas, such as white nationalism and QAnon, especially to right-leaning users. YouTube is one of the most popular social media sites among teens and is what Princeton University sociologist Zeynep Tufekci has called "one of the most powerful radicalizing instruments of the twenty-first century."

I believe it. A good friend of mine recently told me about a time her six-year-old daughter stumbled across a thirty-second YouTube video warning that if she didn't believe in Jesus, she would go to hell, "a terrifying place where you burn in fire forever." My friend and her husband, who are not religious, have since had many conversations with her about what she saw, trying to ease her worries. But even two years later, every time they pass a church or the topic of Jesus comes up, their daughter still insists—with fear in her eyes—that she believes.

What are we, as parents, supposed to do about this? We can limit our kids' exposure to the internet, YouTube, and other forms of social media (for more on that, see chapter 10), but restriction may get us only so far. "I know a lot of parents want to protect their kids from misinformation, and I totally get it—but my experience shows that they see it anyway," said science educator Melanie Trecek-King, the founder of Thinking Is Power, an award-winning course designed to teach kids critical thinking, information literacy, and science literacy skills. Kids may hear or see questionable information at friend's houses, at school, on the radio, and on TV.

Allison Butler, director of the media literacy certificate program in the Department of Communication at the University of Massachusetts Amherst, agreed. "There's no place that we can go, no day that we can get through, without some degree of digital media interaction, either by happenstance, by choice, for entertainment, or for necessity," she said.

If you're thinking, *I don't need to teach my kids these skills because they'll learn them at school*, think again. As of May 2024, according to the nonprofit organization Media Literacy Now, only three states—Georgia, Delaware, and New Jersey—require K–12 students to receive any media literacy education. And while several other states have some kind of media literacy law in place, many are vague and essentially useless—requiring, say, that schools simply include a list of resources on an education department website.

The argument has also been made that perhaps kids today don't really need to be educated about media literacy because they are "digital natives." But experts say this is a myth. "They can figure out how to play advanced YouTube videos or search the internet quickly, but that doesn't mean that they can think critically about it," said Sarah McGrew, a researcher at the University of Maryland who studies young people's civic online reasoning. "People often conflate those two things and assume that kids, even young kids, because they seem better and faster with technology than we are, somehow don't need our help learning to think critically about it."

Teaching Kids Media and Information Literacy

It's unfair and frustrating that the responsibility to teach kids these skills falls squarely on parents' shoulders, but . . . well, here we are. So to the degree that we can, we should try to help our children learn how to evaluate the accuracy and trustworthiness of the information they come across in the media and in their everyday lives. "It's an absolute twenty-first-century survival skill," said Julie Smith, a communications instructor at Webster University and the author of *Master the Media*. "It's everyone's responsibility to teach kids about media literacy. Yes, in the classroom, but also—yes, the kitchen table. Yes, the minivan. Yes, soccer practice. Yes, the couch."

Here's what the research suggests we can do.

1. Become media literate yourself.

Nearly every expert I interviewed for this chapter made this point early on in our conversation: Parents can't teach media literacy if they are not media literate themselves. "Most people think that it's an 'other person' problem—like, *I am good at this, but you all need to work on it*," Trecek-King said.

Sadly, that's often not the case.

My guess is that if you've chosen to read a science-based parenting book, you're better off than most, but media literacy is a complicated skill and few adults have ever received media literacy training. In 2022, the Reboot Foundation, a critical-thinking advocacy organization, conducted a survey among 541 US adults. Only 38 percent of respondents said they had ever had an opportunity in high school to reflect on media messages and how they might affect people's thoughts, beliefs, feelings, or actions. One-quarter of respondents admitted to believing in at least one conspiracy theory, such as that governments add fluoride to drinking water to lower children's IQ.

If you're not sure about your media literacy skills, what can you do? I recommend checking out Crash Course, an educational YouTube channel started by brothers Hank and John Green. It has a free online course, "Navigating Digital Information," created in partnership with MediaWise, the Poynter Institute, and the Stanford History Education Group, which is comprised of a series of YouTube videos on various topics, including understanding social media, engaging in click restraint, evaluating evidence, using Wikipedia, and more. I also enjoyed the book *Verified* by researchers Mike Caulfield and Sam Wineburg.

2. Ask kids questions about what they see and hear.

If the idea of teaching your kids media and information literacy sounds terrifying, here's some reassuring news: You can start by asking questions. A media and information literate person is someone who is always thinking and inquiring about the information they come across, and it's not that hard to teach our kids to be inquisitive about what they encounter.

With little kids, this might be as simple as asking them questions when they're watching shows or videos: *What do you like about this show? Do any of the characters remind you of you or your friends? Why do you think that character just did what they did?* Asking questions about ads can be especially useful, said Seth Ashley, a communications and media literacy researcher at Boise State University. "You can say, *Wow, look at this car ad—why is it the only car on the road? Do you ever see that when we're driving around? Where are they going? Why are they driving to the top of this mountain?*" he suggested. (I am always rolling my eyes at car ads.)

It's especially important to speak up when you are watching something with your child that you find problematic, said Rebecca Hains, a professor of media and communication at Salem State University and the author of *The Princess Problem*. Research finds that when kids and parents watch things together and parents don't speak up about the parts they don't like, children can interpret their silence as tacit approval. We also know from the science that speaking up makes a difference: Research finds, for instance, that when adults express their disapproval of violence portrayed in TV shows, kids are less likely to tolerate violent behavior. If you're in a movie theater or you're watching something at home with others and don't want to press pause, you can, of course, have the conversation afterward. "You can say, *Hey, yesterday, when we were watching that movie, that guy said that thing to that girl that wasn't that nice. I liked that movie. But that kind of bothered me—what did you think?*" Hains suggested.

It may also help to show kids how the sausage is made. When the daughter of an acquaintance of mine admitted that some of the violent scenes in superhero movies scared her, her mom helped her look up behind-the-scenes footage on how the special effects were created. "After that, every time she got a little scared, she would say very loudly, *The animations in this movie are great! They look so real! But they are animations!*" her mom recalled. "This was so useful for her learning that not everything she sees on a screen or online is actually real and encouraging her not to take things at face value."

As kids get older, you can ask deeper questions about the content you and your kids come across, as well as the platforms and apps they use. Here are some potential prompts:

- Who made this?
- Why was this made, and why is it being presented this way?
- What or who is missing from this?
- How might different people interpret this?
- Who might benefit from this?
- Who might be harmed by this?

The goal is to get kids to start automatically reflecting on the stories they see and hear—how and why the stories are being told, who is behind them, and importantly, what and whose stories are *not* being told. Ultimately, Butler explained, what we want to encourage kids to do is to ask the broader question of *How did this get here?*, so that they recognize that all media is constructed and produced by people, most of whom have vested interests. Hains agreed. "To be media literate really requires understanding that the media are created by people who have a goal in our society of selling things," she said.

We and our kids won't necessarily have answers to all the questions we ask, and that's okay—if our kids merely come to understand that these kinds of questions are important, they will become more media literate. It's also important to remember that questioning is not about rejecting. "It's not about hating the media. That'd be like hating oxygen," Smith said. "It's asking questions, just constantly asking questions. To the point of being annoying."

The goal is not to turn our kids into cynics or denialists, either—so we should be careful to strike a balance. At a 2018 talk at the South by Southwest media conference, danah boyd, a Partner Researcher at Microsoft Research and the founder of the nonprofit research organization Data & Society, argued that education teaches kids to question their assumptions, which is good—but that we have to be careful about what happens next. "The hole that opens up, that invites people to look for new explanations . . . that hole can be filled in deeply problematic ways," she said. "When we ask students to challenge their sacred cows but don't give them a new framework through which to make sense of the world, others are often there to do it for us."

According to educational psychologist William Perry of Harvard University, kids go through various stages of learning. First, children are black-and-white thinkers—they think there are right answers and wrong answers. Then they develop into relativists, realizing that knowledge can be contextual. This stage can be dangerous, though, because if kids go too far, they may come to believe there is no truth at all. Ashley explained to me that when students think *everything* is a lie, they also think there is no point in engaging with difficult topics.

The goal is instead to get kids to the third level, "to that place where you can start to see and appreciate the fact that the world is messy, and that's okay," Ashley said when I interviewed him for *Scientific American*. "You have these fundamental approaches to gathering knowledge that you can accept, but you still value uncertainty, and you value ongoing debates about how the world works." Instead of driving students to apathy, the goal is to steer them toward curiosity, awareness, and engagement.

3. Teach kids about logical fallacies.

For kids to be critical thinkers, they should also, ideally, be familiar with common errors in logic that can undermine their (and other people's) reasoning. If you're not keen to teach these to your kids yourself, check out Critikid.com, a website created by science educator Stephanie Simoes that promotes critical thinking. It offers a logical fallacy course, and there are many other online resources, too. But, briefly, here are some key fallacies you might want to be familiar with so you can point them out to your kids when you see or hear them:

1. **Circular reasoning:** When the evidence provided in support of a claim is the claim itself, sometimes repeated in slightly different words. Example: If someone says *You need to wear sunscreen*, and you ask why, and they answer *Because sunscreen is necessary.*

2. **Slippery slope:** When someone assumes a small choice or step will inevitably lead to something much bigger. Example: *If we legalize marijuana, everyone will smoke all the time and never want to work, and our economy will collapse.*

3. **Appeal to ignorance:** When a person argues that a claim is true because it has not been proven false, or argues a claim is false because it hasn't been proven true. Example: *I've never seen an alien, so they can't possibly exist.*

4. **Post hoc fallacy / confusing correlation with causation:** When someone assumes that because Y comes after X, X must have caused Y. Two variables can correlate but not be

causally related. Example: *My daughter's autism symptoms started two days after she got her measles vaccine, therefore vaccines cause autism.* (They do not.)

5. **Straw man:** When a person presents a weak or inaccurate version of a claim or argument and then argues against it. Example: *Feminists want men to have no rights, and that's unconstitutional.* (This is not, in fact, what feminists want.)

6. **Red herring:** When someone veers off course during an argument, presenting a distracting and unrelated side issue to redirect the listener. Example: *Mom, you should let me watch YouTube in the afternoons because homework is dumb.*

7. **False dichotomy:** When a person presents only two possible outcomes or possibilities in a scenario when there are, in fact, more. Example: *Either you let me have Oreos for breakfast, or I'm going to starve.*

8. **Ad hominem:** When someone rejects or argues against a claim because they say the person making the claim is bad. Example: *I know my teacher told you that I am failing math, but she is really mean.*

4. Show your kids how to find trustworthy information, and model that it's okay to not know everything.

Here's a situation that unfolds in our home on a regular basis: One of my kids waltzes into the room and confidently shares some sort of "fact," like that eating vegetables causes cancer. Ninety percent of the time, they have learned this information from YouTube, and I am immediately skeptical. But I know (from plenty of experience!) that if I come back with something like *Did you hear that on YouTube? It's probably not true!*, they will just dig in their heels.

One of the great things about the internet is that information is now always at our fingertips. One of the terrible things about the internet is that information is now always at our fingertips. The internet is a trove of data, some of it useful, but much of it untrustworthy and inaccurate. We need to help our kids understand that just because information is being shared on a large platform doesn't mean it's legitimate. But how do we do that? How do we teach our kids to be mindful of where they get their information, and help them figure out what to trust?

When I asked these questions of experts, they recommended starting, again, with questions. *That's interesting—how did you find that out? Is there a way to check to make sure that's true?* Use a curious, rather than accusatory, tone, said media literacy strategist Faith Rogow, the founding president of the National Association for Media Literacy Education, because you don't want them immediately getting defensive. You want them to invite you into their thinking process. If they answer something like *MrBeast said it, and I trust MrBeast*, you can then start a conversation about expertise, without necessarily dragging MrBeast through the mud. You could say something like *MrBeast is certainly a trustworthy expert on certain things—he knows so much about YouTube!—but when you think about who would be an expert on cancer, would he be the first person who'd come to mind?* One thing that even adults sometimes struggle with, and that we should make clear to our kids, is the fact that experts have specific areas of expertise—that they are not, usually, experts on everything.

When your kids come to you with a "fact" that you're not sure is true, you can also use a technique recommended by Trecek-King: Ask them, on a scale of one to one hundred, how certain they are. This framing helps kids to think of knowledge not as a black-and-white, either-or construct, but as a spectrum in which there can be varying levels of certainty. When you ask this question, Trecek-King explained, you also help kids consider the gaps in their knowledge. If your child answers anything other than one hundred, you can then ask: *Why aren't you more confident?* This puts the ball in their court and lets *them* consider potential reasons why they might be wrong.

Another great way to teach kids about sourcing is to research topics together when questions arise. I don't know about your kids, but mine are always coming to me with out-of-the-blue questions like *Who invented sausages?* In these situations, a great response is something along the lines of *That's a great question—I don't know! Let's try to find out!* This kind of response does two things: First, it shows kids that it's okay to not know everything—and more important, that it's okay to *admit* that you don't know everything. "One of the most important aspects of critical thinking is an awareness of what you know and an awareness of what you don't know," Trecek-King said. "Be curious, be skeptical, be humble." Research suggests a link between curiosity and intellectual humility—the more excited we are to learn new things, the more willing we are to acknowledge the limitations of our knowledge. (For more on fostering curiosity, see chapter 7.)

Doing research together also gives you the opportunity to show your child how to search for and find trustworthy information. "I would recommend actually going on the internet with your kids and demonstrating smart internet use," Simoes said. There are many steps in the online research process that may seem easy and obvious to us but aren't for kids, such as what to type into the Google search bar. When you submit your search request, explain to your child why you've chosen the words you've chosen.

It's also important for kids to understand what Google is—and what it isn't, McGrew said. Many kids (and adults, too) think that Google itself is a source of information, when it's just an aggregator. And it's biased, too: As University of Washington researcher Mike Caulfield and Stanford education researcher Sam Wineburg wrote in their book *Verified*, "Google is out to please, trying to determine what you want—even if doing so means giving you a dubious answer but one you want to hear." Although the temptation is often to click on the first or second search result, those are often ads or sponsored or AI-generated content; it's much better to engage in what's called "click restraint" and to scroll down the page (and sometimes even go to the second page) to find the most reliable and relevant source, McGrew explained, and to explain what you're doing and why to your kids as you do it.

For instance, when I search *Who invented sausages?*, I see results from sausage companies, Reddit, and Quora, among other sources. I should ideally scroll past those and click on the result from the *Encyclopaedia Britannica*, which I know is a trusted source.

What if you're not sure if a website is trustworthy? The internet is chock-full of websites that seem credible, but often are not. Discerning website credibility is an incredibly important skill, but not one that many kids get the opportunity to practice, because often, they are using digital devices at school that allow only "trusted" sources. When schools do this, they don't give students the opportunity to learn how to differentiate between sources that are more and less credible, McGrew said, and kids may even come to assume that *all* online information is accurate.

When kids are explicitly asked to evaluate website credibility, they often look at the wrong things, too. In a small 2021 study, McGrew asked eleventh and twelfth graders to evaluate various websites, finding that students often judged a website's credibility based on whether it looked good and had the information they wanted. This is . . . well, not great. But McGrew and her colleagues have identified an approach that teaches kids better source evaluation skills, known as "lateral reading," and have even developed media literacy courses based on it.

Lateral reading is based on a strategy used by journalism fact-checkers when they evaluate claims. In a study published in 2019, McGrew and Wineburg compared how ten history professors, ten fact-checkers, and twenty-five Stanford undergraduates evaluated websites and information on social and political issues. They found that whereas historians and students were often fooled by manipulative websites, journalism fact-checkers were not. In addition, their methods of analysis differed significantly: Historians and students tried to assess the validity of websites and information by reading "vertically," navigating within a particular website to learn more about it (such as by going to the "About" page). Fact-checkers, on the other hand, read "laterally," opening new browser tabs and running Google searches to judge the original website's credibility.

If you're doing research online with your kids, you can easily model lateral reading. Let's say you find a potential source of information after searching on Google and it's a website you don't recognize. Your inclination might be to spend time clicking around the website itself to gauge its trustworthiness, but there are plenty of slick, legitimate-looking websites backed by advocacy groups with vested interests, and they are very good at making websites look credible. It's far better to instead search for the name of the organization or website on Google to see if there are other credible sources that have written about it, including, yes, Wikipedia. (Teachers often frown up on Wikipedia, claiming it's not trustworthy, but experts reassured me it typically is.)

Take the website of the American College of Pediatricians. On the surface, it looks legitimate, describing itself as "a national organization of pediatricians and other healthcare professionals dedicated to the health and well-being of children." But if you Google "American College of Pediatricians," you discover from sources including Wikipedia, *Wired* magazine, and the Southern Poverty Law Center that the ACP is, in fact, a hate-spewing anti-LGBTQ organization.

Once kids start to recognize that information can be more or less credible depending on where it comes from—and once they develop the skills to identify the most trustworthy sources—they become more worldly and media literate. In a 2022 study, Wineburg, McGrew, and their colleagues found that high school students who learned lateral reading skills became better able to evaluate websites and the credibility of online claims, such as Facebook posts, compared with students who did not receive these lessons. It's a skill that we should be teaching all kids—and it doesn't take long to master.

KEY POINTS

1. The first step to instilling kids' media literacy is ensuring that you're media literate yourself.
2. Parents should ask kids questions about what they see and hear in the world and in the media.
3. Teach kids to recognize common logical fallacies.
4. Research questions and claims with your kids, emphasizing the importance of accurate, relevant sourcing.
5. Teach kids how to evaluate website credibility through lateral reading.

10

"How Many Likes Did I Get?"

Managing Tech and Social Media

In early 2024, when my kids' dad and I were considering giving our son an iPhone for his thirteenth birthday, I asked my newsletter subscribers to tell me about the rules they had in place regarding their kids' phones. I wanted to crowdsource and understand what other parents were doing in terms of rules and monitoring.

Instead, what I got were lots of strongly worded comments telling me what parents *should* do about technology and why. I had never seen my subscribers so prescriptive or divided on a parenting topic, and at that point, I'd been writing my newsletter for more than three years.

I'm not sure there's any issue in the parenting sphere that elicits stronger feelings than digital technology. It's not just that parents have different opinions on the topic; it's that these opinions have become intertwined with morals and values in ways that turn technology into an "us versus them" issue, making it difficult to discuss the topic with others without evoking feelings of shame, moral righteousness, or rage.

I'm sure you're waiting with bated breath to see where I come down on the topic. I'm afraid you might be disappointed, because my stance is not easily summarized in a fearmongering sound bite or a pro-screen slogan. I've analyzed the research and the answer is simply not clear-cut—despite what you may have recently heard. Technology can bring both benefits and harms, and how your child is affected depends on many variables, including what exactly they are doing on their screens, their individual personality and psychology, and your parenting style. The good news is that as parents, we can make choices that go a long way toward mitigating harm and encouraging healthy boundaries—so when our kids grow up, they can safely and confidently navigate the tech-steeped world.

Screens Can Both Harm and Help

There are good reasons to worry about the impact of screens and social media on kids. Nearly half of all US teens said they experienced cyberbullying in 2022, and the risks are even higher for LGBTQ youth. Many experts fear the impact of social media on body image and self-esteem, considering that teens—both boys and girls—compare themselves to (often retouched) peers and influencers at a time when their brains are most sensitive to social feedback. Social media can also promote misinformation and polarization (for more on polarization, see chapter 8).

Pornography is easily accessible now, too, and often, it's violent: In a 2022 Pew Research Center survey, more than half of teens who'd seen porn said they had seen it depicting rape, choking, or someone in pain. It's frightening to consider how these portrayals might affect kids' perceptions of sex, consent, and body image. And even if our kids aren't seeing anything potentially worrying when they go online, there's still the opportunity cost problem: When kids spend more time on screens, they must spend less time on other, potentially more enriching, activities, such as playing outdoors. There are, after all, only twenty-four hours in a day.

Technology can offer benefits, though, too. It's a powerful tool for self-expression and identity exploration. Plenty of kids—mine included—use their digital devices to create art and music. Kids can bolster so many skills online, too, including cooking, math, reading, coding, crafting, and building. (My daughter has learned how to bake thanks to YouTube.)

Research also finds that many tweens and teens use online communication to bolster their budding or existing in-person relationships. When my then twelve-year-old was making the case for having a phone, I told him I was worried that a phone might cause him to spend less time with his friends. He looked genuinely baffled. "I think it will do the exact opposite—it will make it easier for me to make plans to see them," he replied. Sure enough, he's since become a kind of organizational ringleader, planning group trips to the movies on Friday nights and the like.

The benefits of technology can be especially salient for teens with mental health struggles or who are otherwise marginalized, ostracized, or stigmatized, due to factors such as their socioeconomic status, ethnic or racial background, sexual orientation, or gender identity. Yes, some of these kids are at a higher risk for being bullied online, but technology and social media can also connect these teens with online resources as well as peers they identify with and communities that support them. Research has found that online relationships are especially meaningful for teens who have contemplated suicide.

Teasing Out the Effects of Tech

Given the potential of technology to both harm and help kids, researchers have been trying to sort out the net effects. Overall, do screens add to or detract from kids' lives? It's been difficult to arrive at a consensus because the research truly is challenging to interpret. In my twenty years as a science journalist, I have thrown myself headfirst into a bunch of meaty and convoluted scientific controversies, and usually, with enough time and effort, I've been able to come out the other side with a clear sense of what the science says. Not so with the research on the overall impacts of technology and social media on kids, because many studies are flawed or unable to get at this central question, and because effects likely vary depending on the context and the child.

Take, for instance, a 2018 study based on results from the University of Michigan's Monitoring the Future study. This was a correlational study based on surveys that asked adolescents, at a single point in time, to estimate how much time they spent on smartphones and social media as well as how they were doing psychologically. Among other things, the researchers found that eighth and tenth graders who spent more than ten hours a week on social media were more likely to be unhappy than those who used social media for one to two hours a week.

Media coverage of this study made it out to be incontrovertible proof of the harms of screens. It formed the basis for an article that went viral in *The Atlantic*, titled "Have Smartphones Destroyed a Generation?". Penned by psychologist Jean Twenge—who had conducted the study with her colleague Gabrielle N. Martin and University of Georgia social psychologist W. Keith Campbell—the article was one of the key instigators of the ongoing parental fear over screens and social media. "The results could not be clearer: Teens who spend more time than average on screen activities are more likely to be unhappy," Twenge wrote.

Yet this was a correlational study, meaning it found only an association between social media use and depression symptoms; scientists can't conclude from this that social media causes depression. "The fact that two trend lines increase together does not mean that one phenomenon causes the other," researchers explained in a 2020 paper on the relationship between social media and teen depression in the *Journal of Child Psychology and Psychiatry*. It could instead be that depression causes teens to spend more time on social media, which some research has, among girls at least, suggested. Or it could be that a separate unknown variable is involved: Maybe teens with neglectful parents spend more time on social media, and teens with neglectful parents are also more likely to have symptoms of depression. In this scenario, the social media use has nothing to do with the depression; what drives both outcomes is neglectful parenting. Importantly, even if the relationship between technology and depression *is* causal, several studies suggest it would account for less than 1 percent of the overall variation in teens' depression symptoms.

Research shows, too, that kids with difficult temperaments, developmental delays, and behavioral issues are more likely to use devices—and many correlational studies do not control for these kinds of important family- and social-related factors. Kids can also do many different things on screens and even on social media, and each choice may have a different impact—yet studies like Twenge's typically lump all these activities together into a single measure of "screen use" or "screen time." Letting your toddler watch *Bluey* is probably quite different from letting them watch *Deadpool*. Letting your tween use their iPad to draw is very different from letting them use their iPad to scroll through Instagram. Even what they do on social media might matter: Some research suggests that the "active" use of social media, which involves kids chatting with each other and "liking" posts, may have different effects than the "passive" use of social media, such as browsing through news feeds or profiles. Active use may promote feelings of connectedness, while passive use could ramp up feelings of FOMO—fear of missing out—and envy.

Different kids react to experiences differently, too, of course. A video that might upset one child may have absolutely no effect on another. (Like me, my daughter loves scary shows and movies; my son does not.) One teen may be quite upset to see a group of friends hanging out without her, while another may be able to shrug it off. And yet, the research on screens typically lumps all different kinds of kids and all different kinds of screen and social media use together under one umbrella—and then averages the results and spits out one single potentially misleading result.

Importantly, too, the correlation between social media and depression has been challenged by other recent studies. In a 2019 study, researchers surveyed nearly six hundred middle schoolers each year for two years and over eleven hundred college students each year for six years to identify associations between social media use and depression symptoms over time—a study design that can tease out cause-and-effect relationships a lot better than studies that survey kids at a single point in time. The researchers found that, on average, kids and young adults who used social media a lot more were no more likely to experience worsening depression symptoms compared with those who used social media very little or not at all. And they did find some evidence of reverse causality: Teen girls who were depressed were more likely to use social media.

Two years later, researchers at Columbia University, UC Irvine, and the University of Michigan reanalyzed data from the Monitoring the Future study and published their results in the *Journal of Adolescent Health*. With additional statistical controls, they found no overall relationship between social media use and depressive symptoms. "Our results suggest that, in the face of other known risk factors for adolescent depression," they wrote, "the risk conferred by social media use is not meaningful."

Searching for Cause and Effect

To date, there have now been hundreds of correlational studies trying to tease out the relationship between digital technology and kids' mental health. As I've explained, however, we can't glean all that much from correlational studies—results conflict and are difficult to interpret. Thankfully, researchers have been working to tease out the relationship in other ways, too. Yet studies that are designed to give a clearer picture of cause and effect are still rare. Here's why.

By far the best way to assess causality is to conduct what's called a randomized controlled trial, in which a large group of similar people are split into smaller groups that are then assigned to experience different things. Imagine a study that involves teens, and some of those teens are randomly selected to be in an "Instagram group." They are told they must use Instagram for three hours a day. Other teens are randomly selected to be in the "control group" and told to spend three hours a day doing something else, like perusing the internet but not Instagram. In such a study, the researchers might follow the two groups of teens over time and periodically give them tests to assess their mental health to see if the Instagram teens fared better or worse than the control group. If their mental health suffered, the researchers could reasonably conclude that using Instagram worsens mental health compared with merely using the internet.

Randomized controlled trials are extremely expensive (which is why they are often conducted by companies, not academic researchers) and take a very long time. They can also be rejected by research ethics boards, and for good reason: If researchers suspect that social media could be harmful for teens, then forcing teens to do it just so they can be studied would be ethically dubious. (I sure wouldn't want to sign my kid up for that.)

So we don't have many randomized controlled trials, but researchers have gotten creative in their study design in recent years, and some have found clever ways to get at causality without needing to treat kids like guinea pigs. Even so, results are hard to interpret.

In one small 2018 study that has been covered by the media as clear evidence of the harms of social media, researchers randomly assigned 143 college students to either use Facebook, Instagram, and Snapchat as they usually did, or to limit their use of those apps to ten minutes on each platform per day. After three weeks, those who limited their use said they felt less lonely and depressed than those who didn't limit their use—but, importantly, the reductions in depression scores were clinically meaningful only among those who'd started with moderate to high levels of depression. And, interestingly, the students who limited their social media use, as well as those who didn't, experienced drops over time in anxiety and feelings of FOMO. It could be that the study period was too brief to see lasting differences between the two groups, or it could be that limiting social media use really doesn't, on average, have a marked effect on young adults. (Other studies in 2019, 2020, and 2022 reported contradictory results when it came to social media's effects on young adult mental health, too. My point: The results of these studies, like with the correlational studies, are mixed.)

It's also important to note that only a handful of these kinds of experimental studies have included kids and teens. Most studies have involved adults, and many haven't looked specifically at mental health or psychological well-being but instead at other tangentially related things—like whether using Facebook for a few minutes puts adults in a bad mood (one study suggests it does), whether Instagram compared with Facebook makes adult women feel less satisfied with their bodies (one study suggests it does), and whether a weeklong break from social media improves sleep quality (one study suggests it doesn't).

Stoking Anxiety Doesn't Help

One reason I'm discussing the limitations of the research in such detail is because some activists in this space are, I believe, misrepresenting the science in ways that are disingenuous and causing unnecessary anxiety. I think that parents should absolutely be informed of what the research says on parenting-relevant issues, even when it might make us uncomfortable—hence my writing this book. But I also think that this research should be communicated carefully, and with nuance, so as to avoid stoking excessive fear. Parenting is infinitely harder when we are terrified, especially when we can't easily solve the problems we are terrified about.

One scientist who has recently caused a lot of panic is NYU social psychologist Jonathan Haidt, who studies the development of morality. In his Substack, *After Babel*, and in his 2024 bestselling book, *The Anxious Generation*, he argues not only that the research is cut-and-dried and shows that social media is always harmful (I disagree) but also that the rise in phone use is largely responsible for the epidemic of mental illness occurring among teens (I disagree on that, too).

Haidt wrote in his book that "social media use does not just correlate with mental illness; it causes it." His beliefs, he explained in his newsletter, are largely based on sixteen experimental studies that he said "found significant evidence of harm." I looked up these sixteen studies as well as twenty more that have since been published, and I discovered that only one of the thirty-six actually evaluated the impact of technology or social media on the psychological health of kids or young teens. This study found that a two-week drop in recreational screen use improved kids' emotional symptoms and led to increases in prosocial behavior. Nearly all the other experimental studies involved people over the age of seventeen, while one involving fourteen- to eighteen-year-olds evaluated the impact of social media on teen body image, not mental health.

I'm not the only one who feels that Haidt misrepresents the science. UC Irvine quantitative and developmental psychologist Candice Odgers, who has been studying the impact of technology on adolescent mental health for twenty years, wrote in a review in *Nature* magazine that "the book's repeated suggestion that digital technologies are rewiring our children's brains and causing an epidemic of mental illness is not supported by science." The University of Cambridge's Amy Orben and Oxford's Andrew Przybylski, both of whom have spent much of their research careers studying the issue, have expressed concerns about his take, too. Nathan Walter, a media psychologist at Northwestern University, summarized his opinion on CNN this way: "Although you can cherry-pick a study or ten studies that show exactly what you want to show—for or against screen use—when you get the bird's eye view of the entire corpus of work, there's just so many questions," he said. "To think of screens as something that is inherently negative is not very accurate."

To be fair, there are a lot of things I agree with in Haidt's book and his newsletter. Haidt talks about some of the potential ways phones could disrupt healthy brain development, including by reducing the amount of sleep kids get and creating opportunity costs whereby kids who are constantly staring at their phones will then have less time for other developmentally important experiences, such as in-person social interactions. There are also the potential risks that come from being exposed via the internet to porn, worrisome influencers like Andrew Tate, and other dangerous ideas and social trends.

These and the other risks I mentioned at the beginning of this chapter are very real potential harms, and I agree with Haidt that parents should create structures and limits around technology so that we can ensure that kids experience more benefits from technology than drawbacks (more on how to do that shortly!). I also agree with his suggestion to delay kids' access to phones and social media for as long as possible (he suggests high school for phones, and age sixteen for social media), but I also think that these decisions must be context-dependent. YouTube may well pose risks, but when you're the only kid in your friend group who doesn't have access and you're being left out or bullied because of it, that also poses risks.

Still, I think there is a big difference between expressing concern about the potential risks of technology and saying that science has proven that technology is the key reason kids are struggling today. To argue the latter is dishonest, alarmist, and, frankly, harmful. I strongly believe that people who support the institution of science should talk about it with integrity and accuracy. Otherwise, the public loses trust in science and in everything essential that stems from it.

Reconceptualizing Risk

Misrepresenting the science is also a real disservice because it may cause parents, researchers, and policymakers to focus on technology at the expense of other important factors. It's tempting to point fingers at simple and obvious scapegoats, but the science suggests that the reality is much more complex.

It's important to keep in mind that parents—and adults in general—have *always* panicked over the potential dangers of new forms of technologies (there's even a term for it: "techno-panic"). "Anytime kids have a new form of entertainment, or a new way of relating, people freak out and think this is going to wreck the new generation," explained Devorah Heitner, an expert on children's relationships with media and technology and the author of *Growing Up in Public*. People panicked over the printing press, novels, pinball machines, comic books, telephones, beepers, video games, and televisions. These and other new technologies have been blamed for various societal ills including obesity, addiction, disengagement, cultural vacuity, and solipsism. As sociologist James Walsh argued in a 2020 paper in the *International Journal of Cultural Studies*, these reactions "encapsulate deep-seated anxieties about social change and the type of people it begets," and new technologies are a convenient thing to blame. This doesn't mean that concerns about technology today are unfounded—just that we should keep in mind that our beliefs may also be shaped by biased psychological tendencies.

In her book *Worried About the Wrong Things*, Jacqueline Ryan Vickery, director of research for the Youth Media Lab at the University of North Texas, explained that much of society harbors what she calls "harm-driven expectations" about digital media, which are rooted in fear and anxiety and the assumption that technology is, overall, more bad than good. These fear-based expectations are used to rationalize restrictive, often paternalistic policies that consider young people as passive victims who need to be protected—even if that means reducing their agency and their opportunities to learn how to navigate risk.

Vickery contrasts harm-driven expectations with what she calls "opportunity-driven expectations," which, in her words, "start with the assumption that digital media practices, policies, and narratives ought to be designed to maximize benefits and positive opportunities for youth." Instead of being driven by assumptions that technology is bad and must be controlled, opportunity-driven expectations consider the issue more neutrally, are rooted in evidence and lived experiences, and give voice to youth.

I prefer this more opportunity-driven approach. I think it can be empowering for parents to recognize that the impacts of technology are not predetermined, all negative, and inevitable—that there are plenty of things we as parents can do to shape kids' experiences and relationships with tech so that our children enjoy more benefits than harms. And, just as we've seen in other areas of life, we shouldn't protect our kids from *all* risks around tech, because learning how to safely navigate risk is a crucial skill they need to learn. Even if we could create laws or house rules that fully protected kids from online harms, they would lose these protections as young adults—and then where would they be? It's far better for them to learn these skills at age sixteen than at age twenty-six.

"Youth is a time of learning and preparing for adulthood, and that means helping young people identify and navigate risks, not avoid them," Vickery wrote. Here's what the research suggests we can do to help our kids develop a healthy relationship with technology.

1. Try not to panic.

Parenting advice is usually (though not always!) rooted in good intentions. But it's crucial to weigh the potential benefits of recommendations against the potential risks. When it comes to the fear-driven messages parents are given about technology, these risks are often overlooked. When recommendations are hard to follow or stoke too much fear, they can induce stress and guilt in parents and harm the parent-child relationship.

When my kids were toddlers, the American Academy of Pediatrics (AAP) advised parents that kids under the age of two should spend no time in front of screens at all. (They have since slightly softened the recommendations, encouraging parents of kids under the age of eighteen months to "minimize or eliminate" media exposure other than video chatting.) When I first came across this recommendation, I assumed it existed because there was evidence suggesting that even a small amount of screen exposure was harmful for babies and toddlers. Then I thought about the fact that I'd occasionally plopped my babies in front of Classical Baby videos so that I could clean the house or make dinner. Ugh—was I messing them up for life? Sometimes I felt painful pangs of guilt and turned off the TV, only to become became so frazzled by my attempts to do eight things at once that I would yell at my kids or not notice when they were doing potentially unsafe things.

When these AAP guidelines were first set, there were a couple of studies suggesting that babies and toddlers who were exposed to screens were more likely to develop language delays and attention problems. But when other researchers reanalyzed this data, they found that these attention problems arose only among young kids who used screens for more than seven hours a day. And some of the language-related findings could not be replicated. The AAP notes that no longitudinal studies have determined the long-term effects of media use on infants and young toddlers, and that the question of whether screens actually contribute to these issues "remains unanswered."

Why, then, did the AAP set such a conservative recommendation? According to the AAP policy statement, it's because there is a *potential* for screens to have negative effects, and no proven positive effects. Experts say it may also have stemmed from assumptions the AAP held about what parents would do if they weren't sufficiently warned. "It was a little bit of a paternalistic approach on the AAP's part of *If we tell parents that some is safe, then too many of them will overdo it, and so we should just say none*," said Morgan Ellithorpe, a communications professor at the University of Delaware who studies how media use affects health. "But that's not helpful or realistic."

Every recommendation and intervention has potential benefits and potential risks. The potential benefit of cautious recommendations is that kids may be protected from potentially harmful things. But overly cautious, unrealistic recommendations can have a major downside: Studies show they make parents feel guilty and add to family stress and conflict.

In a 2024 study, researchers at the University of Amsterdam, Leibniz-Institut für Wissensmedien in Germany, UC Santa Barbara, and Northwestern University conducted a longitudinal study that involved surveying parents of children between the ages of two and seventeen in 2020 and again in 2021. They asked parents how they felt about their relationship with their children, how many hours of screen time their kids had on an average recent day, and how much guilt and stress they felt regarding their kids' screen time. The scientists found no relationship between the amount of time the kids spent on screens and the quality of parent-child relationships. They also found no consistent relationship between the amount of guilt parents felt over the kids' screen use and how much time kids spent on screens. But, interestingly, parents who felt more guilt over their kids' technology use reported having a more fraught parent-child relationship a year later.

We can't be certain that parents' guilt caused these relationship woes (although the longitudinal design does hint at a causal relationship). But the idea does seem reasonable: The researchers found that parental guilt is linked with greater parental stress over time, which could undermine the parent-child relationship. This, I think, comes as no surprise to a parent who has ever parented: It's hard to be a patient, thoughtful caregiver when totally stressed out. And with regard to technology, stress-induced conflict arises frequently. Studies find that negotiating boundaries around screen time regularly leads to conflicts and frustration, both between little kids and their parents and adolescents and their parents. In one study, 37 percent of parents of toddlers and preschoolers said that "screen time almost always ends with a fight."

It makes sense. If we believe something is terrible, we may be unable to communicate calmly and rationally about it, and we may also experience more bad feelings when we are exposed to it (or see our kids exposed to it). Those feelings may incite more conflict. They also make it difficult to evaluate how technology (or taking breaks from technology) affects us or our kids. If we believe screen time is harmful, we may feel better after taking screen breaks, or feel worse after heavy screen days, in part because this is how we *expect* we should feel. In medicine, such bias is known as the placebo effect, and medical studies use sugar pills to control for it. It is much harder to control for such biases in studies of technology, and some researchers have pointed out that our negative beliefs about screen time may be skewing research results, causing studies to overestimate its potential harms.

Another danger of overly harsh anti-screen messaging is that it can cause us to fall into the trap of what's called "technological determinism"—the belief that technology has predetermined and inevitable effects—and forget that there are so many other factors that shape our kids' relationships with their devices and how they will be affected by them. As researcher Katie Davis, co-director of the University of Washington's Digital Youth Lab, put it in her book *Technology's Child*: "Children's technology use happens in a broader context, and this context may matter just as much—sometimes more—than the technology itself." If our kids are struggling at school and spending too much time on screens, we'll assume technology use is driving the problem, when it could be a symptom rather than a cause. It's far easier to point fingers at TikTok than to consider the role of hormones, stress, peer conflict, or early school start times. Technology is the easiest scapegoat.

Our beliefs and perceptions about technology can shape so many things: our experiences with it ourselves, our reactions to our kids' use of it, the way we talk to our kids and partners about it, and our willingness to listen to other perspectives on it. It's impossible, of course, to eliminate all our beliefs and perceptions—to simply decide to consider the issue fresh and without prejudice. But by being aware of these psychological biases, we may be able to soften our opinions and perceptions, even if just slightly, and become more open-minded.

None of this means that the research linking technology to bad outcomes is irrelevant or invalid. It also doesn't mean that our kids won't benefit from limits surrounding technology use. But we should remember that our fear, guilt, shame, and stress about technology can impact us, our kids, and the research—so taking some deep breaths, trying to quell our panic, and reminding ourselves of the big picture may actually mitigate some of the harm that is supposedly coming from those dastardly screens.

2. Consider your child and what they're able to handle. Introduce tech slowly.

One question I regularly get from parents is this: *When is my kid ready for a phone?*

Sadly, research can't give us a simple answer. In 2023, the nonprofit organization Sapien Labs published the results of a study in which they surveyed nearly twenty-eight thousand young adults between the ages of eighteen and twenty-four from forty-one countries. The researchers gave the young adults a mental health questionnaire and asked them the age at which they first got a smartphone or tablet with internet access. They found that the younger the subjects were when they received their first devices, the worse their mental health tended to be in young adulthood—and that the relationship between the two was more pronounced among girls than boys. On the flip side, a 2022 Stanford study that tracked low-income kids over the course of five years as they transitioned to phone ownership—a longitudinal approach that can better tease out cause-and-effect patterns—found no relationship between the age at which kids got their first device and their well-being as measured through their grades, sleep habits, and depression symptoms.

Once I learned about this conflicting research, I wondered if there were other metrics besides age that parents could use to help them gauge when the risk/benefit calculation of phone ownership tipped more toward benefits. To find out, I reached out to Jacqueline Nesi, a Brown University psychologist who studies how social media affects adolescents' mental health. She suggested that parents consider four R's: responsibility, rules, risks, and reasons.

The first R, responsibility, refers to whether your child understands what it means and requires to be responsible with a phone. Do they easily lose things, or are they generally able to keep track of their possessions? Do they come to you when they encounter new problems? Do they generally show good judgment, or are they impulsive?

The second R, rules, refers to whether your child understands and respects rules you plan to set surrounding phone use, such as when, where, and for what purpose phones can be used. In our family, for instance, phones have to be charged every night in the kitchen starting at eight, and nobody can download new apps without permission.

The third R, risks, involves determining if your child understands the potential risks of having a phone and what to do if they encounter those risks. It involves considering whether you've had conversations about how you hope to help your child mitigate risks, for instance through monitoring their texts or setting up certain app limits or content restrictions.

Finally, the fourth R is reasons. What are the reasons you are considering getting your kid a phone? Is it so that they can reach you in emergencies? Or so they can stay in touch with their friends? Is it mostly just a status symbol? Reflecting on these reasons can, among other things, help families determine the right kind of phone to get for their child, and whether they need a phone at all. If the phone is just for emergencies or for texting, they might not need a smartphone. If it's primarily for game playing, perhaps they can instead play on their iPad or on a console. The psychologist Lisa Damour has argued that kids don't need phones unless they are explicitly asking for them, and even then, their needs and desires may sometimes be better served by other devices. Remember, too, that you can absolutely get your kid a phone without giving them access to social media. Damour suggests that parents give kids access to as little technology as is required to maintain their friendships.

When we are making decisions about technology, we should also consider the ways in which our kids' personalities, characteristics, strengths, and weaknesses might shape their interactions with it and responses to it—because all kids do not react the same way.

In the early twentieth century, many people worried that mass media—and in particular, movies—had powerful and uniformly harmful effects on kids. During the 1920s, many teens went to movie theaters at least once a week, and parents feared how the adult themes depicted in films—drinking, smoking, driving fast cars—would shape their kids' moral identities.

In 1928, these concerns led William Short, the director of the Motion Picture Research Council, to initiate a series of studies now known as the Payne Fund project to assess the impact of motion pictures on children and teens. One of its studies analyzed the content and themes of fifteen hundred movies and studied the effects of these films on one thousand teens by analyzing their behavior. Much to their surprise, the researchers did *not* find that movies had consistent effects on teens. Instead, they found that movies' effects largely depended on the individual.

"That the movies exert an influence, there can be no doubt," researchers wrote in a concluding summary in 1933. "But it is our opinion that this influence is specific for a given child and a given movie. The same picture may influence different children in distinctly opposite directions."

Other research has largely confirmed this notion. "Individual differences are absolutely crucial," Ellithorpe told me. Some kids will be more likely than others to develop problems in how they manage technology use, respond to the content they come across, and engage with others online—and some kids will also be more likely than others to derive benefits from technology in terms of building more connections with others, absorbing more educational information, and engaging in healthy forms of self-expression.

Although it's impossible to predict how any one child will engage with and respond to technology, the emerging research does suggest some general themes. Kids who struggle with impulse control—including kids with ADHD—are more at risk for excessive technology use, including problematic use that could interfere with their ability to engage in other activities. Because of this, parents of kids who are especially impulsive may want to set careful limits and structure around screen use (more on how to do that shortly).

Although age is always not the best metric, some research does suggest it can make a difference when it comes to how kids are affected by social media in particular. In a 2022 study, researchers Amy Orben, Andrew Przybylski, Sarah-Jayne Blakemore, and Rogier Kievit analyzed data involving more than eighty thousand people, including longitudinal data that tracked more than seventeen thousand kids between the ages of ten and twenty-one over time. They were looking to see whether and how the use of social media affected kids' life satisfaction one year later. They found that in girls, social media use between the ages of eleven and thirteen was linked with future drops in life satisfaction, while a similar drop was seen in boys who used social media at ages fourteen and fifteen. Interestingly, too, use at age nineteen was linked with issues one year later.

In addition to considering our kids' age, temperament, and personality, we should also pay close attention to how kids seem to be doing when they use technology. Many of us think of the risks associated with technology as being insidious and invisible—that there's just no way to know if our kids are experiencing negative effects from screen use. But often, if there are problems, there are clear signs. So instead of coming at the issue with the overarching assumption of harm, we should tune in to our senses and observations. Have they lost interest in other activities? Are they suddenly struggling at school? Have they become socially or emotionally withdrawn?

"I can't tell you how many parents have come up to me at workshops and said, *I'm worried about X, Y, or Z related to screens.* And I'll say, *So what's your kid doing that makes you concerned?*" said media literacy scholar Faith Rogow, the founding president of the National Association for Media Literacy Education. Often, in response, Rogow said, parents say that they're seeing nothing concerning—their kids have lots of friends and are doing well in school. She follows up with: *Then what are you worried about?*

Put another way, given that the impact of screens on kids is shaped by what kids are doing and who those kids are, parents, not researchers, are probably the best equipped to assess how screens affect their kids—because the impact largely depends on context and observations that only parents know and have. In her book *Autonomy-Supportive Parenting*, clinical psychologist Emily Edlynn explained that she switched from thinking about technology through the anxious lens of *too much time on the phone will be harmful* to a more curious approach driven by the question *Am I seeing any evidence of the phone causing problems?* This framing can minimize the scary noise and help us focus on the reason we ask such questions in the first place: We want to ensure our kids are okay.

3. Monitoring and restriction shouldn't replace two-way conversations, especially with tweens and teens.

With all the fear and angst parents have today over kids' tech use, it's no wonder that we are quick to sign up for services that promise to keep our children safe. The Life360 app, which tracks kids' whereabouts and experiences online and claims to have been used by one in eight US smartphone users in 2024, promises parents "location safety," "driving safety," and "digital safety." Bark, a company that sells apps as well as phones, reassures parents that its products help to preserve kids' mental health.

These products can certainly provide useful services, and I know parents who swear by them. But experts warn that these products are neither comprehensive nor fail-safe. As Nesi explained to me, these apps are limited in the kinds of content and language they can detect and block. For instance, they may be able to prevent kids from downloading new apps, but they typically can't block worrisome in-app content—and, moreover, kids often find ways around their limits. "They're far from perfect," she said. Julie Smith, a communications instructor at Webster University and the author of *Master the Media*, agrees. "The kid will have a workaround, whatever thing you try," she warned.

In 2024, researchers at the London School of Economics and Political Science and the University of Colorado Boulder published an evidence review analyzing the overall benefits and drawbacks of parental monitoring tools. They concluded that they "found little support for advocating parental controls as a stand-alone strategy." In a 2018 study, kids said that parental monitoring apps also negatively affected their relationship with their parents.

It can be far more helpful to engage with our children directly and help them learn necessary skills. In one study, researchers found that teens whose parents used parental control software tended to encounter more, not fewer, online risks, but that kids were protected when parents were more involved and aware of what their kids were doing online. In her 2024 book *The Screentime Solution*, technology consultant Emily Cherkin argued that kids don't need parental controls; kids need parenting. Parental monitoring apps are one potentially useful tool, she wrote, but their use "does not exempt us from teaching our children about how to be safe online, how to deal with scary situations or images, or how to balance tech use intentionally."

When parents ease up on surveillance, kids often make better choices, too, Heitner told me. As she wrote in her book *Growing Up in Public*, kids think: "I know you can surveil me, but I appreciate that you don't, so I will honor your trust by not doing things we've agreed I'm not supposed to."

If you do want to track your kids, it's best to be candid about it—let them know exactly what you're monitoring and why. Parents may also want to consider using only the surveillance tools they really need: Maybe they track their kids' location because they walk home from school alone, but they don't need to read all the kids' texts.

The same can be said for restriction and rules: They can certainly be helpful, but they are not a panacea—especially as kids get older. Experts told me that, when kids are younger than eight or nine, rules designed to restrict the use of devices or specific features do help to protect them from online risks and harmful content. But with tweens and teens, restriction doesn't always work as well, and it can sometimes backfire.

In one study, Ohio State University communication researcher Amy Nathanson surveyed college students—mostly women—and at least one of their parents about the students' experiences in high school. Students who had parents who'd tried to restrict exposure to violent or sexual television content reported having worse relationships with their parents and more positive attitudes toward explicit content compared with students whose parents had not been as restrictive. The students with more restrictive parents were also more likely to have viewed explicit content with friends in what researchers have termed a "forbidden fruit response."

And in a 2023 longitudinal study conducted in China and involving more than 2,100 adolescent-parent pairs, researchers found that youth whose parents tried to restrict their media use through rules and time limits ended up using their phones more frequently and in riskier ways compared with teens whose parents tried to limit their use through respectful conversations about media-related risks.

Restricting a child's tech use can, when done in the wrong ways, damage their relationship with their parents without actually improving their relationship with technology, Ellithorpe explained to me. "This is a pretty consistent finding," she said. In a 2022 paper, researchers found that strict, harsh parenting actually caused kids to spend *more* time online, and the researchers theorized kids may gravitate to screens in an attempt to comfort themselves. As I mentioned earlier, it's important to consider the potential harms that various "risk-reducing" interventions can pose; there are always potential drawbacks.

What scientists have concluded from the research is that, with adolescents, parental communication often works a lot better than parental control—and that if you're going to take control, you need to do it carefully. With tweens and teens, instead of setting what may seem to them like arbitrary rules and restrictions, we will make more headway if we talk to our kids about our concerns and expectations as well as the rationale behind them. It is through conversations with our kids that we can impart knowledge and wisdom about media literacy, online communication, privacy, and other important issues. And granting kids autonomy can inspire them to make more informed and respectful choices, helping to create healthy habits that could last a lifetime.

This idea aligns with the research on parenting styles, which has consistently found that kids of respectful, boundary-setting parents who are willing to negotiate fare better in many ways than kids of parents who bark orders, set strict rules, and dole out harsh punishments. When we engage with our kids respectfully and ensure that they feel some freedom and independence, they are more likely to listen to us, learn from us, and behave in thoughtful ways.

This doesn't mean we can't have *any* media restrictions in place—but it does mean that when we set rules, we should be mindful of our children's autonomy. In their book *Plugged In*, Patti M. Valkenburg, a professor of Media, Youth and Society at the University of Amsterdam, and Jessica Taylor Piotrowski, a media psychologist at the University of Amsterdam, explained that parents will likely be most successful setting restrictions with tweens and teens if they consider their child's perspective, present alternative options and ideas, and involve their children in the decision-making. If your kid comes to you asking after a new video game, perhaps you sit down with them to learn about the game, then start a conversation about your family values and how the game does or doesn't align with them. You can also talk through other safety settings and why you have them.

Likewise, when your kid comes to you and says, *I want TikTok—*

all my friends have it, you could research the app together and discuss its benefits and drawbacks. Kids often don't understand why we have strong opinions about what they perceive to be harmless social media platforms, so it can help to explain where we're coming from and why—and listen to their point of view, too. Afterward, you can decide on a course of action: Perhaps the answer is no—they can't have TikTok yet, and here's why. Or you can arrive at a compromise, like *Okay, we'll let you use TikTok for an hour a day this week, and then let's check in on Sunday to see what you've noticed and are feeling about it.* You might explain that you'll be monitoring their viewing history (you can do this through the app's Family Pairing feature) or the videos they're posting themselves, if you're allowing that.

As our kids use technology, we should stay curious, regularly asking questions about what they're up to and how it's going. What do they enjoy doing online and what are they doing to ensure they're getting more positives than negatives? In *Technology's Child*, Davis pointed out that because so many kids stray from the averages we might glean from the research, it's helpful to consider contextual factors. Is your child becoming more obsessed with body image because she's been scrolling through photos and comparing herself to other people? Does your teen seem to be feeling increasingly left out because he keeps seeing evidence of friends hanging out without him?

Through these observations and conversations, we can help our kids learn what their own needs and limits are regarding technology—a skill that will help them forever. When we uniformly restrict, and especially when we do so without open communication, we don't give kids the chance to understand the value of this self-knowledge or the opportunity to develop it through practice—

until they are much older, when the stakes are often much higher. Plus, checking in regularly gives you the opportunity to identify signs that they're struggling. If you notice they're not okay, you may well want to step up your online supervision, perhaps with more online monitoring and rules, to help them achieve a healthy balance.

Generally speaking, experts define "problematic media use" not based on how much time kids spend on screens, but on whether their use interferes with their daily functioning. If screens start getting in the way of your child's ability to engage in other normal and healthy activities, or if you observe symptoms of depression (sleep or appetite changes, irritability, difficulty concentrating, loss of interest in things they used to find enjoyable) or anxiety (excessive worrying, irritability, headaches, stomachaches, sleep problems), consult with your child's doctor or a mental health professional.

4. Be intentional about your own device use.

I'm sure this will come as a surprise to absolutely none of you, but how we engage with our phones shapes how kids will engage with their phones. If I berate my son for being glued to his device while I'm stealing glances at my own, I can assure you that the message is not going to get through (and, moreover, my son might start to resent my hypocrisy). Some studies have found that the more time parents spend on their devices around their kids, the more likely kids are to excessively use theirs.

Yet the effects of our own tech use could extend beyond merely setting a bad example. For one thing, we may threaten our children's privacy and agency when we post photos or videos of them, which is why we should always ask for consent first. (We should also consider whether our kids are actually old enough to provide informed consent—do they understand the value of privacy?) In *Growing Up in Public*, Heitner implores parents to be cautious. "After years of talking with kids who feel violated and exposed by their parents, I've come to believe in erring on the side of privacy. If it could be problematic later, don't share."

Frequent device use may also make us less responsive caregivers. In a 2020 study, researchers in Norway and the Netherlands observed fifty-three parents and their kids on playgrounds and in waiting rooms. They found that the odds of a parent responding in a timely fashion to their child's bid for attention was five times lower when the parent was engrossed in their phone than when they were not, and that these phone-focused parents were also less likely to prioritize their child's needs. And now for some good news: The researchers also found that parents who only *occasionally* glanced at their phones were no less attentive to their kids. Phew!

Our relationships with our phones could also affect our relationships with our kids in other ways. In one study, Jenny Radesky, a pediatrician at the University of Michigan, and her colleagues at Boston Medical Center conducted in-depth interviews with thirty-five caregivers, including moms, dads, and grandmothers, about how they felt their device use affected their interactions with their kids and grandkids. Some subjects admitted that when they were glued to their phones, kids often resorted to annoying attention-seeking behaviors, which then led to conflict. "I get mad and then I actually guilt for a minute and I'm like, *Whoa, I'm getting pissed off at him because I want to make a post, like is it really that important?*" one mother expressed in the study.

It's easy to see how this could turn into a vicious cycle: kids act out to get their parents' attention; frustrated parents feel compelled to turn to their phones as a means to escape; the parent-child relationship suffers.

In a 2021 study, researchers interviewed tweens about how frequently their parents' technology use disrupted their interactions. The more these disruptions happened, the more the tweens said they fought with their parents, the less frequently they reported going to their parents with their problems, and the less fun they said they had with their parents.

But how do we actually pull ourselves away from our phones? Many of us reflexively check Instagram when we have a moment to ourselves, and it can be hard to quit a habit we hardly even notice ourselves doing. In her book *How to Break Up with Your Phone*, the journalist Catherine Price offers a thirty-day plan to change habits that involves activity tracking, settings changes, and mindfulness exercises—it might be worth checking out.

All this said, we shouldn't panic. If we use our phones excessively, it's probably not great for our kids, and we may want to ease up. But this doesn't mean we should never use our phones around our kids or that we should feel guilty every time we check Instagram. As with everything else, it's all about striving for balance. And we know that excessive guilt doesn't help.

KEY POINTS

1. Research on the effects of technology use and social media on youth is difficult to interpret. Technology has the potential for harm and for good, and its effects seem to depend on the child and what they are doing.
2. Parental anxiety over screens can have a negative impact on kids and on the parent-child relationship, so try not to panic.
3. Introduce tech slowly, and remember who your child is. Kids with impulse control problems are at a higher risk for developing problems with technology.
4. Remember that the harms of screens aren't invisible, so keep an eye out for them. If everything seems okay, you may not need to worry.
5. Keep in mind that monitoring and restriction can reduce risks, but they are not fail-safe. With teens and tweens, especially, it's important to grant kids some autonomy and have regular conversations about technology use so they can build skills.

Epilogue

After I settled on the framework for *Hello, Cruel World!*, I soon started panicking. Addiction, resilience, relationships, media literacy—people have written entire books about each of these topics. How was I going to cover, in a single book, everything parents needed to know about *ten* of them? What if the science on one topic suggested strategies that contradicted what the science recommended on another topic?

I had no idea what I was going to find out and how I was going to organize so much potentially contradictory and confusing information into a coherent whole.

You can imagine my surprise and relief when the exact opposite happened. I started to uncover common, somewhat simple themes rather than frustrating complexities. Although the researchers who study how to talk to kids about money don't necessarily share their findings with the researchers who study how to help kids safely navigate social media, I found that they often made similar suggestions based on the science in their fields. This delighted me—and made me feel so relieved not only about this book, but also about parenting in general.

Parenting is the hardest job in the world. But as it turns out, the science on what truly helps kids isn't *all* that hard to grasp or understand. I can't tell you the number of times I went into an interview and found myself smiling and nodding along as I heard a researcher tell me something I'd heard two weeks ago, and also two months ago, when I was reporting on different topics for two different chapters.

I'm sure you noticed some of this overlap while reading the book, and I hope you also found it reassuring rather than frustrating or annoying. I mean, yes—repetition *can* be annoying. It's why, if I'm honest, I often avoid reading self-help books. But when solidifying parenting skills, I think repetition is essential; sometimes we have to hear the same ideas and strategies over and over again before they sink and start to shape our everyday choices.

What I thought was fascinating, too, was that although some of the approaches and strategies were similar across different topics, the reasons they were helpful often differed. In other words, some parenting approaches seem to help kids on multiple levels, for multiple reasons, through multiple pathways.

I know it can be next to impossible to keep the big picture in mind when putting out the near constant fires of day-to-day parenting. So to make this a little bit easier, I've organized the big, common themes from this book into three simple recommendations. They certainly don't cover everything in the book—there are lots of nuances, as well as certain strategies that zero in on specific skills—so I encourage you to revisit the chapters over the years to remind yourself of the details and discover how various strategies can be tailored to different ages.

1. Prepare more than you protect.

When I ask myself what my number one job is as a parent, I settle on the idea that my job is to help my kids become independent and well-adjusted adults. I want them to grow into human beings who can take care of themselves, as well as others, and who can manage all kinds of situations—including ones they've never come across before.

Ironically, though, many common parenting trends and instincts work against this goal.

For instance, we often think we should protect our kids from hard experiences and curate their environments so they are always comfortable—yet both of these approaches take away opportunities for kids to learn new skills and work through challenges and discomfort. What makes you better at hard things? Practice. We need to give our kids lots of opportunities to practice problem-solving and deal with frustration and disappointment.

We often step in and do things for our kids to ensure that they succeed, too. We take over their science projects, pay them for good grades, hire private baseball coaches, and put them in intensive acting classes. We do it because we love them and we worry about their future, but this kind of overprotection and pressure can backfire, ironically putting kids' futures at risk. The pressure parents put on kids to excel increases the chance kids will have low self-esteem, use substances, and suffer from mental health problems.

We also sometimes fear for our kids' physical safety when we shouldn't. We don't let them walk to school or find items on their own in the grocery store because we have been fed misleading statistics about stranger danger. We don't let them play or goof off with friends because we believe that scheduled, adult-led activities are more appropriate or helpful. But by constantly hovering, intervening, and protecting, we rob our kids of opportunities to build social skills and resilience and to discover on their own what they truly enjoy doing—essential information they will need throughout their lives.

Sometimes we overprotect our kids by not talking to them—by intentionally shielding them from what we consider to be "adult" topics. We think our kids are too young or innocent for conversations about drugs, money, racism, or pornography. But it's possible to have an age-appropriate conversation with kids about pretty much anything. And, because they are such observant little scientists, children are typically more aware of important societal issues than we give them credit for. If *we* don't talk to them, all we are doing is ensuring that the information they get on these issues comes from someone else.

Whenever I'm faced with a difficult parenting decision, I try to remember to ask myself *What will help them grow into the adults I want them to be?* Often, we need to pull ourselves out of the present and consider what will help prepare our kids for the future.

2. Listen more than you lecture.

One strategy I recommend over and over again in this book is to ask your kids questions. It's so simple, takes the pressure off, and is a great way to start a conversation about pretty much anything. Asking your child a question gives you a moment to breathe, gives them the chance to share their perspective before you jump in, and can help clarify the aspects of the topic you may want to zero in on next.

Asking questions also models a curious mindset, which is so important for kids to see in us. We want our kids to learn that life isn't about always having the answers, that everyone is a lifelong learner, and that it is okay to make mistakes. Asking questions tells kids that we, as adults, are still curious and willing to learn—and that as they grow up, they should be, too.

When you ask kids questions, you also then have the opportunity to listen to them. Listening to our children—really, truly listening to them—is crucial. When kids feel heard and understood, they feel valued, they feel loved, they feel calm. They become more connected to us and more willing to listen to our perspective. They learn through our modeling to listen to their friends and other loved ones as well, which helps them build stronger relationships over the course of their lives.

Listening to our kids benefits humanity more broadly, too. From the research, we know that when people feel listened to, they become more self-reflective and humble and less extreme in their beliefs. When we deeply listen to our kids, in other words, we are helping to build a less polarized, more open-minded, and more respectful society.

This is yet another example of the way in which parenting is a form of activism: We can build a better, more humane world based on how we raise our kids.

3. Comfort more than you chide.

Kids—toddlers, tweens, and teens especially—have lots of big feelings. Emotions are part of the human condition, so we *all* have them, although some of us are more attuned to them than others. Feelings are useful, too, because they provide us with essential information about our wants and needs.

For a long time, parents were encouraged to ignore, diminish, or chide their kids for their emotions. *Children should be seen and not heard.* My best friend encounters this belief every time she goes to the grocery store with her toddler, who invariably loses her mind in the yogurt aisle because she doesn't have the emotional regulation or delayed gratification skills to manage seeing a tub of Chobani without eating it *right this second*. When my friend's toddler becomes upset, there's often a customer or employee who snaps at her child for having big feelings or chides my friend for not admonishing her daughter herself.

Look, I get it. Screaming children aren't my cup of tea, either. But when we communicate to kids that their feelings aren't welcome, a number of unfortunate things can happen. Kids may instead learn to suppress or repress their feelings, which makes it harder for them to learn emotional regulation skills and to listen to and interpret the sometimes very useful information their feelings offer. When kids perceive that we are uncomfortable around feelings, they may stop coming to us when they are upset and in need of help or support, because they assume we'd rather not know. And when we don't allow our kids to sit with their feelings—and we don't have conversations about them—our kids may not develop crucial emotional literacy and social skills.

So the next time your kid is totally losing their mind, take a deep breath to help regulate your *own* emotions and then at least briefly acknowledge and label theirs. Let them air their grievances (but don't problem-solve unless you know that's what they want). Regularly talk about what emotions look and feel like and what can be done to manage them, and let them know they're not alone in their struggles. These strategies will not only support your kids' mental health but will help your kids become more thoughtful, resilient, and compassionate humans, too.

* * *

With these three themes in mind, I also want you to remember that perfection is never the goal. Have I overprotected my kids, lectured my kids, and told my kids to calm the heck down? Absolutely. So many times I can't even count. It doesn't matter how much you know; we're all still human, which means we are all sometimes ruled by our emotions, and we will make lots of mistakes.

That's okay. That's *good*. It's important for our kids to see us screw up, take responsibility for our actions, and revise our strategies. Our children are growing up in a messy and challenging world—it's helpful for them to see that floundering is an okay and sometimes necessary part of the survival process.

We don't want to—and cannot—raise our kids to be perfect human beings. The best we can do is to raise them to be compassionate, hopeful, and resilient enough to take care of themselves and fight for the things that really matter. And we should remind ourselves that, through the activism of our thoughtful daily parenting, we are fighting for the things that really matter, too.

Acknowledgments

When you write a book inspired by your deepest fears—how *are* our children going to handle this crazy world?—you need all the support you can get. This book came about in a tumultuous period in my personal life, too, and I am deeply grateful to everyone who helped me along the way.

I considered abandoning this book early on, and if it weren't for my amazing agents, Larry Weissman and Sascha Alper, you might not be reading it at all. Thank you for always (somehow) understanding and supporting my creative vision. To my editor, Michelle Howry: Thank you for being fiercely on board the minute we came to you with the idea, and for supporting me at every juncture, along with the rest of the fantastic Putnam team, including Ashley Hewlett, Ashley Di Dio, and Brennin Cummings.

For the conceit of this book, I once again must thank Michael Moyer, who (again while we were out to dinner!!) originally suggested the topic and framework. You have an uncanny ability to distill ideas and sharpen my thinking. I am grateful for the many ways you supported me throughout this process, even when things weren't easy.

For the title of this book and so many other important things, I am eternally indebted to Dan Blank. Our phone calls got me through the hardest parts of the reporting and writing process. Thank you for your wisdom and for always making me laugh.

Karen Simring and Meredith Knight: Thank you for your boundless wisdom, humor, and love—and for sending me the four thousand texts per day I needed to keep going. (Sorry that I always sent you a factor of ten more in return.) Karen, thank you for your incisive edits on my hardest chapters, which have made me sound a gazillion times smarter and more clearheaded than I actually am.

Virginia Sole-Smith, who is apparently on the same life path as me but just a few strides ahead: I'm endlessly grateful for your takeout, your pool, your edits, and your love.

Tracy Bunye, Bernard Bunye, and Rachel Moody: Thank you for always being there for me—often by text at odd hours!—even when I don't realize I need it. I'm so grateful for your generosity and your kindness.

I'm not sure what I would do without Molly Webster, Rachele Lenehan, and Andrea Anderson. From our days together at SHERP—and far before that for Rachele—you have believed in me, and I feel it in my bones when I most need it. I've already started packing for girls' weekend 2026.

Emily Krieger, Wudan Yan, and Brad Sciber: Thank you for fact-checking my book with such care and thoughtfulness. You have no idea the peace of mind you have given me.

Heidi and Michael Bender and everyone at Split Rock Books: I can't count the ways in which you've helped and supported me as an author. I will always be grateful.

Gabrielle Gerard, thank you for always making me look amazing in my author photos!

Phil Benante: Thank you for your thoughts, ideas, and sage perspective.

Emily Edlynn and Yael Schonbrun: You two hold a special place in my heart and always will; sometimes I forget we connected through our work and then became friends, rather than the other way around.

I have so much gratitude for all the parenting and social science writers and creators who have helped and supported me along the way these past few years: Carla Naumburg, Adam Grant, Emily Oster, Cara Natterson, Vanessa Kroll Bennett, Eve Rodsky, Aliza Pressman, Devorah Heitner, Lisa Damour, Jessi Gold, Kelly Fradin, Claire Zulkey, Kathryn Barbash, Cara Goodman, Clare Lerner, Sara Petersen, Catherine Price, Christopher Pepper, Kate Manne, Amy Palanjian, Amanda Montei, Elissa Strauss, Ruth Whippman, Niobe Way, Katie Hurley, Tovah Klein, Phyllis Fagell, Tina Payne Bryson, Michele Borba, Elise Loehnen, Lyz Lenz, Anne Helen Petersen, Zibby Owens, Krupa Playforth, Jo-Ann Finkelstein, Ron Lieber, Robyn Silverman, Madeline Levine, Ryan Holiday, and many more.

My sources: Thank you for the crucial work you do. Thank you trusting me, making time for me, and sharing your wisdom and insights with me.

My parents, Marilyn and Dave; my sister, Bethany; my aunt, Wendy; and my nieces and nephews: Thank you for always being there for me, challenging me in all the right ways, and encouraging me to follow my dreams.

My two children, who have been so patient with me as I've been writing this book: Although you don't always know what I'm doing in my office, I want you to know that with every interview I conduct, every study I read, and every word I write, I'm thinking of you. I love you.

Notes

Introduction

2 **According to the Centers for Disease Control and Prevention:** "Youth Risk Behavior Survey: Data Summary & Trends Report: 2011–2021," CDC, accessed August 9, 2024, https://www.cdc.gov/healthyyouth/data/yrbs/pdf/YRBS_Data-Summary-Trends_Report2023_508.pdf.

2 **Deaths due to drug overdoses:** Joseph Friedman and Scott E. Hadland, "The Overdose Crisis Among U.S. Adolescents," *New England Journal of Medicine* 390, no. 2 (January 11, 2024): 97–100; "Unintentional Drug Overdose Death Rates Among US Youth Aged 15-19," National Institute on Drug Abuse, accessed September 28, 2024: https://nida.nih.gov/research-topics/trends-statistics/infographics/unintentional-drug-overdose-death-rates-among-us-youth-aged-15-19.

2 **Anxiety rates and sleep deprivation:** "Anxiety in Teens Is Rising: What's Going On?" Healthychildren.org, November 20, 2019, https://www.healthychildren.org/English/health-issues/conditions/emotional-problems/Pages/Anxiety-Disorders.aspx; "Youth Online," CDC, accessed August 9, 2024, https://nccd.cdc.gov/Youthonline/App/Results.aspx.

2 **In a large 2023 survey:** "Youth Right Now: Full Survey Results 2023," Boys and Girls Clubs of America, accessed August 9, 2024, https://www.bgca.org/wp-content/uploads/2024/02/YouthRightNow2023_FullSurveyResults.pdf.

3 **As US Surgeon General Vivek H. Murthy:** "Protecting Youth Mental Health," US Surgeon General's Advisory, 2021, accessed August 9, 2024, https://www.hhs.gov/sites/default/files/surgeon-general-youth-mental-health-advisory.pdf.

4 **When author Ryan Holiday:** Ryan Holiday, host, *The Daily Stoic* (podcast), "Melinda Moyer on Changing the World by Raising Curious Kids," July 12, 2023, https://dailystoic.com/melinda-moyer-on-changing-the-world-by-raising-curious-kids/.

8 **In a 2019 study, sociologist Patrick Ishizuka:** Patrick Ishizuka, "Social Class, Gender, and Contemporary Parenting Standards in the United States: Evidence from a National Survey Experiment," *Social Forces* 98, no. 1 (September 2019): 31–58.

9 In a recent study, researchers conducted in-depth interviews: Sarah Hubert and Isabelle Aujoulat, "Parental Burnout: When Exhausted Mothers Open Up," *Frontiers in Psychology* 9 (June 2018): 1021.

1
"I Hate Myself!"

14 First, let me define self-compassion: Kristin Neff, "What Is Self-Compassion?" self-compassion.org, accessed August 11, 2024, https://self-compassion.org/what-is-self-compassion/#what-is-self-compassion.

15 Studies have found that self-compassionate adolescents: Karen Bluth, Michael Mullarkey, and Christine Lathren, "Self-Compassion: A Potential Path to Adolescent Resilience and Positive Exploration," *Journal of Child and Family Studies* 27, no. 9 (September 2018): 3037–47; Karen Bluth and Tory A. Eisenlohr-Moul, "Response to a Mindful Self-Compassion Intervention in Teens: A Within-Person Association of Mindfulness, Self-Compassion, and Emotional Well-Being Outcomes," *Journal of Adolescence* 57 (June 2017): 108–18; Karen Bluth, Patricia N. E. Roberson, Susan A. Gaylord, Katurah R. Faurot, Karen M. Grewen, Samantha Arzon, and Susan S. Girdler, "Does Self-Compassion Protect Adolescents from Stress?" *Journal of Child and Family Studies* 25, no. 4 (April 2016): 1098–109.

15 Self-compassionate kids are also less likely: Karen Bluth, Susan A. Gaylord, Rebecca A. Campo, Michael C. Mullarkey, and Lorraine Hobbs, "Making Friends with Yourself: A Mixed Methods Pilot Study of a Mindful Self-Compassion Program for Adolescents," *Mindfulness (NY)* 7, no. 2 (March 2016): 479–92; Kristin Neff and Christopher Germer, "Self-Compassion and Psychological Well-Being," in *The Oxford Handbook of Compassion Science*, ed. E. M. Seppälä, E. Simon-Thomas, S. L. Brown, M. C. Worline, C. D. Cameron, and J. R. Doty (Oxford University Press, 2017): 371–85.

15 Adults high in self-compassion: Mark R. Leary, Eleanor B. Tate, Claire E. Adams, Ashley Batts Allen, and Jessica Hancock, "Self-Compassion and Reactions to Unpleasant Self-Relevant Events: The Implications of Treating Oneself Kindly," *Journal of Personality and Social Psychology* 92, no. 5 (May 2007): 887–904; Kristin D. Neff, "Self-Compassion: Theory, Method, Research, and Intervention," *Annual Review of Psychology* 74 (2023): 193–218.

16 we can treat other people well, too: Sarah L. Marshall, Joseph Ciarrochi, Philip D. Parker, and Balijinder K. Sahdra, "Is Self-Compassion Selfish? The Development of Self-Compassion, Empathy, and Prosocial Behavior in Adolescence," *Journal of Research on Adolescence* 30, suppl. 2 (February 2020): 472–84.

17 Over the years, Neff and her colleagues: Neff, "Self-Compassion."

19 In her wonderful book: Carla Naumburg, *You Are Not a Sh*tty Parent: How to Practice Self-Compassion and Give Yourself a Break* (Workman, 2022).

20 **In 1953, pediatrician Donald Winnicott:** D. W. Winnicott, *Playing and Reality* (Tavistock, 1971), 7.

21 **Research suggests that many adults lack the ability:** Lisa Feldman Barrett and Eliza Bliss-Moreau, "Affect as a Psychological Primitive," *Advances in Experimental Social Psychology* 41 (2009): 167–218.

22 **Research suggests that when you name the emotion:** Matthew D. Lieberman, Naomi I. Eisenberger, Molly J. Crockett, Sabrina M. Tom, Jennifer H. Pfeifer, and Baldwin M. Way, "Putting Feelings into Words: Affect Labeling Disrupts Amygdala Activity in Response to Affective Stimuli," *Psychological Science* 18, no. 5 (May 2007): 421–28.

24 **A 2023 study found that when:** Emily C. Willroth, Gerald Young, Maya Tamir, and Iris B. Mauss, "Judging Emotions as Good or Bad: Individual Differences and Associations with Psychological Health," *Emotion* 23, no. 7 (October 2023): 1876–90.

26 **Often, we assume that our kids know this already:** Lucia Ciciolla, Alexandria S. Curlee, Jason Karageorge, and Suniya Luthar, "When Mothers and Fathers Are Seen as Disproportionately Valuing Achievements: Implications for Adjustment Among Upper Middle Class Youth," *Journal of Research in Adolescence* 46, no. 5 (May 2017): 1057–75.

2
"I Give Up."

31 **In 2023, according to the CDC:** "Youth Risk Behavior Survey: Data Summary & Trends Report, 2013–2023," CDC, accessed February 24, 2025, https://www.cdc.gov/yrbs/dstr/index.html.

31 **In a 2021 meta-analysis of twenty-nine studies:** Nicole Racine, Brae Anne McArthur, Jessica E. Cooke, Rachel Eirich, Jenney Zhu, and Sheri Madigan, "Global Prevalence of Depressive and Anxiety Symptoms in Children and Adolescents During Covid-19," *JAMA Pediatrics* 175, no. 11 (November 2021): 1142–50.

35 **Sociologists such as Anthony Giddens:** Anthony Giddens, "Risk and Responsibility," *Modern Law Review* 62, no. 1 (January 1999): 1–10.

35 **When writing about the idea:** Ulrich Beck, *Risk Society: Towards a New Modernity* (Sage, 1992), 23.

35 **In her book *Worried About the Wrong Things*:** Jacqueline Ryan Vickery, *Worried About the Wrong Things: Youth, Risk, and Opportunity in the Digital World* (MIT Press, 2018), 62.

37 **That's in part because:** Lisa Damour, *The Emotional Lives of Teenagers: Raising Connected, Capable, and Compassionate Adolescents* (Ballantine, 2023), xxi.

37 **Research on college students has found:** Holly H. Schiffrin, Miriam Liss, Haley Miles-McLean, Katherine A. Geary, Mindy J. Erchull, and Taryn

Tashner, "Helping or Hovering? The Effects of Helicopter Parenting on College Students' Well-Being," *Journal of Child and Family Studies* 23, no. 3 (February 2013): 548–57; Ming Cui, Jeffery W. Allen, Frank D. Fincham, Ross W. May and Hayley Love, "Helicopter Parenting, Self-Regulatory Processes, and Alcohol Use Among Female College Students," *Journal of Adult Development* 26, no. 2 (June 2019): 97–104; Terri LeMoyne and Tom Buchanan, "Does 'Hovering' Matter? Helicopter Parenting and Its Effect on Well-Being," *Sociological Spectrum* 31, no. 4 (June 2011): 399–418.

37 **Young adults of hyper-involved parents:** Holly H. Schiffrin and Miriam Liss, "The Effects of Helicopter Parenting on Academic Motivation," *Journal of Child and Family Studies* 26, no. 5 (2017): 1472–80; Aaron M. Luebbe, Kathryn J. Mancini, Elizabeth J. Kiel, Brooke R. Spangler, Julie L. Semlak, and Lauren M. Fussner, "Dimensionality of Helicopter Parenting and Relations to Emotional, Decision-Making, and Academic Functioning in Emerging Adults," *Assessment* 25, no. 7 (October 2018): 841–57.

38 **As childhood-independence advocate Lenore Skenazy:** Camilo Ortiz and Lenore Skenazy, "This Simple Fix Could Help Anxious Kids," *New York Times*, September 4, 2023, https://www.nytimes.com/2023/09/04/opinion/anxiety-depression-teens.html.

38 **When researchers at the University of Illinois:** Eva M. Pomerantz and Missa Murry Eaton, "Developmental Differences in Children's Conceptions of Parental Control: 'They Love Me, but They Make Me Feel Incompetent,'" *Merrill-Palmer Quarterly* 46, no. 1 (January 2000): 140–67.

38 **In her book *The Emotional Lives of Teenagers*:** Damour, *Emotional Lives of Teenagers*, 21–22.

39 **In a 2021 study, researchers observed:** Rachel E. White, Rachel B. Thibodeau-Nielsen, Francisco Palermo, and Ariana M. Mikulski, "Engagement in Social Pretend Play Predicts Preschoolers' Executive Function Gains Across the School Year," *Early Childhood Research Quarterly* 56, no. 3 (2021): 103–13.

40 **In a 2017 study, researchers asked:** Rachel E. White, Emily O. Prager, Catherine Schaefer, Ethan Kross, Angela L. Duckworth, and Stephanie M. Carlson, "The 'Batman Effect': Improving Perseverance in Young Children," *Child Development* 88, no. 5 (September/October 2017): 1563–71.

41 **In one small study, University of Illinois psychologist:** Lynn A. Barnett, "Research Note: Young Children's Resolution of Distress Through Play," *Journal of Child Psychology and Psychiatry* 25, no. 3 (July 1984): 477–83.

43 **In one small study, Stanford psychologists:** Kyla Haimovitz and Carol S. Dweck, "Parents' Views of Failure Predict Children's Fixed and Growth Intelligence Mind-Sets," *Psychological Science* 27, no. 6 (April 2016): 859–69.

44 **Dweck's research has shown:** Claudia M. Mueller and Carol S. Dweck, "Praise for Intelligence Can Undermine Children's Motivation and Performance," *Journal of Personality and Social Psychology* 75, no. 1 (July 1998): 33–52.

44 **One study in particular, published in 1998:** Mueller and Dweck, "Praise for Intelligence."

46 **In October 2023, researchers:** "Promoting Children's Independence: What Parents Say vs Do," *Mott Poll Report* 44, no. 2, C.S. Mott Children's Hospital, October 16, 2023: https://mottpoll.org/sites/default/files/documents/101623_Independence.pdf.

49 **As Michelle Icard wrote:** Michelle Icard, *Fourteen Talks by Age Fourteen: The Essential Conversations You Need to Have with Your Kids Before They Start High School* (Rodale, 2023).

51 **"Whenever there's evidence of resilience":** "*The Brain Architects* Podcast: Building Resilience Through Play," Center on the Developing Child, Harvard University, accessed August 9, 2024: https://developingchild.harvard.edu/resources/podcast-resilience-play/.

51 **In a 2022 study, researchers investigated:** Eva Kallay and Lavinia Cheie, "'Can I Still Blame My Parents?' Links Between Perceived Parenting, Cognitive Emotion Regulation Strategies, and Adolescent Mental Health," *Current Psychology* 42, no. 31 (October 2022): 27259–74.

51 **In one small but fascinating study, researchers recruited:** Simone Schnall, Kent D. Harber, Jeanine K. Stefanucci, and Dennis R. Profitt, "Social Support and the Perception of Geographical Slant," *Journal of Experimental Social Psychology* 44, no. 5 (September 1, 2008): 1246–55.

3
"Everyone Else Is Doing It."

60 **In 1997, the year I graduated from high school:** Richard A. Miech, Lloyd D. Johnston, Megan E. Patrick, Patrick M. O'Malley, Jerald G. Bachman, and John E. Schulenberg, "Monitoring the Future: National Survey Results on Drug Use, 1975–2022: Secondary School Students," Institute for Social Research, University of Michigan, June 2023, https://files.eric.ed.gov/fulltext/ED627366.pdf.

60 **Between 2019 and 2023:** Lauren J. Tanz, Amanda T. Dinwiddie, Christine L. Mattson, Julie O'Donnell, and Nicole L. Davis, "Drug Overdose Deaths Among Persons Aged 10–19 Years—United States, July 2019–December 2021," *Morbidity and Mortal Weekly Report* 71, no. 50 (December 16, 2022): 1576–82.

60 **The Drug Enforcement Administration (DEA) reported:** "Public Safety Alert: DEA Laboratory Testing Reveals That 6 out of 10 Fentanyl-Laced Fake Prescription Pills Now Contain a Potentially Lethal Dose of Fentanyl," DEA.gov, accessed July 31, 2024, https://www.dea.gov/alert/dea-laboratory-testing-reveals-6-out-10-fentanyl-laced-fake-prescription-pills-now-contain.

60 **In work published in 2019:** Suniya S. Luthar, Phillip J. Small, and Lucia Ciciolla, "Adolescents from Upper Middle Class Communities: Substance Misuse and Addiction Across Early Childhood," *Development and Psychopathology* 30, no. 1 (February 2018): 315–35.

61 **Teens are more likely than adults:** Laurence Steinberg, "A Social Neuroscience Perspective on Adolescent Risk-Taking," *Developmental Review* 28, no. 1 (March 2008): 78–106.

61 Researchers believe that teens: Steinberg, "A Social Neuroscience."

62 We all know the trope: Anthony D. Pellegrini and Jeffrey D. Long, "A Sexual Selection Theory Longitudinal Analysis of Sexual Segregation and Integration in Early Adolescence," *Journal of Experimental Child Psychology* 85, no. 3 (July 2003): 257–78.

62 One thing we know: Steinberg, "A Social Neuroscience."

62 Making matters worse, animal studies suggest: Elena I. Varlinskaya and Linda P. Spear, "Acute Ethanol Withdrawal (Hangover) and Social Behavior in Adolescent and Adult Male and Female Sprague-Dawley Rats," *Alcohol: Clinical & Experimental Research* 28, no. 1 (January 2004): 40–50.

63 Alcohol damages cells: "Alcohol and the Adolescent Brain," National Institute on Alcohol Abuse and Alcoholism, accessed July 31, 2024, https://www.niaaa.nih.gov/publications/alcohol-and-adolescent-brain.

63 Back in 1980: "Cannabis Potency Data," National Institute on Drug Abuse, accessed July 31, 2024, https://nida.nih.gov/research/research-data-measures-resources/cannabis-potency-data.

63 Whereas today's pot: Brianna Wise, "When Is THC Potency Considered 'High'?" SunMed Growers, January 15, 2024, https://www.sunmedgrowers.com/education-resources/blog/post/when-is-thc-potency-considered-high/.

63 The other thing that's important to note: Denise Kandel and Kazuo Yamaguchi, "From Beer to Crack: Developmental Patterns of Drug Involvement," *American Journal of Public Health* 83, no. 6 (June 1993): 851–55.

63 The good news, however: Stephen Nkansah-Amankra and Mark Minelli, "'Gateway Hypothesis' and Early Drug Use: Additional Findings from Tracking a Population-Based Sample of Adolescents to Adulthood," *Preventive Medicine Reports* 4 (December 2016): 134–41.

67 Unfortunately, these programs: Steven L. West and Keri K. O'Neal, "Project D.A.R.E. Outcome Effectiveness Revisited," *American Journal of Public Health* 94, no. 6 (June 2004): 1027–29.

69 Research has shown that children: Fahimeh Rezai Niaraki and Hassan Rahimi, "The Impact of Authoritative, Permissive and Authoritarian Behavior of Parents on Self-Concept, Psychological Health and Life Quality," *European Online Journal of Natural and Social Sciences* 2, no. 1 (2013); Kathy Newman, Lynda Harrison, Carol Dashiff, and Susan Davies, "Relationships Between Parenting Styles and Risk Behaviors in Adolescent Health: An Integrative Literature Review," *Revista Latino-Americana de Enfermagem* 16, no. 1 (2008): 142–50; Laura M. Padilla-Walker, Gustavo Carlo, Katherine J. Christensen, and Jeremy B. Yorgason, "Bidirectional Relations Between Authoritative Parenting and Adolescents' Prosocial Behavior," *Journal of Research on Adolescence* 22, no. 3 (September 2012): 400–08.

69 In a 1991 paper: Diana Baumrind, "The Influence of Parenting Style on Adolescent Competence and Substance Use," *Journal of Early Adolescence* 11, no. 1 (1991): 56–95.

70 In 2014, researchers evaluated: Amador Calafat, Fernando García, Montse Juan, Elisardo Becoña, and José Ramón Fernández-Hermida, "Which Parenting Style Is More Protective Against Adolescent Substance Use? Evidence Within the European Context," *Drug and Alcohol Dependence* 138 (May 1, 2014): 185–92.

70 In a separate review: Elisardo Becoña, Ursula Martinez, Amador Calafat, Montse Juan, José Ramón Fernández-Hermida, and Roberto Secades-Villa, "Parental Styles and Drug Use: A Review," *Drugs: Education, Prevention, and Policy* 19, no. 1 (2012): 1–10.

70 For instance, a 2020 study found: Ina Koning, Margaretha de Looze, and Zeena Harakeh, "Parental Alcohol-Specific Rules Effectively Reduce Adolescents' Tobacco and Cannabis Use: A Longitudinal Study," *Drug and Alcohol Dependence* 216 (November 1, 2020): 108226.

70 Another study found that: Margaretha E. de Looze, Saskia A. F. M. van Dorsselaer, Karin Monshouwer, and Wilma A. M. Vollebergh, "Trends in Adolescent Alcohol Use in the Netherlands, 1992–2015: Differences Across Sociodemographic Groups and Links with Strict Parental Rule-Setting," *International Journal of Drug Policy* 50 (December 2017): 90–101.

71 The truth is, European kids: "15-19 Years Old Heavy Episodic Drinking (Population), Past 30 Days by Country," World Health Organization, accessed August 2, 2024, https://apps.who.int/gho/data/node.main.A1048?lang=en&showonly=GISAH.

71 One study conducted by Kristina: Kristina M. Jackson, Nancy P. Barnett, Suzanne M. Colby, and Michelle L. Rogers, "The Prospective Association Between Sipping Alcohol by the Sixth Grade and Later Substance Use," *Journal of Studies on Alcohol and Drugs* 76, no. 2 (March 2015): 212–21.

72 Recent data suggest: "Cannabis and Teens," CDC, accessed August 1, 2024: https://www.cdc.gov/cannabis/health-effects/cannabis-and-teens.html.

72 In a 2013 study: Leenke Visser, Andrea F. de Winter, Wilma A. M. Vollebergh, Frank C. Verhulst, and Sijmen A. Reijneveld, "The Impact of Parenting Styles on Adolescent Alcohol Use: The TRAILS Study," *European Addiction Research* 19, no. 4 (2013): 165–72.

73 Here's a more specific example: Melissa J. Cox, Joy Gabrielli, Tim Janssen, and Kristina M. Jackson, "Parental Restriction of Movie Viewing Prospectively Predicts Adolescent Alcohol and Marijuana Initiation: Implications for Media Literacy Programs," *Prevention Science* 19, no. 7 (October 2018): 914–26.

74 Although the research conflicts on this issue, some studies suggest: Melissa J. Cox, Tim Janssen, Hector Lopez-Vergara, Nancy P. Barnett, and Kristina M. Jackson, "Parental Drinking as Context for Parental Socialization of Adolescent Alcohol Use," *Journal of Adolescence* 69 (December 2018): 22–32.

74 Other research has found: Cox et al., "Parental Drinking as Context for Parental Socialization of Adolescent Alcohol Use"; Christine Jackson, Susan T. Ennett, Denise M. Dickinson, and J. Michael Bowling, "Attributes That

Differentiate Children Who Sip Alcohol from Abstinent Peers," *Journal of Youth and Adolescence* 42, no. 11 (November 2013): 1687–95.

74 **There is less research:** Bertha K. Madras, Beth Han, Wilson M. Compton, Christopher M. Jones, Elizabeth I. Lopez, and Elinore F. McCance-Katz, "Associations of Parental Marijuana Use with Offspring Marijuana, Tobacco, and Alcohol Use and Opioid Misuse," *JAMA Network Open* 2, no. 11 (November 2019): e1916015.

75 **Since 40 to 60 percent of a person's risk:** Joseph D. Deak and Emma C. Johnson, "Genetics of Substance Use Disorders: A Review," *Psychological Medicine* 51, no. 13 (October 2021): 2189–200.

4
"I Have Too Much to Do!"

80 **During the 2018–2019 school year, Challenge Success:** "Give Teens More Downtime and Support with Time Management," ACSD, May 9, 2019, https://ascd.org/el/articles/give-teens-more-downtime-and-support-with-time-management.

80 **When Challenge Success resurveyed:** "Kids Under Pressure: A Look at Student Well-Being and Engagement During the Pandemic," Challenge Success, February 2021, https://challengesuccess.org/wp-content/uploads/2021/02/CS-NBC-Study-Kids-Under-Pressure-PUBLISHED.pdf; "The Children We Mean to Raise: The Real Messages Adults Are Sending About Values," Making Caring Common Project, Harvard Graduate School of Education, July 2014, https://mcc.gse.harvard.edu/reports/children-mean-raise.

80 **As Jennifer Breheny Wallace:** Jennifer Breheny Wallace, *Never Enough: When Achievement Culture Becomes Toxic—and What We Can Do About It* (Portfolio, 2023).

81 **Research conducted by psychologist Suniya Luthar:** Suniya S. Luthar, Nina L. Kumar, and Nicole Zillmer, "High-Achieving Schools Connote Risks for Adolescents: Problems Documented, Processes Implicated, and Directions for Interventions," *American Psychologist* 75, no. 7 (October 2020): 983–95.

82 **Heck, I wrote a feature about it:** Melinda Wenner, "The Serious Need for Play," *Scientific American*, February 1, 2009, https://www.scientificamerican.com/article/the-serious-need-for-play/.

82 **We know from research that play helps kids:** Emma Newton and Vickii Jenvey, "Play and Theory of Mind: Associations with Social Competence in Young Children," *Early Child Development and Care* 181, no. 6 (2011): 761–73; A. D. Pellegrini, "Rough-and-Tumble Play and Social Problem Solving Flexibility," *Creativity Research Journal* 5 (1992): 13–26; Lynn A. Barrett, "Research Note: Young Children's Resolution of Distress Through Play," *Journal of Child Psychology and Psychiatry* 25, no. 3 (July 1984): 477–83.

83 **In a 2014 study, adults who reported:** Werner Greve, Tamara Thomsen, and Cornelia Dehio, "Does Playing Pay? The Fitness-Effect of Free Play During Childhood," *Evolutionary Psychology* 12, no. 2 (April 2014): 434–47.

83 **As one academic paper put it:** Linda L. Caldwell and Peter A. Witt, "Leisure, Recreation, and Play from a Developmental Context," *New Directions for Youth Development* 130 (Summer 2011): 13–27.

83 **In a documentary filmed in 1975:** *Two Ball Games*, directed by David H. Gluck (Cornell University Department of Psychology and New York State College of Human Ecology, 1976), https://media.library.cornell.edu/media/Two+Ball+Games/1_hkvip27v.

84 **In a 2014 Harvard University survey:** "The Children We Mean to Raise."

84 **As Amherst College sociologist Pawan Dhingra:** Pawan Dhingra, *Hyper Education: Why Good Schools, Good Grades, and Good Behavior Are Not Enough* (NYU Press, 2020).

85 **In a 2017 study, researchers interviewed:** Lucia Ciciolla, Alexandria S. Curlee, Jason Karageorge, and Suniya Luthar, "When Mothers and Fathers Are Seen as Disproportionately Valuing Achievements: Implications for Adjustment Among Upper Middle Class Youth," *Journal of Youth and Adolescence* 46, no. 5 (May 2017): 1057–75.

85 **In a follow-up study published in 2020:** Kelsey Stiles, Steve S. Lee, and Suniya S. Luthar, "When Parents Seek Perfection: Implications for Psychological Functioning Among Teens at High-Achieving Schools," *Journal of Child and Family Studies* 29, no. 11 (September 2020): 3117–28.

87 **In a 2016 study, researchers surveyed:** Elizabeth H. Weybright, Linda L. Caldwell, Nilam Ram, Edward A. Smith, and Lisa Wegner, "Trajectories of Adolescent Substance Use Development and the Influence of Healthy Leisure: A Growth Mixture Modeling Approach," *Journal of Adolescence* 49 (June 2016): 158–69.

87 **In her book *Real Self-Care*:** Pooja Lakshmin, *Real Self-Care: A Transformative Program for Redefining Wellness (Crystals, Cleanses, and Bubble Baths Not Included)* (Penguin Life, 2023).

89 **In her aptly titled book *Quit*:** Annie Duke, *Quit: The Power of Knowing When to Walk Away* (Portfolio, 2022).

90 **In one small study published in 2017:** Ajay S. Padaki, Christopher S. Ahmad, Justin L. Hodgins, David Kovacevic, Thomas Sean Lynch, and Charles A. Popkin, "Quantifying Parental Influence on Youth Athlete Specialization: A Survey of Athletes' Parents," *Orthopedic Journal of Sports Medicine* 5, no. 9 (September 2017): 2325967117729147.

90 **The sad truth is, though:** "NCAA Recruiting Facts," NCAA, December 2023: https://ncaaorg.s3.amazonaws.com/compliance/recruiting/NCAA_RecruitingFactSheet.pdf.

90 **Also, successful athletes:** "The Path to Excellence: A View on the Athletic Development of U.S. Olympians Who Competed from 2000–2012," Initial Re-

port: Results of the Talent Identification and Development Questionnaire to U.S. Olympians, ed. Suzie Riewald, 2014, https://www.scribd.com/document/415205347/Path-to-Excellence-A-View-on-the-Athletic -Development-of-U-S-Olympians.

92 **In one study, researchers in Canada:** Margo Hilbrecht, Jiri Zuzanek, and Roger C. Mannell, "Time Use, Time Pressure and Gendered Behavior in Early and Late Adolescence," *Sex Roles* 58, no. 5 (March 2008): 342–57.

93 **Another study found that when teen girls:** Susan M. Shaw, Linda L. Caldwell, and Douglas A. Kleiber, "Boredom, Stress and Social Control in the Daily Activities of Adolescents," *Journal of Leisure Research* 28, no. 4 (1996): 274–92.

93 **Kids notice household inequality:** Allegra J. Midgette, Danyang Ma, Lucy M. Stowe, and Nadia Chernyak, "US and Chinese Preschoolers Normalize Household Labor Inequality," *PNAS* 120, no. 38 (September 19, 2023): e2301781120.

5
"That's Her Problem, Not Mine."

100 **With each passing month, though:** Audun Dahl and Celia A. Brownell, "The Social Origins of Human Prosociality," *Current Directions in Psychological Science* 28, no. 3 (June 2019): 274–79.

100 **Then, between ages two and three, kids also start:** Audun Dahl and Markus Paulus, "From Interest to Obligation: The Gradual Development of Human Altruism," *Child Development Perspectives* 13, no. 1 (March 2019): 10–14.

101 **Kinder, more compassionate people:** Lee Rowland and Oliver Scott Curry, "A Range of Kindness Activities Boost Happiness," *Journal of Social Psychology* 159, no. 3 (2018): 340–43; Francis Vergunst, Richard E. Tremblay, Daniel Nagin, Yann Algan, et al. "Association Between Childhood Behaviors and Adult Employment Earnings in Canada," *JAMA Psychiatry* 76, no. 10 (June 2019): 1044–51.

101 **In his book *Against Empathy*:** Paul Bloom, *Against Empathy: The Case for Rational Compassion* (Ecco, 2016).

101 **In one study, researchers recruited soccer fans:** Grit Hein, Giorgia Silani, Kerstin Preuschoff, C. Daniel Batson, and Tania Singer, "Neural Responses to Ingroup and Outgroup Members' Suffering Predict Individual Differences in Costly Helping," *Neuron* 68, no 1 (October 6, 2010): 149–60.

103 **Studies have found, for instance, that emotional empathy:** Simone G. Shamay-Tsoory, Judith Aharon-Peretz, and Daniella Perry, "Two Systems for Empathy: A Double Dissociation Between Emotional and Cognitive Empathy in Inferior Frontal Gyrus Versus Ventromedial Prefrontal Lesions," *Brain* 132, no. 3 (March 2009): 617–27.

104 **In a 2024 study published in the journal *Child Development*:** Jessica A. Stern, Natasha A. Bailey, Meghan A. Costello, Amanda F. Hellwig, Jennifer Mitchell, and Joseph P. Allen, "Empathy Across Three Generations: From Ma-

ternal and Peer Support in Adolescence to Adult Parenting and Child Outcomes," *Child Development* 95, no. 5 (September/October 2024): 1628–40.

104 **Compared with other, less securely attached kids:** Richard A. Fabes, Nancy Eisenberg, Mariss Karbon, Debra Troyer, and Galen Switzer, "The Relations of Children's Emotion Regulation to Their Vicarious Emotional Responses and Comforting Behaviors," *Child Development* 65, no. 6 (December 1994): 1678–93.

104 **Studies find that one of the strongest predictors of secure attachment:** Esther M. Leerkes, "Maternal Sensitivity During Distressing Tasks: A Unique Predictor of Attachment Security," *Infant Behavior and Development* 34, no. 3 (June 2011): 443–46.

105 **Secure attachments are also thought to help kids:** Jessica A. Stern and Jude Cassidy, "Empathy from Infancy to Adolescence: An Attachment Perspective on the Development of Individual Differences," *Developmental Review* 47 (March 2018): 1–22.

105 **In 1979, researchers conducted a landmark study:** Everett Waters, Judith Wippman, and L. Alan Sroufe, "Attachment, Positive Affect, and Competence in the Peer Group: Two Studies in Construct Validation," *Child Development* 50, no. 3 (September 1979): 821–29.

105 **In another study:** Roberta Kestenbaum, Ellen A. Farber, and L. Alan Sroufe, "Individual Differences in Empathy Among Preschoolers: Relation to Attachment History," *New Directions for Child and Adolescent Development* 44 (1989): 51–64.

105 **In a 2019 study, researchers found:** Nancy Eisenberg, Tracy L. Spinrad, Zoe E. Taylor, and Jeffrey Liew, "Relations of Inhibition and Emotion-Related Parenting to Young Children's Prosocial and Vicariously Induced Distress Behavior," *Child Development* 90, no. 3 (May/June 2019): 846–58.

106 **In an experimental study published in 2019:** Nils Schuhmacher, Moritz Köster, and Joscha Kärtner, "Modeling Prosocial Behavior Increases Helping in 16-Month-Olds," *Child Development* 90, no. 5 (September/October 2019): 1789–801.

106 **similar patterns among older kids:** Ervin Staub, "A Child in Distress: The Influence of Nurturance and Modeling on Children's Attempts to Help," *Developmental Psychology* 5, no. 1 (1971): 124–32.

106 **In one fascinating study, Celia Brownell:** Celia A. Brownell, Margarita Svetlova, Ranita Anderson, Sara R. Nichols, and Jesse Drummond, "Socialization of Early Prosocial Behavior: Parents' Talk About Emotions Is Associated with Sharing and Helping in Toddlers," *Infancy* 18 (January 1, 2013): 91–119.

107 **Researchers found in one study:** Zoe E. Taylor, Nancy Eisenberg, Tracy L. Spinrad, Natalie D. Eggum, and Michael J. Sulik, "The Relations of Ego-Resiliency and Emotion Socialization to the Development of Empathy and Prosocial Behavior Across Early Childhood," *Emotion* 13, no. 5 (October 2013): 822–31.

108 **Research has linked theory of mind skills:** Kana Imuta, Julie D. Henry, Virginia Slaughter, Bilge Selcuk, and Ted Ruffman, "Theory of Mind and Prosocial Behavior in Childhood: A Meta-Analytic Review," *Developmental Psychology* 52, no. 8 (August 2016): 1192–205.

108 **In her book *Bad Therapy***: Abigail Shrier, *Bad Therapy: Why the Kids Aren't Growing Up* (Sentinel, 2024); Abigail Shrier, "Stop Constantly Asking Your Kids How They Feel," *Wall Street Journal*, March 8, 2024, https://www.wsj.com/health/wellness/stop-constantly-asking-your-kids-how-they-feel-d36cf32e.

109 **In one brain-imaging study, for instance, researchers at UCLA found:** Matthew D. Lieberman, Naomi I. Eisenberger, Molly J. Crockett, Sabrina M. Tom, Jennifer H. Pfeifer, and Baldwin M. Way, "Putting Feelings into Words: Affect Labeling Disrupts Amygdala Activity in Response to Affective Stimuli," *Psychological Science* 18, no. 5 (May 2007): 421–28.

109 **Hoffman and Saltzstein found:** Martin L. Hoffman and Herbert D. Saltzstein, "Parent Discipline and the Child's Moral Development," *Journal of Personality and Social Psychology* 5, no. 1 (1967): 47–57.

110 **In one study, researchers surveyed mothers:** Julia Krevans and John C. Gibbs, "Parents' Use of Inductive Discipline: Relations to Children's Empathy and Prosocial Behavior," *Child Development* 67, no. 6 (December 1996): 3263–77.

110 **In one study, third- and fourth-grade kids:** Nancy Eisenberg-Berg and Elizabeth Geisheker, "Content of Preachings and Power of the Model/Preacher: The Effect on Children's Generosity," *Developmental Psychology* 15, no. 2 (1979): 168–75.

111 **As developmental psychologists aptly noted:** Stuart I. Hammond and Jeremy I. M. Carpendale, "Helping Children Help: The Relation Between Maternal Scaffolding and Children's Early Help," *Social Development* 24, no. 2 (May 2015): 367–83.

111 **Perhaps this is why researchers have observed:** Harriet L. Rheingold, "Little Children's Participation in the Work of Adults, a Nascent Prosocial Behavior," *Child Development* 53, no. 1 (February 1982): 114–25.

111 **In a 2017 study, researchers split:** Audun Dahl, Emma S. Satlof-Bedrick, Stuart I. Hammond, Jesse Drummond, Whitney E. Waugh, and Celia A. Brownell, "Explicit Scaffolding Increases Simple Helping in Younger Infants," *Developmental Psychology* 53, no. 3 (March 2017): 407–16.

112 **In one study, kids of moms who scaffolded:** Dahl et al., "Explicit Scaffolding Increases Simple Helping."

112 **In one fascinating study:** Lucía Alcalá, Barbara Rogoff, Rebeca Mejía-Arauz, Andrew D. Coppens, and Amy L. Dexter, "Children's Initiative in Contributions to Family Work in Indigenous-Heritage and Cosmopolitan Communities in Mexico," *Human Development* 57, no. 2/3 (2014): 96–115.

113 **As researchers explained:** Andrew D. Coppens and Lucía Alcalá, "Supporting Children's Initiative: Appreciating Family Contributions or Paying Chil-

dren for Chores," *Advances in Child Development and Behavior* 49 (2015): 91–112.

113 **In a 2014 study, researchers interviewed:** Andrew D. Coppens, Lucía Alcalá, Rebeca Mejía-Arauz, and Barbara Rogoff, "Children's Initiative in Family Household Work in Mexico," *Human Development* 57, no. 2/3 (2014): 116–30.

6
"I Am So Lonely!"

118 **As two of the scientists involved in the study wrote:** Robert Waldinger and Marc Schulz, "What the Longest Study on Human Happiness Found Is the Key to a Good Life," *The Atlantic*, January 19, 2023.

118 **Youth who felt lonely during the pandemic:** Ann H. Farrell, Irene Vitoroulis, Mollie Eriksson, and Tracy Vaillancourt, "Loneliness and Well-Being in Children and Adolescents During the COVID-19 Pandemic: A Systematic Review," *Children (Basel)* 10, no. 2 (February 2023): 279.

118 **Kids who feel more connected with others:** P. Qualter, S. L. Brown, K. J. Rotenberg, J. Vanhalst, R. A. Harris, L. Goossens, M. Bangee, and P. Munn, "Trajectories of Loneliness During Childhood and Adolescence: Predictors and Health Outcomes," *Journal of Adolescence* 36, no. 6 (December 2013): 1283–93; Erin E. Bonar, Maureen A. Walton, Patrick M. Carter, Lewei A. Lin, Lara N. Coughlin, and Jason E. Goldstick, "Longitudinal Within- and Between-Person Associations of Substance Use, Social Influences, and Loneliness Among Adolescents and Emerging Adults Who Use Drugs," *Addiction Research & Theory* 30, no. 4 (2022): 262–67; Rebecca A. Harris, Pamela Qualter, and Sarita J. Robinson, "Loneliness Trajectories from Middle Childhood to Pre-Adolescence: Impact on Perceived Health and Sleep Disturbance," *Journal of Adolescence* 36, no. 6 (December 2013): 1295–1304.

118 **One longitudinal study found:** Emily L. Loeb, Alida Davis, Meghan Costello, and Joseph P. Allen, "Autonomy and Relatedness in Early Adolescent Friendships As Predictors of Short- and-Long-Term Academic Success," *Social Development* 29, no. 3 (August 2020): 818–36.

119 **Studies find that when teens feel lonely:** Lily Verity, Keming Yang, Rebecca Nowland, Aparna Shankar, Michelle Turnbull, and Pamela Qualter, "Loneliness from the Adolescent Perspective: A Qualitative Analysis of Conversations About Loneliness Between Adolescents and Childline Counselors," *Journal of Adolescent Research* 39, no. 5 (September 2024): 1413–43.

119 **In the 2023 State of American Men survey:** "State of American Men: From Crisis and Confusion to Hope," Equimundo, accessed August 24, 2024, https://www.equimundo.org/resources/state-of-american-men/.

119 **Eighty percent of deaths by suicide happen among men:** "Suicide Data and Statistics," CDC, accessed September 21, 2024, https://www.cdc.gov/suicide/facts/data.html; Andrea Miranda-Mendizabal, Pere Castellví, Oleguer Parés-Badell, et al. "Gender Differences in Suicidal Behavior in

Adolescents and Young Adults: Systematic Review and Meta-Analysis of Longitudinal Studies," *International Journal of Public Health* 64, no. 2 (March 2019): 265–83.

120 **Over the course of two years:** Judy Y. Chu, *When Boys Become Boys: Development, Relationships, and Masculinity* (NYU Press, 2014).

121 **Niobe Way, an applied psychologist:** Niobe Way, Alisha Ali, Carol Gilligan, and Pedro Noguera, eds. *The Crisis of Connection: Roots, Consequences, and Solutions* (NYU Press, 2018).

121 **"By middle to late adolescence, the boys and young men":** Niobe Way, *Rebels with a Cause: Reimagining Boys, Ourselves, and Our Culture* (Dutton, 2024).

122 **Research suggests that the more strongly boys and young men adhere:** Carlos E. Santos, Kathrine Galligan, Erin Pahlke, and Richard A. Fabes, "Gender-Typed Behaviors, Achievement, and Adjustment Among Racially and Ethnically Diverse Boys During Early Adolescence," *American Journal of Orthopsychiatry* 83, no. 2, pt 3 (April–July 2013): 252–64; Adam A. Rogers, Kimberly Updegraff, Carlos E. Santos, and Carol Martin, "Masculinity and School Adjustment in Middle School," *Psychology of Men and Masculinity* 18, no. 1 (January 2017): 50–61.

122 **Brown and Gilligan conducted extensive interviews:** Lyn Mikel Brown and Carol Gilligan, *Meeting at the Crossroads: Women's Psychology and Girls' Development* (Harvard University Press, 1992).

124 **For her book *Girlfighting*, Brown interviewed:** Lyn Mikel Brown, *Girlfighting: Betrayal and Rejection Among Girls* (NYU Press, 2003).

125 **In her book *On Our Best Behavior*:** Elise Loehnen, *On Our Best Behavior: The Seven Deadly Sins and the Price Women Pay to Be Good* (Dial Press, 2023).

125 **America Ferrera's character Gloria:** *Barbie*, directed by Greta Gerwig (Warner Bros. Pictures, 2023).

125 **More than half of all girls report symptoms of depression:** "U.S. Teen Girls Experiencing Increased Sadness and Violence," CDC, press release, February 13, 2023, https://www.cdc.gov/media/releases/2023/p0213-yrbs.html.

125 **Although a higher proportion of boys and men:** "Youth Risk Behavior Survey Data Summary & Trends Report: 2011–2021," CDC, accessed August 9, 2024: https://www.cdc.gov/healthyyouth/data/yrbs/pdf/YRBS_Data-Summary-Trends_Report2023_508.pdf.

126 **And as they grow up, women are nearly twice as likely:** Olivia Remes, Carol Brayne, Rianne van der Linde, and Louise Lafortune, "A Systematic Review of Reviews on the Prevalence of Anxiety Disorders in Adult Populations," *Brain and Behavior* 6, no. 7 (June 2016): e00497.

128 **And yet, Itzchakov said, the research suggests:** Einat Lavee and Guy Itzchakov, "Good Listening: A Key Element in Establishing Quality in Qualitative Research," *Qualitative Research* 23, no. 3 (June 2023): 614–31.

131 **I was there to observe the Listening Project:** "The Listening Project," Science of Human Connection Lab, accessed August 24, 2024, https://niobewaylab.squarespace.com/listening-project.

132 **University Neighborhood Middle School, where I was observing:** "University Neighborhood Middle School," InsideSchools, accessed August 24, 2024, https://insideschools.org/school/01M332.

135 **Emerging findings suggest:** Niobe Way and Joseph D. Nelson, "The Listening Project: Fostering Curiosity and Connection in Middle Schools," in *The Crisis of Connection: Roots, Consequences, and Solutions*, ed. Niobe Way, Alisha Ali, Carol Gilligan, and Pedro Noguera (New York University Press, 2018), 274–98.

138 **In one study, Way and her colleagues repeatedly interviewed:** Niobe Way, Jessica Cressen, Samuel Bodian, Justin Preston, Joseph Nelson, and Diane Hughes, "'It Might Be Nice to Be a Girl . . . Then You Wouldn't Have to Be Emotionless': Boys' Resistance to Norms of Masculinity During Adolescence," *Psychology of Men and Masculinity* 15, no. 3 (July 2014): 241–52.

139 **Studies have shown that parents talk about emotions:** Susan Adams, Janet Kuebli, Patricia A. Boyle, and Robyn Fivush, "Gender Differences in Parent-Child Conversations About Past Emotions: A Longitudinal Investigation," *Sex Roles* 33, nos. 5–6 (September 1995): 309–23.

139 **When mothers actually *do* talk:** Robyn Fivush, "Exploring Sex Differences in the Emotional Content of Mother-Child Conversations About the Past," *Sex Roles* 20, no. 11/12 (June 1989): 675–91.

140 **fathers of preschoolers:** Patricia K. Kerig, Philip A. Cowan, and Carolyn Pape Cowan, "Marital Quality and Gender Differences in Parent-Child Interaction," *Developmental Psychology* 29, no. 6 (1993), 931–39.

140 **As Boston University psychologist Leslie Brody concluded:** Leslie Brody, *Gender, Emotion, and the Family* (Harvard University Press, 1999).

140 **Moms smile less at their infant sons:** Klaudia Kosiak, "Sex Differences in Mother-Infant Interaction" (dissertation, Seton Hall University, 2013), https://scholarship.shu.edu/dissertations/1914; Richard Fabes, "Physiological, Emotional, and Behavioral Correlates of Gender Segregation," in *Childhood Gender Segregation: Causes and Consequences. New Directions for Child Development* 65, ed. Campbell Leaper (Jossey-Bass, 1994), 19–34.

140 **When she interviewed mothers for her book:** Kate Stone Lombardi, *The Mama's Boy Myth: Why Keeping Our Sons Close Makes Them Stronger* (Avery, 2012).

140 **Compared with females, male babies cry more often:** Eleanor Emmons Maccoby and Carol Nagy Jacklin, *The Psychology of Sex Differences* (Stanford University Press, 1974).

140 **In one study, researchers:** M. Katherine Weinberg, Edward Z. Tronick, Jeffrey F. Cohn, and Karen L. Olson, "Gender Differences in Emotional Expressivity and Self-Regulation During Early Infancy," *Developmental Psychology* 35, no. 1 (1999): 175–88.

140 **This is in part because the part of the brain:** Allan N. Schore, "All Our Sons: The Developmental Neurobiology and Neuroendocrinology of Boys at Risk," *Infant Mental Health Journal* 38, no. 1 (January 2017): 15–52.

141 **Compared with younger boys:** Nancy Eisenberg, Richard A. Fabes, M. Schaller, and P. A. Miller, "Sympathy and Personal Distress: Development, Gender Differences, and Interrelations of Indexes," in *Empathy and Related Emotional Responses: New Directions for Child Development* 44, ed. Nancy Eisenberg (Jossey-Bass, 1989), 107–26.

142 **In a 2024 study, researchers:** Jessica A. Stern, Natasha A. Bailey, Meghan A. Costello, Amanda F. Hellwig, Jennifer Mitchell, and Joseph P. Allen, "Empathy Across Three Generations: From Maternal and Peer Support in Adolescence to Adult Parenting and Child Outcomes," *Child Development* 95, no. 5 (September/October 2024): 1628–40.

143 **One clever study illustrated this phenomenon:** Catharine Evers, Agneta H. Fischer, Patrician M. Rodriguez Mosquera, and Antony S. R. Manstead, "Anger and Social Appraisal: A 'Spicy' Sex Difference?" *Emotion* 5, no. 3 (September 2005): 258–66.

144 **In her 1985 book *The Dance of Anger*:** Harriet Lerner, *The Dance of Anger: A Woman's Guide to Changing the Patterns of Intimate Relationships* (Harper & Row, 1985).

145 **In her book *Girls on the Brink*:** Donna Jackson Nakazawa, *Girls on the Brink: Helping Our Daughters Thrive in an Era of Increased Anxiety, Depression, and Social Media* (Harmony, 2022).

147 **In her book *Under Pressure*:** Lisa Damour, *Under Pressure: Confronting the Epidemic of Stress and Anxiety in Girls* (Ballantine, 2019).

7
"Those People Are Dumb."

154 **Research suggests that open-minded, curious people:** Thomas Gatzka, "Aspects of Openness as Predictors of Academic Achievement," *Personality and Individual Differences* 170 (February 2021): 110422; Todd B. Kashdan and Michael F. Steger, "Curiosity and Pathways to Well-Being and Meaning in Life: Traits, States, and Everyday Behaviors," *Motivation and Emotion* 31 (September 2007): 159–73.

155 **In a 2015 study, researchers found:** Marjorie Rhodes, Sarah-Jane Leslie, Katya Saunders, Yarrow Dunham, and Andrei Cimpian, "How Does Social Essentialism Affect the Development of Inter-Group Relations?" *Developmental Science* 21, no. 1 (January 2018): e12509.

155 **Kids who have essentialist ideas about race:** Kristin Pauker, Nalini Ambady, and Evan P. Apfelbaum, "Race Salience and Essentialist Thinking in Racial Stereotype Development," *Child Development* 81, no. 6 (November–December 2010): 1799–1813.

156 **Essentialist thinking is often used to rationalize:** Tara M. Mandalaywala, David M. Amodio, and Marjorie Rhodes, "Essentialism Promotes Racial Prejudice by Increasing Endorsement of Social Hierarchies," *Social Psychological and Personality Science* 9, no. 4 (May 2018): 461–69.

156 **In a 2023 paper, Stanford political scientists:** Matthew Tyler and Shanto Iyengar, "Learning to Dislike Your Opponents: Political Socialization in the Era of Polarization," *American Political Science Review* 117, no. 1 (February 2023): 347–54.

157 **Research has found that social media posts:** William J. Brady, Julian A. Wills, Dominic Burkart, John T. Jost, and Jay J. Van Bavel, "An Ideological Asymmetry in the Diffusion of Moralized Content on Social Media Among Political Leaders," *Journal of Experimental Psychology: General* 148, no. 10 (October 2019): 1802–13.

157 **In a 2022 study, Ike Silver:** Ike Silver and Alex Shaw, "When and Why 'Staying Out of It' Backfires in Moral and Political Disagreements," *Journal of Experimental Psychology: General* 151, no. 10 (October 2022): 2542–61.

158 **Studies show that most angry:** Brady et al., "Ideological Asymmetry."

159 **As Goodall has said:** Claire Elise Thompson, "Jane Goodall's Legacy of Empathy, Curiosity, and Courage," *Grist*, April 3, 2024, https://grist.org/looking-forward/jane-goodalls-legacy-of-empathy-curiosity-and-courage/.

160 **In a 2018 study, researchers invited:** Yue Yu, Asheley R. Landrum, Elizabeth Bonawitz, and Patrick Shafto, "Questioning Supports Effective Transmission of Knowledge and Increased Exploratory Learning in Pre-Kindergarten Children," *Developmental Science* 21, no. 6 (November 2018): e12696.

161 **In one study, researchers invited:** Anne Park, Joseph Colantonio II, Lourdes Delgado Reyes, Sophie Sharp, Elizabeth Bonawitz, and Allyson Mackey, "Question Asking Fosters Curiosity and Learning in Children," PsyArXiv Preprints, accessed August 10, 2024, https://osf.io/preprints/psyarxiv/qzekc.

161 **The same has been found to be true for teens:** Shelby Clark, Allen G. Harbaugh, and Scott Seider, "Fostering Adolescent Curiosity Through a Question Brainstorming Intervention," *Journal of Adolescence* 75 (August 2019): 98–112.

162 **Research suggests that a far better approach:** Emily Kubin, Curtis Puryear, Chelsea Schein, and Kurt Gray, "Personal Experiences Bridge Moral and Political Divides Better than Facts," *PNAS* 118, no. 6 (January 2021): e2008389118.

162 **Research suggests that while most mothers:** Alexis A. Adams-Clark, Angela H. Lee, Christina Gamache Martin, Arianna Zarosinski, and Maureen Zalewski, "Characterizing Maternal Apology Attitudes and Behaviors," *Journal of Child and Family Studies* 30, no. 10 (October 2021): 2379–91.

164 **More broadly, research has shown:** Marta Miklikowska and Helena Hurme, "Democracy Begins at Home: Democratic Parenting and Adolescents' Support for Democratic Values," *European Journal of Developmental Psychology* 8, no. 5 (May 2011): 541–57.

164 **In a 2024 essay for *The Cut*:** Kathryn Jezer-Morton, "Can Parents Prevent Their Sons from Sliding to the Right?" *The Cut*, February 17, 2024, https://www.thecut.com/article/can-we-keep-our-sons-from-conservative-politics.html.

166 **In one of Itzchakov's studies, published in 2023:** Guy Itzchakov, Netta Weinstein, Mark Leary, Dvori Saluk, and Moty Amar, "Listening to Understand: The Role of High-Quality Listening on Speakers' Attitudes During Disagreements," *Journal of Personality and Social Psychology* 126, no. 2 (February 2024): 213–39.

166 **In another of his studies:** Guy Itzchakov, "Why Listening Well Can Make Disagreements Less Damaging," *Psyche*, February 19, 2024, https://psyche.co/ideas/why-listening-well-can-make-disagreements-less-damaging.

168 **In a 2014 study, researchers at Bar-Ilan University:** Gili Segall, Dana Birnbaum, Inas Deeb, and Gil Diesendruck, "The Intergenerational Transmission of Ethnic Essentialism: How Parents Talk Counts the Most," *Developmental Science* 18, no. 4 (July 2015): 543–55.

169 **In one study, researchers at NYU and Princeton:** Marjorie Rhodes, Sarah-Jane Leslie, and Christina M. Tworek, "Cultural Transmission of Social Essentialism," *PNAS* 109, no. 32 (August 2012): 13526–531.

171 **Among other things, they notice hierarchies:** Tara M. Mandalaywala, Christine Tai, and Marjorie Rhodes, "Children's Use of Race and Gender as Cues to Social Status," *PLoS One* 15, no. 6 (June 2020): e0234398.

171 **Indeed, multiple studies have found:** Nadia Chernyak, "The Emergence of Young Children's Tolerance for Inequality: With Age, Children Stop Showing Numerically Sensitive Fairness," *Journal of Experimental Child Psychology* 238 (2024): 105785; Larisa J. Hussak and Andrei Cimpian, "An Early-Emerging Explanatory Heuristic Promotes Support for the Status Quo," *Journal of Personality and Social Psychology* 109, no. 5 (November 2015): 739–52.

171 **Kids are especially likely to perpetuate:** Michael T. Rizzo, Steven O. Roberts, and Marjorie Rhodes, "The Effect of Group Status on Children's Hierarchy-Reinforcing Beliefs," *Developmental Science* 26, no. 6 (November 2023): e13393.

172 **Research finds that educating kids about discrimination:** Julie M. Hughes, Rebecca S. Bigler, and Sheri R. Levy, "Consequences of Learning About Historical Racism Among European American and African American Children," *Child Development* 78, no. 6 (November–December 2007): 1689–705.

172 **In another small study, researchers presented elementary-aged:** Michael T. Rizzo, Tobias C. Britton, and Marjorie Rhodes: "Developmental Origins of Anti-Black Bias in White Children in the United States: Exposure to and Beliefs About Racial Inequality," *PNAS* 119, no. 47 (November 2022): e2209129119.

173 **In fact, research suggests that approaches that foster color-blindness:** Brigitte Vittrup and George W. Holden, "Exploring the Impact of Educational

Television and Parent-Child Discussions on Children's Racial Attitudes," *Analyses of Social Issues and Public Policy (ASAP)* 11, no. 1 (December 2011): 82–104.

174 **In 1954, psychologist Gordon Allport proposed:** Gordon W. Allport, *The Nature of Prejudice* (Addison-Wesley, 1954).

174 **One powerful illustration of the importance of these conditions:** "Interview with Elliot Aronson, PhD," MentorCoach, accessed August 10, 2024, https://www.mentorcoach.com/positive-psychology-coaching/interviews/interview-with-elliot-aronson-phd/.

175 **After the "jigsaw" classrooms:** Elliot Aronson and Diane Bridgeman, "Jigsaw Groups and the Desegregated Classroom: In Pursuit of Common Goals," *Personality and Social Psychology Bulletin* 5, no. 4 (1979): 438–46.

175 **When Aronson climbed to the roof:** Susan Gilbert, "A Conversation with Elliot Aronson; No One Left to Hate: Averting Columbines," *New York Times*, March 27, 2001, https://www.nytimes.com/2001/03/27/health/a-conversation-with-elliot-aronson-no-one-left-to-hate-averting-columbines.html.

175 **In a 2023 study, University of Notre Dame political scientist:** Erin Rossiter, "The Similar and Distinct Effects of Political and Non-Political Conversation in Affective Polarization," working paper, January 22, 2023, https://erossiter.com/files/conversations.pdf.

176 **A similar study conducted by Rhodes:** Michael T. Rizzo, Emily R. Green, Yarrow Dunham, Emile Bruneau, and Marjorie Rhodes, "Beliefs About Social Norms and Racial Inequalities Predict Variation in the Early Development of Racial Bias," *Developmental Science* 25, no. 2 (March 2022): e13170.

177 **In a 2021 study, University of British Columbia economist:** Matt Lowe, "Types of Contact: A Field Experiment on Collaborative and Adversarial Caste Integration," *American Economic Review* 111, no. 6 (June 2021): 1807–44.

177 **Researchers have even looked at what happens:** João F. Guassi Moreira, Jay J. Van Bavel, and Eva H. Telzer, "The Neural Development of 'Us and Them,'" *Social Cognitive and Affective Neuroscience* 12, no. 2 (February 2017): 184–96.

8
"Are We Rich?"

182 **According to a 2023 Pew Research Center survey:** "Parenting in America Today," Pew Research Center, January 24, 2023, https://www.pewresearch.org/social-trends/2023/01/24/parenting-in-america-today.

182 **Studies have found that when parents regularly talk to:** Jill M. Norvilitis and Michael G. MacLean, "The Role of Parents in College Students' Financial Behaviors and Attitudes," *Journal of Economic Psychology* 31, no. 1 (February 2010): 55–63; Ashley B. LeBaron, Erin K. Holmes, Bryce L. Jorgensen, and Roy A. Bean, "Parental Financial Education During Childhood and Financial

Behaviors of Emerging Adults," *Journal of Financial Consulting and Planning* 31, no. 1 (June 2020): 42–54.

182 **Yet surveys find that money is also a topic:** Michelle Fox, "Who Should Teach Kids About Money? Americans Say Parents, but Many Don't Talk to Their Own Children About It: CNBC + Acorns Survey," April 6, 2022, https://www.cnbc.com/2022/04/06/americans-think-parents-should-teach-kids-about-money-yet-many-dont.html.

182 **A 2024 Pew survey found:** "Parents, Young Children, and the Transition to Adulthood," January 25, 2024.

183 **Kids notice inequality from a very young age:** Jessica A. Somerville, "Infants' Understanding of Distributive Fairness as a Test Case for Identifying the Extents and Limits of Infants' Sociomoral Cognition and Behavior," *Child Development Perspectives* 12, no. 3 (September 2018): 141–45.

184 **By age eight, kids can accurately rank jobs:** Julie Dickinson, Patrick J. Leman, and Matthew J. Easterbrook, "Children's Developing Understanding of Economic Inequality and Their Place Within It," *British Journal of Developmental Psychology* 41, no. 2 (June 2023): 81–98.

185 **Studies have indeed shown that young kids:** Kristin Shutts, Elizabeth L. Brey, Leah A. Dornbusch, Nina Slywotzky, and Kristina R. Olson, "Children Use Wealth Cues to Evaluate Others," *PLoS One* 11, no. 3 (2016): e0149360.

187 **In a 2022 poll of over one thousand parents:** Fox, "Who Should Teach Kids About Money?"

187 **In a 2020 study, researchers:** LeBaron et al., "Parental Financial Education."

188 **In another 2020 study, a different group of researchers:** Rimantas Vosylis and Rasa Erentaitė, "Linking Family Financial Socialization with Its Proximal and Distal Outcomes: Which Dimensions Matter Most for Emerging Adults' Financial Identity, Financial Behaviors, and Financial Anxiety?" *Emerging Adulthood* 8, no. 6 (December 2020): 464–75.

190 **In a 2019 study involving nearly ten thousand high school students:** Rebecca G. Chambers, Carlos J. Asarta, and Elizabeth N. Farley-Ripple, "Gender, Parental Characteristics, and Financial Knowledge of High School Students: Evidence from Multicountry Data," *Journal of Financial Consulting and Planning* 30, no. 1 (June 2019): 97–109.

192 **Researchers have theorized that children:** Andrew D. Coppens and Lucía Alcalá, "Supporting Children's Initiative: Appreciating Family Contributions or Paying Children for Chores," *Advances in Child Development and Behavior* 49 (2015): 91–112.

194 **Research suggests that as kids get older:** Nadia Chernyak, "The Emergence of Young Children's Tolerance for Inequality: With Age, Children Stop Showing Numerically Sensitive Fairness," *Journal of Experimental Child Psychology* 238 (February 2024): 105785.

194 **Interestingly, some research suggests that Western children:** Marie Schäfer, Daniel B. M. Haun, and Michael Tomasello, "Fair Is Not Fair Everywhere," *Psychological Science* 26, no. 8 (August 2015): 1252–60.

195 **Research has shown that young children tend to believe:** Shutts et al., "Children Use Wealth Cues."

195 **Kids tend to believe that girls are less intelligent than boys:** Lin Bian, Sarah-Jane Leslie, and Andrei Cimpian, "Gender Stereotypes About Intellectual Ability Emerge Early and Influence Children's Interests," *Science* 355, no. 6323 (January 2017): 389–91; Kristin Pauker, Yiyuan Xu, Amanda Williams, and Ashley M. Biddle, "Race Essentialism and Social Contextual Differences in Children's Racial Stereotyping," *Child Development* 87, no. 5 (September 2016): 1409–22.

195 **Kids who harbor these racist ideas:** Michael T. Rizzo, Tobias C. Britton, and Marjorie Rhodes, "Developmental Origins of Anti-Black Bias in White Children in the United States: Exposure to and Beliefs About Racial Inequality," *PNAS* 119, no. 47 (November 2022): e2209129119.

195 **In a 2015 study, Larisa Hussak, then a psychologist:** Larisa J. Hussak and Andrei Cimpian, "An Early-Emerging Explanatory Heuristic Promotes Support for the Status Quo," *Journal of Personality and Social Psychology* 109, no. 5 (November 2015): 739–52.

196 **Research suggests that when we seek to explain things:** Andrei Cimpian and Erika Salomon, "The Inherence Heuristic: An Intuitive Means of Making Sense of the World, and a Potential Precursor to Psychological Essentialism," *Behavioral and Brain Sciences* 37, no. 5 (October 2014): 461–80.

196 **In one study, children between the ages of three and eight:** Michael T. Rizzo, Laura Elenbaas, and Kimberly E. Vanderbilt, "Do Children Distinguish Between Resource Inequalities with Individual Versus Structural Origins?" *Child Development* 91, no. 2 (March 2020): 439–55.

199 **One 2024 study illustrated the power:** Jamie Amemiya and Lin Bian, "Why Are There No Girls? Increasing Children's Recognition of Structural Causes of the Gender Gap in STEM," *Cognition* 245 (April 2024): 105740.

200 **In a 2023 study, researchers surveyed three- to ten-year-old kids:** Allegra J. Midgette, Danyang Ma, Lucy M. Stowe, and Nadia Chernyak, "US and Chinese Preschoolers Normalize Household Labor Inequality," *PNAS* 120, no. 38 (September 19, 2023): e2301781120.

200 **It's long been documented in psychology that people, including kids, often confuse:** Steven O. Roberts, Susan A. Gelman, and Arnold K. Ho, "So It Is, So It Shall Be: Group Regularities License Children's Prescriptive Judgments," *Cognitive Science* 41, suppl. 3 (April 2017): 576–600.

200 **In a 2014 study, researchers at the University of British Columbia:** Alyssa Croft, Toni Schmader, Katharina Block, and Andrew Scott Baron, "The Second Shift Reflected in the Second Generation: Do Parents' Gender Roles at Home Predict Children's Aspirations?" *Psychological Science* 25, no. 7 (July 2014): 1418–28.

9
"I Learned It from YouTube."

203 **A few years ago, for a story I wrote:** Melinda Wenner Moyer, "Schoolkids Are Falling Victim to Disinformation and Conspiracy Fantasies," *Scientific American*, February 1, 2022, https://www.scientificamerican.com/article/schoolkids-are-falling-victim-to-disinformation-and-conspiracy-fantasies/.

204 **Research suggests that many kids now start believing:** Daniel Jolley, Karen M. Douglas, Yvonne Skipper, Eleanor Thomas, and Darel Cookson, "Measuring Adolescents' Beliefs in Conspiracy Theories: Development and Validation of the Adolescent Conspiracy Beliefs Questionnaire (ACBQ)," *British Journal of Developmental Psychology* 39, no. 3 (September 2021): 499–520.

204 **In a 2016 study, Stanford University researchers analyzed 7,804 responses:** "Evaluating Information: The Cornerstone of Civic Online Reasoning," Stanford History Education Group, accessed August 24, 2024, https://stacks.stanford.edu/file/druid:fv751yt5934/SHEG%20Evaluating%20Information%20Online.pdf

204 **In 2022, researchers at the University of California, Davis, reported:** Muhammad Haroon, Magdalena Wojcieszak, Anshuman Chhabra, Xin Liu, et al. "Auditing YouTube's Recommendation System for Ideologically Congenial, Extreme, and Problematic Recommendations," *PNAS* 120, no. 50 (December 2023): e2213020120.

204 **YouTube is one of the most popular social media sites:** Zeynep Tufekci, "YouTube, the Great Radicalizer," *New York Times*, March 10, 2018, https://www.nytimes.com/2018/03/10/opinion/sunday/youtube-politics-radical.html.

205 **As of May 2024:** "Putting Media Literacy on the Public Policy Agenda," Media Literacy Now, accessed August 24, 2024, https://medialiteracynow.org/impact/current-policy/.

207 **In 2022, the Reboot Foundation:** "Science Fictions: Low Science Knowledge, Poor Critical Thinking Linked to Conspiracy Beliefs," Reboot, September 5, 2022, https://reboot-foundation.org/research/science-fictions-low-science-knowledge-poor-critical-thinking-linked-to-conspiracy-beliefs/.

208 **Research finds, for instance, that when adults express their disapproval of violence:** Charles R. Corder-Bolz, "Mediation: The Role of Significant Others," *Journal of Communication* 30, no. 3 (Summer 1980): 106–18.

210 **At a 2018 talk at the South by Southwest:** "What Hath We Wrought?" SXSW Conference 2018, accessed August 25, 2024, https://www.sxswedu.com/news/2018/watch-danah-boyd-keynote-what-hath-we-wrought-video/.

210 **According to educational psychologist William Perry:** "Overview of Perry Scheme," Perry Network, accessed August 25, 2024, http://perrynetwork.org/?page_id=2.

214 **Research suggests a link between curiosity:** Mark R. Leary, Kate J. Diebels, Erin K. Davisson, Katrina P. Jongman-Sereno, Jennifer C. Isherwood, Katlin

T. Raimi, Samantha A. Deffler, and Rick H. Hoyle, "Cognitive and Interpersonal Features of Intellectual Humility," *Personality and Social Psychology Bulletin* 43, no. 6 (March 2017): 793–813.

215 **As University of Washington researcher Mike Caulfield:** Mike Caulfield and Sam Wineburg, *Verified: How to Think Straight, Get Duped Less, and Make Better Decisions About What to Believe Online* (University of Chicago Press, 2023).

215 **In a small 2021 study, McGrew asked eleventh and twelfth graders:** Sarah McGrew, "Skipping the Source and Checking the Contents: An In-Depth Look at Students' Approaches to Web Evaluation," *Computers in the Schools* 38, no. 2 (July 2021): 75–97.

216 **In a study published in 2019, McGrew and Wineburg:** Sam Wineburg and Sarah McGrew, "Lateral Reading and the Nature of Expertise: Reading Less and Learning More When Evaluating Digital Information," *Teachers College Record: The Voice of Scholarship in Education* 121, no. 11 (November 2019): 1–40.

217 **In a 2022 study, Wineburg, McGrew, and their colleagues found:** Sam Wineburg, Joel Breakstone, Sarah McGrew, Mark Smith, and Teresa Ortega, "Lateral Reading on the Open Internet: A District-Wide Field Study in High School Government Classes," *Journal of Educational Psychology* 114, no. 5 (April 2022): 893–909.

10
"How Many Likes Did I Get?"

220 **Nearly half of all U.S. teens:** "Teens and Cyberbullying 2022," Pew Research Center, December 15, 2022, https://www.pewresearch.org/internet/2022/12/15/teens-and-cyberbullying-2022/.

220 **In a 2022 Pew Research Center survey:** "Teens and Pornography," Pew Research Center, accessed September 24, 2024, https://www.commonsensemedia.org/sites/default/files/research/report/2022-teens-and-pornography-final-web.pdf.

221 **Research also finds that many tweens:** "Connection, Creativity and Drama: Teen Life on Social Media in 2022," Pew Research Center, November 16, 2022, https://www.pewresearch.org/internet/2022/11/16/connection-creativity-and-drama-teen-life-on-social-media-in-2022/.

221 **Research has found that online relationships:** Maya Massing-Schaffer, Jacqueline Nesi, Eva H. Telzer, Kristen A. Lindquist, and Michelle J. Prinstein, "Adolescent Peer Experiences and Prospective Suicidal Ideation: The Protective Role of Online-Only Friendships," *Journal of Clinical Child and Adolescent Psychology* 51, no. 1 (January–February 2022): 49–60.

222 **Take, for instance, a 2018 study:** Jean M. Twenge, Gabrielle N. Martin, and W. Keith Campbell, "Decreases in Psychological Well-Being Among American Adolescents After 2012 and Links to Screen Time During the Rise of Smartphone Technology," *Emotion* 18, no. 6 (January 2018): 765–80.

223 "The fact that two trend lines increase together": Candice L. Odgers and Michaeline R. Jensen, "Adolescent Mental Health in the Digital Age: Facts, Fears and Future Directions," *Journal of Child Psychology and Psychiatry* 61, no. 3 (March 2020): 336–48.

223 It could instead be that depression: Taylor Heffer, Marie Good, Owen Daly, Elliott MacDonell, and Teena Willoughby, "The Longitudinal Association Between Social-Media Use and Depressive Symptoms Among Adolescents and Young Adults: An Empirical Reply to Twenge et al. (2018)," *Clinical Psychological Science* 7, no. 3 (January 2019): 462–70.

224 In a 2019 study: Heffer et al., "Longitudinal Association."

224 Two years later, researchers at Columbia: Noah Kreski, Jonathan Platt, Caroline Rutherford, Mark Olfson, Candice Odgers, John Schulenberg, and Katherine M. Keyes, "Social Media Use and Depressive Symptoms Among United States Adolescents," *Journal of Adolescent Health* 68, no. 3 (March 2021): 572–79.

226 In one small 2018 study: Melissa G. Hunt, Rachel Marx, Courtney Lipson, and Jordyn Young, "No More FOMO: Limiting Social Media Decreases Loneliness and Depression," *Journal of Social and Clinical Psychology* 37, no. 10 (December 2018): 751–68.

226 Other studies in 2019, 2020, and 2022: Jeffrey A. Hall, Chong Xing, Elaina M. Ross, and Rebecca M. Johnson, "Experimentally Manipulating Social Media Abstinence: Results of a Four-Week Diary Study," *Media Psychology* 24, no. 2 (November 2019): 259–75; Julia Brailovskaia, Fabienne Ströse, Holger Schillack and Jürgen Margraf, "Less Facebook Use—More Well-Being and a Healthier Lifestyle? An Experimental Intervention Study," *Computers in Human Behavior* 108 (July 2020): 106332; Avinash Collis and Felix Eggers, "Effects of Restricting Social Media Usage on Wellbeing and Performance: A Randomized Control Trial Among Students," *PLoS One* 17, no. 8 (August 2022): e0272416.

227 In his Substack, *After Babel*: Jon Haidt, "Yes, Social Media Really Is a Cause of the Epidemic of Teenage Mental Illness," After Babel, April 9, 2024, https://www.afterbabel.com/p/phone-based-childhood-cause-epidemic; Jonathan Haidt, *The Anxious Generation: How the Great Rewiring of Childhood Is Causing an Epidemic of Mental Illness* (Penguin Press, 2024).

228 His beliefs, he explained in his newsletter: Haidt, "Yes, Social Media."

228 UC Irvine quantitative and developmental psychologist: Candice L. Odgers, "The Great Rewiring: Is Social Media Really Behind an Epidemic of Teenage Mental Illness?" *Nature*, March 29, 2024, https://www.nature.com/articles/d41586-024-00902-2.

228 The University of Cambridge's Amy Orben: David Wallace-Wells, "Are Smartphones Driving Our Teens to Depression?" *New York Times*, May 1, 2024, https://www.nytimes.com/2024/05/01/opinion/smartphones-social-media-mental-health-teens.html; Zoë Schiffer, "Inside the Debate Over *The*

Anxious Generation," *Platformer*, April 11, 2024, https://www.platformer.news/anxious-generation-jonathan-haidt-debate-critique/.

228 **Nathan Walter, a media psychologist:** Matt Villano, "Parents Should Let Go of Guilt Over Screens, an Expert Explains," CNN, June 19, 2024, https://www.cnn.com/2024/06/19/health/children-screen-time-guilt-wellness/.

230 **Anytime kids have a new form of entertainment:** Devorah Heitner, *Growing Up in Public: Coming of Age in a Digital World* (TarcherPerigee, 2023).

230 **As sociologist James Walsh argued:** James P. Walsh, "Social Media and Moral Panics: Assessing the Effects of Technological Change on Societal Reaction," *International Journal of Cultural Studies* 23, no. 6 (November 2020): 840–59.

231 **In her book *Worried About the Wrong Things*:** Jacqueline Ryan Vickery, *Worried About the Wrong Things: Youth, Risk, and Opportunity in the Digital World* (MIT Press, 2018).

232 **When my kids were toddlers:** Ari Brown, "Media Use by Children Younger Than 2 Years," *Pediatrics* 128, no. 5 (November 2011): 1040–45.

232 **They have since slightly softened the recommendations:** "Where We Stand: Screen Time," Healthychildren.org, last updated December 13, 2023, https://www.healthychildren.org/English/family-life/Media/Pages/Where-We-Stand-TV-Viewing-Time.aspx.

232 **When these AAP guidelines were first set:** Dimitri A. Christakis, Frederick J. Zimmerman, David L. DiGiuseppe, and Carolyn A. McCarty, "Early Television Exposure and Subsequent Attentional Problems in Children," *Pediatrics* 113, no. 4 (April 2004): 708–13; Frederick J. Zimmerman, Dimitri A. Christakis, and Andrew N. Meltzoff, "Television and DVD/Video Viewing in Children Younger Than 2 Years," *Archives of Pediatrics and Adolescent Medicine* 161, no. 5 (May 2007): 473–79.

233 **But when other researchers reanalyzed this data:** E. Michael Foster and Stephanie Watkins, "The Value of Reanalysis: TV Viewing and Attention Problems," *Child Development* 81, no. 1 (January–February 2010): 368–75; Christopher J. Ferguson and M. Brent Donnellan, "Is the Association Between Children's Baby Video Viewing and Poor Language Development Robust? A Reanalysis of Zimmerman, Christakis, and Meltzoff (2007)," *Developmental Psychology* 50, no. 1 (January 2014): 129–37.

233 **The AAP notes that no longitudinal studies have determined:** Brown, "Media Use."

233 **In a 2024 study, researchers at the University of Amsterdam:** Lara N. Wolfers, Robin L. Nabi, and Nathan Walter, "Too Much Screen Time or Too Much Guilt? How Child Screen Time and Parental Screen Guilt Affect Parental Stress and Relationship Satisfaction," *Media Psychology* 28, no. 1 (2025): 102–33.

234 **In one study, 37 percent of parents:** Alexis Hiniker, Hyewon Suh, Sabina Cao, and Julia A. Kientz, "Screen Time Tantrums: How Families Manage Screen

Media Experiences for Toddlers and Preschoolers," CHI '16: Proceedings of the 2016 CHI Conference on Human Factors in Computing Systems (May 2016).

235 **It is much harder to control for such biases in studies of technology:** Jeffrey A. Hall, Chong Xing, Elaina M. Ross, and Rebecca M. Johnson, "Experimentally Manipulating Social Media Abstinence: Results of a Four Week Diary Study," *Media Psychology* 24, no. 2 (2021): 259–75.

235 **As researcher Katie Davis:** Katie Davis, *Technology's Child: Digital Media's Role in the Ages and Stages of Growing Up* (MIT Press, 2023).

236 **In 2023, the nonprofit organization Sapien Labs:** "Age of First Smartphone/Tablet and Mental Wellbeing Outcomes," Sapien Labs, May 15, 2023, https://www.sapienlabs.org/age-of-first-smartphone-tablet-and-mental-wellbeing-outcomes-report.

236 **On the flip side, a 2022 Stanford study:** Xiaoran Sun, K. Farish Haydel, Donna Matheson, Manisha Desai, and Thomas N. Robinson, "Are Mobile Phone Ownership and Age of Acquisition Associated with Child Adjustment? A 5-Year Prospective Study Among Low-Income Latinx Children," *Child Development* 94, no. 1 (January/February 2023): 303–14.

237 **The psychologist Lisa Damour:** Lisa Damour, "Beyond All-or-Nothing: A Pragmatic Approach to Kids and Social Technologies," Sesame Workshop Joan Ganz Cooney Center, March 25, 2024, https://joanganzcooneycenter.org/2024/03/25/beyond-all-or-nothing/.

238 **In the early twentieth century, many people worried:** Patti M. Valkenberg and Jessica Taylor Piotrowski, *Plugged In: How Media Attract and Affect Youth* (Yale University Press, 2017).

238 **In 1928, these concerns led William Short:** Patti M. Valkenburg, "The Limited Informativeness of Meta-Analyses of Media Effects," *Perspectives on Psychological Science* 10, no. 5 (September 2015): 680–82.

239 **Kids who struggle with impulse control:** Tycho J. Dekkers and Jorien van Hoorn, "Understanding Problematic Social Media Use in Adolescents with Attention Deficit/Hyperactivity Disorder (ADHD): A Narrative Review and Clinical Recommendations," *Brain Sciences* 12, no. 12 (December 2022): 1625.

239 **In a 2022 study, researchers:** Amy Orben, Andrew K. Przybylski, Sarah-Jayne Blakemore, and Rogier A. Kievit, "Windows of Developmental Sensitivity to Social Media," *Nature Communications* 13 (2022): 1649.

240 **In her book *Autonomy-Supportive Parenting*:** Emily Edlynn, *Autonomy-Supportive Parenting: Reduce Parental Burnout and Raise Competent, Confident Children* (Familius, 2023).

241 **In 2024, researchers:** Mariya Stoilova, Monica Bulger, and Sonia Livingstone, "Do Parental Control Tools Fulfill Family Expectations for Child Protection? A Rapid Evidence Review of the Contexts and Outcomes of Use," *Journal of Children and Media* 18, no. 1 (October 2024): 29–49.

241 **In a 2018 study, kids said:** Arup Kumar Ghosh, Karla Badillo-Urquiola, Shion Guha, Joseph J. LaViola Jr., and Pamela J. Wisniewski, "Safety vs. Surveillance: What Children Have to Say About Mobile Apps for Parental Control," CHI '18: Proceedings of the 2018 CHI Conference on Human Factors in Computing Systems, paper no. 124: 1–14.

242 **teens whose parents used:** Arup Kumar Ghosh, Karla Badillo-Urquiola, Mary Beth Rosson, Heng Xu, John M. Carroll, and Pamela J. Wisniewski, "A Matter of Control or Safety?: Examining Parental Use of Technical Monitoring Apps on Teens' Mobile Devices," CHI '18: Proceedings of the 2018 CHI Conference on Human Factors in Computing Systems, paper no. 194: 1–14, https://dl.acm.org/doi/10.1145/3173574.3173768.

242 **In her 2024 book *The Screentime Solution*:** Emily Cherkin, *The Screentime Solution: A Judgment-Free Guide to Becoming a Tech-Intentional Family* (Greenleaf, 2024).

242 **In one study, Ohio State University communication researcher:** Amy I. Nathanson, "The Unintended Effects of Parental Mediation of Television on Adolescents," *Media Psychology* 4, no. 3 (2002): 207–30.

243 **And in a 2023 longitudinal study:** Shunsen Huang, Xiaoxiong Lai, Yajun Li, Wenrong Wang, Xinmei Zhao, Xinran Dai, Hunalei Wang, and Yun Wang, "Does Parental Media Mediation Make a Difference for Adolescents? Evidence from an Empirical Cohort Study of Parent-Adolescent Dyads," *Heliyon* 9, no. 4 (March 2023): e14897.

243 **In a 2022 paper, researchers found:** Wei Ren and Xiaowen Zhu, "Parental Mediation and Adolescents' Internet Use: The Moderating Role of Parental Style," *Journal of Youth and Adolescence* 51 (2022): 1483–96.

244 **In their book *Plugged In*:** Patti M. Valkenburg and Jessica Taylor Piotrowski, *Plugged In: How Media Attract and Affect Youth* (Yale University Press, 2017).

246 **Some studies have found that the more time parents spend on their devices:** Lu Qiao and Qinxue Liu, "The Effect of Technoference in Parent-Child Relationships on Adolescent Smartphone Addiction: The Role of Cognitive Factors," *Children and Youth Services Review* 118 (November 2020): 105340; Jason M. Nagata, Angel Paul, Felicia Yen, Zacariah Smith-Russack, et al. "Associations Between Media Parenting Practices and Early Adolescent Screen Use," *Pediatric Research* 97, no. 1 (January 2025): 403–10.

247 **In a 2020 study, researchers in Norway and the Netherlands:** Mariek M. P. Vanden Abeele, Monika Abels, and Andrew T. Hendrickson, "Are Parents Less Responsive to Young Children When They Are on Their Phones? A Systematic Naturalistic Observation Study," *Cyberpsychology, Behavior, and Social Networking* 23, no. 6 (June 2020): 363–70.

247 **In one study, Jenny Radesky, a pediatrician:** Jenny S. Radesky, Caroline Kistin, Staci Eisenberg, Jamie Gross, Gabrielle Block, Barry Zuckerman, and Michael Silverstein, "Parent Perspectives on their Mobile Technology Use: The Excitement and Exhaustion of Parenting While Connected," *Journal of De-*

velopmental and Behavioral Pediatrics 37, no. 9 (November/December 2016): 694–701.

248 In a 2021 study, researchers interviewed tweens: Anneleen Meus, Lennert Coenen, Steven Eggermont, and Kathleen Beullens, "Family Technoference: Exploring Parent Mobile Device Distraction from Children's Perspectives," *Mobile Media & Communication* 9, no. 3 (February 2021): 584–604.

248 In her book *How to Break Up with Your Phone*: Catherine Price, *How to Break Up with Your Phone: The 30-Day Plan to Take Back Your Life* (Ten Speed Press, 2018).

Index

Index

About the Author

Melinda Wenner Moyer is an award-winning contributing editor at *Scientific American*, a regular contributor to *The New York Times*, and a former faculty member at NYU's Arthur L. Carter Journalism Institute. She also writes the popular Substack parenting newsletter *Now What?*.

Visit Melinda Online

melindawennermoyer.com

melindawmoyer.substack.com

𝕏 Lindy2350

MelindaWMoyer

RAISING READERS
Books Build Bright Futures

Dear Reader,

We'd love your attention for one more page to tell you about the crisis in children's reading, and what we can all do.

Studies have shown that reading for fun is the **single biggest predictor of a child's future life chances** – more than family circumstance, parents' educational background or income. It improves academic results, mental health, wealth, communication skills, ambition and happiness.[1]

The number of children reading for fun is in rapid decline. Young people have a lot of competition for their time. In 2024, 1 in 10 children and young people in the UK aged 5 to 18 did not own a single book at home.[2]

Hachette works extensively with schools, libraries and literacy charities, but here are some ways we can all raise more readers:

- Reading to children for just 10 minutes a day makes a difference
- Don't give up if children aren't regular readers – there will be books for them!
- Visit bookshops and libraries to get recommendations
- Encourage them to listen to audiobooks
- Support school libraries
- Give books as gifts

There's a lot more information about how to encourage children to read on our website: **www.RaisingReaders.co.uk**

Thank you for reading.

hachette UK

[1] OECD, '21st-Century Readers: Developing Literacy Skills in a Digital World', 2021, https://www.oecd.org/en/publications/21st-century-readers_a83d84cb-en.html

[2] National Literacy Trust, 'Book Ownership in 2024', November 2024, https://literacytrust.org.uk/research-services/research-reports/book-ownership-in-2024